T0044171

PRAISE FOR

# LANGUAGES
## OF TRUTH

––––––

"Stretches from blazing manifesto to nostalgic reminiscence, close-focus review to . . . podium utterance. . . . Rushdie pays heed to the music of chance."　　　　　　　　　　　*—The Wall Street Journal*

"Powerful . . . essential reading . . . reminding us that the stories we have told each other over millennia are universal, even if this shared heritage is often lost or forgotten in today's angry, fractured world."
　　　　　　　　　　　　　　　　　　　*—Financial Times*

"The venerable novelist Salman Rushdie's *Languages of Truth* has big ambitions. . . . These essays are at their best when he trains his attention on literature."　　　　　　　　　*—The New York Times*

"Rushdie is vital, expansive, the critic as storyteller, championing his subjects with gusto. . . . A writer to be reckoned with."
　　　　　　　　　　　　　　　*—Times Literary Supplement*

"Mesmerizing . . . Rushdie's writing is erudite and full of sympathy, brimming with insight and wit. . . . Fans will be delighted."
　　　　　　　　　　　　　*—Publishers Weekly* (starred review)

"A grand array of subjects . . . prose that is, by turns, erudite, caustic, and funny . . . engrossing and provocative testimony to our need for the 'languages of truth.'"　　　　　　　　　　*—Booklist*

"Superlative nonfiction."　　　　　　　　　　　*—The Guardian*

"Wide-ranging nonfiction pieces by the distinguished novelist, unified by his commitment to artistic freedom and his adamant opposition to censorship in any form . . . This collection . . . showcases his generous spirit, dedicated to illuminating the work of fellow artists and defending their right to unfettered creativity. Formidably erudite, engagingly passionate, and endlessly informative: a literary treat."                —*Kirkus Reviews* (starred review)

"Superb . . . highly recommended for Rushdie fans, as well as readers interested in art, literature, or creative writing."
—*Library Journal* (starred review)

"This master of magical realism approaches giants of storytelling from the world's classical cultural hegemons . . . as they relate to his own early memories of discovering the written word, first as a boy in private schools in old Bombay and England, and then as a young writer. . . . With commentary on censorship, bravery, betrayal, politics, transnationalism, language, and more, Rushdie takes the reader on a journey equal parts coolly cerebral, heavily contemplative, and appropriately fantastical."                —*Avenue*

"Ranging from the . . . idiosyncratic to the polemical . . . the pieces are a pleasure to read for their variety, sharpness, and literary brio. . . . This is the universe that Rushdie has sought to capture in his fiction. *Languages of Truth* illuminates some of the choices, influences and beliefs that have driven this lifelong venture."     —*Telegraph India*

# BY SALMAN RUSHDIE

### FICTION
*Grimus*
*Midnight's Children*
*Shame*
*The Satanic Verses*
*Haroun and the Sea of Stories*
*East, West*
*The Moor's Last Sigh*
*The Ground Beneath Her Feet*
*Fury*
*Shalimar the Clown*
*The Enchantress of Florence*
*Luka and the Fire of Life*
*Two Years Eight Months and Twenty-Eight Nights*
*The Golden House*
*Quichotte*
*Victory City*

### NONFICTION
*Joseph Anton: A Memoir*
*The Jaguar Smile: A Nicaraguan Journey*
*Imaginary Homelands: Essays and Criticism 1981–1991*
*Step Across This Line: Collected Nonfiction 1992–2002*
*Languages of Truth: Essays 2003–2020*

### SCREENPLAY
*Midnight's Children*

### ANTHOLOGIES
*Mirrorwork: 50 Years of Indian Writing, 1947–1997* (co-editor)
*Best American Short Stories 2008* (co-editor)

# LANGUAGES OF TRUTH

ESSAYS 2003–2020

# SALMAN RUSHDIE

RANDOM HOUSE

NEW YORK

*Languages of Truth* is a work of nonfiction. Some names
and identifying details have been changed.

2022 Random House Trade Paperback Edition

Copyright © 2021 by Salman Rushdie

All rights reserved.

Published in the United States by Random House,
an imprint and division of Penguin Random House LLC, New York.

RANDOM HOUSE and the HOUSE colophon are
registered trademarks of Penguin Random House LLC.

Originally published in hardcover in the United States by
Random House, an imprint and division of Penguin Random House LLC,
in the United Kingdom by Jonathan Cape, a division of
Penguin Random House UK, London, and in Canada by Knopf Canada,
an imprint of Penguin Random House Canada, Toronto, in 2021.

The essays and speeches in this work originally appeared in different form and most
pieces have been previously published. A source list can be found on page 353.

"I Am Not Yet Dead" from the musical *Monty Python's Spamalot*, written by Eric Idle,
music by John Du Prez. Copyright © 2004. Used with permission.

LIBRARY OF CONGRESS CATALOGING-IN-PUBLICATION DATA
NAMES: Rushdie, Salman, author.
TITLE: Languages of truth: essays 2003–2020 / Salman Rushdie.
DESCRIPTION: | New York: Random House, [2021]
IDENTIFIERS: LCCN 2020028493 (print) | LCCN 2020028494 (ebook) |
ISBN 9780593133194 | ISBN 9780593133187 (ebook) |
SUBJECTS: LCGFT: Essays.
CLASSIFICATION: LCC PR6068.U757 L36 2021 (print) |
LCC PR6068.U757 (ebook) | DDC 824/.914—dc23
LC record available at lccn.loc.gov/2020028493
LC ebook record available at lccn.loc.gov/2020028494

Printed in the United States of America on acid-free paper

randomhousebooks.com

3rd Printing

*Book design by Barbara M. Bachman*

To the next generation
Nabeelah
and
Rose

# CONTENTS

## PART THREE

## PART FOUR

# PART
ONE

# WONDER TALES

———

## 1

BEFORE THERE WERE BOOKS, THERE WERE STORIES. AT FIRST the stories weren't written down. Sometimes they were even sung. Children were born, and before they could speak, their parents sang them songs, a song about an egg that fell off a wall, perhaps, or about a boy and a girl who went up a hill and fell down it. As the children grew older, they asked for stories almost as often as they asked for food. Now there was a goose that laid golden eggs, or a boy who sold the family cow for a handful of magic beans, or a naughty rabbit trespassing on a dangerous farmer's land. The children fell in love with these stories and wanted to hear them over and over again. Then they grew older and found those stories in books. And other stories that they had never heard before, about a girl who fell down a rabbit hole, or a silly old bear and an easily scared piglet and a gloomy donkey, or a phantom tollbooth, or a place where wild things were. They heard and read stories and they fell in love with them, Mickey in the night kitchen with magic bakers who all looked like Oliver Hardy, and Peter Pan, who thought death would be an awfully big adventure, and Bilbo Baggins under a mountain winning a riddle contest against a strange creature who had lost his precious, and the act of falling in love with stories awakened something in the children that would nourish them all their lives: their imagination.

The children fell in love with stories easily and lived in stories too; they made up play stories every day, they stormed castles and conquered nations and sailed the ocean blue, and at night their dreams were full of dragons. They were all storytellers now, makers of stories as well as receivers of stories. But they went on growing up and slowly the stories fell away from them, the stories were packed away in boxes in the attic, and it became harder for the former children to tell and receive stories, harder for them, sadly, to fall in love. For some of them, stories began to seem irrelevant, unnecessary: kids' stuff. These were sad people, and we must pity them and try not to think of them as stupid boring philistine losers.

I believe that the books and stories we fall in love with make us who we are, or, not to claim too much, that the act of falling in love with a book or story changes us in some way, and the beloved tale becomes a part of our picture of the world, a part of the way in which we understand things and make judgments and choices in our daily lives. As adults, falling in love less easily, we may end up with only a handful of books that we can truly say we love. Maybe this is why we make so many bad judgments.

Nor is this love unconditional or eternal. A book may cease to speak to us as we grow older, and our feeling for it will fade. Or we may suddenly, as our lives shape and hopefully increase our understanding, be able to appreciate a book we dismissed earlier; we may suddenly be able to hear its music, to be enraptured by its song. When, as a college student, I first read Günter Grass's great novel *The Tin Drum*, I was unable to finish it. It languished on a shelf for fully ten years before I gave it a second chance, whereupon it became one of my favorite novels of all time: one of the books I would say that I love. It is an interesting question to ask oneself: Which are the books that you truly love? Try it. The answer will tell you a lot about who you presently are.

I grew up in Bombay, India, a city that is no longer, today, at all like the city it once was and has even changed its name to the much less euphonious Mumbai, in a time so unlike the present that it feels impossibly remote, even fantastic: a real-life version of the mythic golden age. Childhood, as A. E. Housman reminds us in "The Land of Lost Content," often also called "Blue Remembered Hills," is the country to which we all once belonged and will all eventually lose:

Into my heart an air that kills
From yon far country blows:
What are those blue remembered hills,
What spires, what farms are those?

That is the land of lost content,
I see it shining plain,
The happy highways where I went
And cannot come again.

In that far-off Bombay, the stories and books that reached me from the West seemed like true tales of wonder. Hans Christian Andersen's "The Snow Queen," with its splinters of magic mirror that entered people's bloodstreams and turned their hearts to ice, was even more terrifying to a boy from the tropics, where the only ice was in the refrigerator. "The Emperor's New Clothes" felt especially enjoyable to a boy growing up in the immediate aftermath of the British Empire. And there was *Huckleberry Finn*, irresistible to a Bombay boy because of its hero's extraordinary freedom of action, though I was puzzled about why, if the runaway slave Jim was trying to escape the world of slavery and get to the non-slave-owning North, did he get onto a raft on the Mississippi, which flows south?

Perhaps tales of elsewhere always feel like fairy tales, and certainly it is one of the great wonders of literature that it opens up many "elsewheres" to us, from the Little Mermaid's underwater world to Dorothy's Oz, and makes them ours. But for me, the real wonder tales were closer to home, and I have always thought it my great good fortune as a writer to have grown up steeped in them.

Some of these stories were sacred in origin, but because I grew up in a nonreligious household, I was able to receive them simply as beautiful stories. This did not mean I did not believe them. When I heard about the *samudra manthan*, the tale of how the great god Indra churned the Milky Way, using the fabled Mount Mandara as his churning stick, to force the giant ocean of milk in the sky to give up its nectar, *amrita*, the nectar of immortality, I began to see the stars in a new way. In that impossibly ancient time, my childhood, a time before light pollution made most of the stars invisible to city dwellers, a boy in a garden in Bombay could still look up at the night sky and hear the music of the spheres and see with humble joy the thick stripe of the galaxy there. I imagined it dripping with magic nectar. Maybe if I opened my mouth, a drop might fall in and then I would be immortal too.

This is the beauty of the wonder tale and its descendant, fiction: that one can simultaneously know that the story is a work of imagination, which is to say *untrue,* and believe it to contain profound truth. The boundary between the magical and the real, at such moments, ceases to exist.

We were not Hindus, my family, but we believed the great stories of Hinduism to be available to us also. On the day of the annual Ganpati festival, when huge crowds carried effigies of the elephant-headed deity Ganesh to the water's edge at Chowpatty Beach to immerse the god in the sea, Ganesh felt as if he belonged to me too; he felt like a symbol of the collective joy and, yes, unity of the city rather than a member of the pantheon of a "rival" faith. When I learned that Ganesh's love of literature was so great that he sat at the feet of India's Homer, the sage Vyasa, and became the scribe who wrote down the great *Mahabharata* epic, he belonged to me even more deeply; and when I grew up and wrote a novel about a boy called Saleem with an unusually big nose, it seemed natural, even though Saleem came from a Muslim family, to associate the narrator of *Midnight's Children* with the most literary of gods, who just happened to have a big trunk of a nose as well. The blurring of boundaries between religious cultures in that old, truly secularist Bombay now feels like one more thing that divides the past from India's bitter, stifled, censorious, sectarian present.

The *Mahabharata* and its sidekick, the *Ramayana,* two of the longest wonder tales of all, are still alive in India, alive in the minds of Indians and relevant to their daily lives, in the way the gods of the Greeks and Romans were once alive in Western imaginations. Once, and not so long ago, it was possible in the lands of the West to allude to the story of the shirt of Nessus, and people would have known that the dying centaur Nessus tricked Deianira, the wife of Heracles or Hercules, into giving her husband his shirt, knowing it was poisoned and would kill him. Once, everyone knew that after the death of Orpheus, greatest of poets and singers, his severed head continued to sing. These images and many others were available, as metaphors, to help people understand the world. Art does not die when the artist dies, said Orpheus's head. The song survives the singer. And the shirt of Nessus warned us that even a very special gift may be dangerous. Another such gift, of course, was the Trojan horse, which taught us all to fear the Greeks, even when they bring gifts. Some metaphors of the wonder tales of the West have managed to survive.

But in India, as I grew up, the wonder tales all lived, and they still do. Nowadays it isn't even necessary to read the full *Ramayana* or *Mahabharata;* some may be grateful for this news, because the *Mahabharata* is the longest poem in world literature, over two hundred thousand lines long, which is to say ten times as long as the *Iliad* and *Odyssey* put together, while the *Ramayana* runs to around fifty thousand lines, merely two and a half times as long as the combined works of Homer. Fortunately for younger readers, the immensely popular comic-book series *Amar Chitra Katha,* "immortal picture stories," offers adept renderings of tales from both. And for adults, a ninety-four-episode TV version of the *Mahabharata* brought the nation to a stop each week when originally screened in the 1990s and found an audience numbering in the hundreds of millions.

It has to be admitted that the influence of these tales is not always positive. The sectarian politics of the Hindu nationalist parties like the BJP uses the rhetoric of the past to fantasize about a return to "Ram Rajya," the "reign of Lord Ram," a supposed golden age of Hinduism without such inconveniences as members of other religions to complicate matters. The politicization of the *Ramayana,* and of Hinduism in general, has become, in the hands of unscrupulous sectarian leaders, a dangerous affair. The attack on the book *The Hindus*—a work of consummate scholarship written by one of the world's greatest Sanskritists, Wendy Doniger—and the regrettable decision of Penguin India to withdraw and pulp copies of it in response to fundamentalist criticism, is a sharp illustration of that fact.

Problems can extend beyond politics too. In some later versions of the *Ramayana,* the exiled Lord Ram and his brother Lakshman leave Sita alone in their forest dwelling one day while they hunt a golden deer, not knowing that the deer is actually a *rakshasa,* a kind of demon, in disguise. To protect Sita in their absence, Lakshman draws a *rekha,* or an enchanted line, around their home; anyone who tries to cross it except Ram, Lakshman, and Sita will be burned to death by flames that erupt from the line. But the demon king Ravana disguises himself as a beggar and comes to Sita's door asking for alms, and she crosses the line to give him what he wants. This is how he captures her and spirits her away to his kingdom of Lanka, after which Ram and Lakshman have to fight a war to get her back. To "cross the *Lakshman rekha*" has become a metaphor for overstepping the boundaries of what is permissible or right, of going too far, of succumbing foolishly to iconoclasm, and bringing down upon yourself dire consequences.

A few years ago in Delhi, there occurred the now notorious assault and gang rape of a twenty-three-year-old student, who afterward died from her horrific injuries. Within days of this awful event, a state minister remarked that if the young woman concerned had not "crossed the *Lakshman rekha*"—in other words, taken a bus with a male friend in the evening instead of staying demurely at home— she would not have been attacked. He later withdrew the remark because of a public outcry, but his use of the metaphor revealed that too many men in India still believe that there are limits and boundaries women should not transgress. It should be said that in most traditional versions of the *Ramayana,* including the original version by the poet Valmiki, the story of the *Lakshman rekha* is not to be found. However, an apocryphal wonder tale can sometimes be as potent as a canonical one.

I want to return, however, to that childhood self, enchanted by tales whose express and sole purpose was enchantment. I want to move away from the grand religious epics to the great hoard of scurrilous, conniving, mysterious, exciting, comic, bizarre, surreal, and very often extremely sexy narratives contained in the rest of the Eastern storehouse, because—not only because, but, yes, because—they show how much pleasure is to be gained from literature once God is removed from the picture. One of the most remarkable characteristics of the stories now gathered in the pages of *The Thousand Nights and One Night*, to take just one example, is the almost complete absence of religion. Lots of sex, much mischief, a great deal of deviousness; monsters, jinnis, giant rocs; at times, enormous quantities of blood and gore; but no God. This is why censorious Islamists dislike it so much.

In Egypt in May 2010, just seven months before the revolt against President Hosni Mubarak, a group of Islamist lawyers got wind of a new edition of *Alf Laylah wa Laylah* (the book's original Arabic title) and brought an action demanding that the edition be withdrawn and the book banned, because it was "a call to vice and sin" that contained several references to sex. Fortunately, they did not succeed, and then larger matters began to preoccupy Egyptian minds. But the fact is, they had a point. There are indeed in that book several references to sex, and the characters seem much more preoccupied with having sex than being devout, which could indeed be, as the lawyers argued, a call to vice, if that's the deformed puritanical way you see the world. To my mind, this call is an excellent thing and well worth responding to, but you can see how people who dislike music, jokes, and pleasure would be upset by it. It is rather wonderful that this ancient text, this wonderful group of wonder tales, retains the power to upset the world's fanatics more than twelve hundred years after the stories first came into the world.

The book that we now usually call *The Arabian Nights* didn't originate in the Arab world. Its probable origin is Indian; Indian story compendiums too have a fondness for frame stories, for Russiandoll-style stories within stories, and for animal fables. Somewhere around the eighth century, these stories found their way into Persian, and according to surviving scraps of information, the collection was known as *Hazar Afsaneh*, "a thousand stories." There's a tenth-century document from Baghdad that describes the *Hazar Afsaneh* and mentions its frame story, about a wicked king who kills a concubine every night until one of these doomed wives manages to stave off her execution by telling him stories. This is where we first see the name "Scheherazade." Sadly, of the *Hazar Afsaneh* itself not a single copy survives. This book is the great "missing link" of world literature, the fabled volume through which the wonder tales of India traveled west to encounter, eventually, the Arabic language and to turn into *The Thousand Nights and One Night,* a book with many versions and no agreed canonical form, and then to move farther west, first into French, in the eighteenth-century version by Antoine Galland, who added a number of stories not included in the Arabic, such as the tales of "Aladdin and the Wonderful Lamp" and "Ali Baba and the Forty Thieves." And from French the stories made it into English, and from English they journeyed to Hollywood, which is a language of its own, and then it's all flying carpets and Robin Williams as The Genie. (It's worth noting, by the way, that there are no flying carpets in *The Arabian Nights.* There are flying carpets elsewhere in the Eastern tradition. For example, there's a legend that King Solomon possessed one that could change its size and become big enough to transport an army: the world's first air force. But in *The Arabian Nights,* all carpets remain passive and inert.)

This great migration of narrative has inspired much of the world's literature, all the way down to the magic realism of the South American fabulists, so that when I, in my turn, used some of those devices, I had the feeling of closing a circle and bringing that story tradition all the way back home to the country in which it began. But I mourn the loss of the *Hazar Afsaneh,* which would, if rediscovered, complete the story of the stories, and what a find that would be. Perhaps it would solve a mystery at the heart of the frame story, or rather at the very end of it, and answer a question I've been asking myself for some years: Did Scheherazade and her sister, Dunyazad, finally, after one thousand nights and one night and more, become murderers and kill their bloodthirsty husbands?

It was, I confess, the bloody aspect of the frame story that first attracted me to *The Arabian Nights*. Let's make a small calculation.

How many women did they actually kill, this king, this Shahryar, the Sassanid monarch of "the island or peninsula of India and China," and his brother, Shah Zaman, sovereign ruler over barbarian Samarkand? It began, or so the story goes, when Shah Zaman found his wife in the arms of a palace cook, whose chief characteristics were that he was (a) black, (b) huge, and (c) covered in kitchen grease. In spite of, or perhaps because of, these characteristics, the queen of Samarkand was obviously having far too much fun, so Shah Zaman chopped her and her lover into several pieces, left them there on the bed of their delight, and headed for his brother's home, where, not long afterward, he chanced to espy his sister-in-law, Shahryar's queen, in a garden, by a fountain, in the company of ten ladies-in-waiting and ten white slaves. The ten and ten were busy gratifying one another; the queen, however, summoned her own lover down from a convenient tree. This hideous fellow was, yes, (a) black, (b) huge, and (c) slobbering! What fun they had, the ten and ten and the queen and her "blackamoor"! Ah, the malice and treachery of womankind, and the unaccountable attraction of huge, ugly, dripping black men! Shah Zaman told his brother what he had seen, whereupon the ladies-in-waiting, the white slaves, and the queen all met their fates, personally executed by Shahryar's chief minister, his vizier (or wazir). The "slobbering" black lover of Shahryar's late queen escaped, or so it seems; how else to explain his absence from the list of the dead?

King Shahryar and King Shah Zaman duly took their revenge on faithless womankind. For three years, they each married, deflowered, and then ordered the execution of a fresh virgin every night. It is not clear how Shah Zaman in Samarkand went about his gory business, but of Shahryar's methods there are things that can be told. It is known, for instance, that the vizier—Scheherazade's father, Shahryar's wise prime minister—was obliged to carry out the executions himself. All those beautiful young bodies, decapitated; all those tumbling heads and bloody, spurting necks. The vizier was a cultured gentleman, not only a man of power but also a person of discernment, even of delicate sensibilities—he must have been, must he not, to have raised such a paragon, such a wondrously gifted, multiply accomplished, heroically courageous, selfless daughter as Scheherazade? And Dunyazad too; let's not forget the kid sister, Dunyazad. Another good, smart, decent girl. What would it do to the soul of the father of such fine girls to be forced to execute young women by the hundreds, to slit girls' throats and see their lifeblood flow? What secret fury might have burgeoned in his subtle breast? We are not told. We do know, however, that Shahryar's subjects began to resent him mightily and to flee his capital city with their womenfolk, so that after three years there were no virgins to be found in town.

No virgins except Scheherazade and Dunyazad.

Three years already: one thousand and ninety-five nights, one thousand and ninety-five dead queens for Shahryar, one thousand and ninety-five more for Shah Zaman, or one thousand and ninety-six each if a leap year was involved. Let's err on the low side. One thousand and ninety-five each let it be. And let us not forget the original twenty-three. By the time Scheherazade entered the story, marrying King Shahryar and ordering her sister, Dunyazad, to sit at the foot of the marital bed and to ask, after Scheherazade's deflowering was complete, to be told a bedtime story . . . By this time, Shahryar and Shah Zaman were already responsible for two thousand, two hundred and thirteen deaths. Only eleven of the dead were men.

Shahryar, upon marrying Scheherazade and being captivated by her tales, stopped killing women. Shah Zaman, untamed by literature, went right on with his vengeful work, slaughtering each morning the virgin he'd ravished the night before, demonstrating to the female sex the power of men over women, the ability of men to separate fornication from love, and the inevitable union, as far as women were concerned, of sexuality and death. In Samarkand the carnage continued for at least another one thousand nights and one night, because it was only at the conclusion of the entire cycle of Scheherazade's tales—when that greatest of storytellers begged to be spared, not in recognition of her genius but for the sake of the three sons she had given Shahryar during the fabled years, and when Shahryar confessed his love for her, the last of his one thousand and ninety-seven wives, and gave up all pretense of murderous intent—that Shah Zaman's project also ended; cleansed at last of bloodlust, he asked for, and received, sweet Dunyazad's hand in marriage.

The minimum total number of the dead by this time was, by my calculation, three thousand, two hundred and fourteen. Only eleven of the dead were men.

Consider Scheherazade, whose name meant "city-born" and who was without a doubt a big-city girl, crafty, wisecracking, by turns sentimental and cynical, as contemporary a metropolitan narrator as one could wish to meet. Scheherazade, who snared the prince in her never-ending story. Scheherazade, telling stories to save her life, setting fiction against death, a Statue of Liberty built not of metal but of words. Scheherazade, who insisted, against her father's will, on taking her place in the procession into the king's deadly boudoir. Scheherazade, who set herself the heroic task of saving her sisters by taming the king. Who had faith, who must have had faith, in the man beneath the murderous monster and in her own ability to restore him to his true humanity, by telling him stories.

What a woman! It's easy to understand how and why King Shahryar fell in love with her. For certainly he did fall, becoming the father of her children and understanding, as the nights progressed, that his threat of execution had become empty, that he could no longer ask his vizier, her father, to carry it out. His savagery was blunted by the genius of the woman who, for a thousand nights and one night, risked her life to save the lives of others, who trusted her imagination to stand against brutality and overcome it not by force but, amazingly, by civilizing it.

Lucky king! But (this is the greatest unanswered question of *The Arabian Nights*) why on earth did she fall in love with him? And why did Dunyazad, the younger sister who sat at the foot of the marital bed for one thousand nights and one night, watching her sister being fucked by the murderous king and listening to her stories—Dunyazad, the eternal listener, but also voyeur—why did she agree to marry

Shah Zaman, a man even deeper in blood than his story-charmed brother?

How can we understand these women? There is a silence in the tale that cries out to be spoken of. This much we are told: After the stories were over, Shah Zaman and Dunyazad were married, but Scheherazade made one condition—that Shah Zaman leave his kingdom and come to live with his brother, so that the sisters might not be parted. This Shah Zaman gladly did, and Shahryar appointed to rule over Samarkand in his brother's stead that same vizier who was now also his father-in-law. When the vizier arrived in Samarkand, he was greeted by the townspeople very joyfully, and all the local grandees prayed that he might reign over them for a long time. Which he did.

My question is this, as I interrogate the ancient story: Was there a conspiracy between the daughter and the father? Is it possible that Scheherazade and the vizier had hatched a secret plan? For, thanks to Scheherazade's strategy, Shah Zaman was no longer king in Samarkand. Thanks to Scheherazade's strategy, her father was no longer a courtier and unwilling executioner but a king in his own right, a well-beloved king, what was more, a wise man, a man of peace, succeeding a bloody ogre. And then, without explanation, Death came, simultaneously, for Shahryar and Shah Zaman. Death, the "Destroyer of Delights and the Severer of Societies, the Desolator of Dwelling Places and the Garnerer of Graveyards," came for them, and their palaces lay in ruins, and they were replaced by a wise ruler, whose name we are not told.

But how and why did the Destroyer of Delights arrive? How was it that both brothers died simultaneously, as the text clearly implies, and why did their palaces afterward lie in ruins? And who was their successor, the Unnamed and Wise?

We are not told. But imagine, once again, the vizier filling up with fury for many years as he was forced to spill all that innocent blood. Imagine the years of the vizier's fear, the one thousand and one nights of fear, while his daughters, flesh of his flesh, blood of his blood, were hidden in Shahryar's bedroom, their fate hanging by a story's thread.

How long will a man wait for his revenge? Will he wait longer than one thousand nights and one night?

This is my theory: that the vizier, now ruler of Samarkand, was the wise king who came home to rule Shahryar's kingdom. And the kings died simultaneously either at their wives' hands or at the vizier's. It's just a theory. Maybe the answer lies in the great lost book. Maybe it doesn't. We can only ... wonder.

At any rate, the final count of the dead was three thousand, two hundred and sixteen. Thirteen of the dead were men.

WHEN I FINISHED MY memoir, *Joseph Anton,* I felt a deep hunger for fiction. And not just any old fiction, but fiction as wildly fantastic as the memoir had been determinedly realistic. My mood swung from one end of the literary pendulum's arc to the other extreme. And I began to remember the stories that had made me fall in love with literature in the first place, tales full of beautiful impossibility, which were not true but by being not true told the truth, often more beautifully and memorably than stories that relied on being true. Those stories didn't have to happen once upon a time either. They could happen right now. Yesterday, today, or the day after tomorrow.

One of these wonder tales is from the Kashmiri Sanskrit compendium, the *Katha Sarit Sagara* or "Ocean of the Streams of Story," whose title inspired my children's book *Haroun and the Sea of Stories.* I confess that I stole this story and put it in a novel. It goes something like this:

"Once upon a time in a faraway place, a merchant was owed money by a local nobleman, really quite a lot of money, and then unexpectedly the nobleman died and the merchant thought, This is bad, I'm not going to get paid. But a god had given him the gift of transmigration—this was in a part of the world in which there were many gods, not just one—so the merchant had the idea of migrating his spirit into the dead lord's body so that the dead man could get up from his deathbed and pay him what he owed. The merchant left his body in a safe place, or so he thought, and his spirit jumped into the dead man's skin, but when he was walking the dead man's body to the bank, he had to pass through the fish market, and a large dead codfish lying on a slab saw him go past and started to laugh. When people heard the dead fish laughing, they knew there was something fishy about the walking dead man and attacked him for being possessed by a demon. The dead nobleman's body quickly became uninhabitable, and the merchant's spirit had to abandon it and make its way back to its own discarded shell. But some other people had found the merchant's empty body and, thinking it the body of a dead man, had set it on fire according to the customs of that part of the world. So now the merchant had no body and had not been paid what he was owed, and his spirit is probably still wandering somewhere in the market. Or maybe he ended up migrating into a dead fish and swam away into the ocean of the streams of story. And the moral of the story is, don't push your fucking luck."

Animal fables—including talking-dead-fish fables—have been among the most enduring tales in the Eastern canon, and the best of them, unlike, say, the fables of Aesop, are amoral. They don't seek to preach about humility or modesty or moderation or honesty or abstinence. They do not guarantee the triumph of virtue. As a result, they seem remarkably modern. The bad guys sometimes win.

The collection known in India as the *Panchatantra* features a pair of talking jackals: Karataka, the good or better guy of the two, and Damanaka, the wicked schemer. At the book's outset they are in the service of the lion king, but Damanaka doesn't like the lion's friendship with another courtier, a bull, and tricks the lion into believing the bull to be an enemy. The lion murders the innocent animal while the jackals watch.

The end.

In the tales of Karataka and Damanaka we also read about a war between crows and owls, in which one crow pretends to be a traitor and joins the owls to discover the location of the cave where they live. Then the crows set fires at all the entrances to the cave, and the owls all suffocate to death.

The end.

In a third story a man leaves his child in the care of his friend, a mongoose, and when he returns he sees blood on the mongoose's mouth and kills it, believing it has attacked his child. Then he discovers the mongoose has actually killed a snake and saved his child. But by now the mongoose is unfortunately deceased.

The end.

Many of Aesop's little morality tales about the victory of dogged slowness (the tortoise) over arrogant speed (the hare), or the foolishness of crying "wolf" when there is no wolf, or of killing the goose that laid the golden eggs, seem positively soppy when compared to this Quentin Tarantino savagery. So much for the cliché of the peaceful, mystical East.

As a migrant myself, I have always been fascinated by the migration of stories, and these jackal tales traveled almost as far as the *Arabian Nights* narratives, ending up in both Arabic and Persian versions, in which the jackals' names have mutated into Kalila and Dimna. They also ended up in Hebrew and Latin and eventually, as *The Fables of Bidpai*, in English and French. Unlike the *Arabian Nights* stories, however, they have faded from modern readers' consciousness, perhaps because their insufficient attention to happy endings made them unattractive to the Walt Disney Company.

Yet their power endures; and it does so, I believe, because for all their cargo of monsters and magic, these stories are entirely truthful about human nature (even when in the form of anthropomorphic animals). All human life is here, brave and cowardly, honorable and dishonorable, straight-talking and conniving, and the stories ask the greatest and most enduring question of literature: How do ordinary people respond to the arrival in their lives of the extraordinary? And they answer: Sometimes we don't do so well, but at other times we find resources within ourselves we did not know we possessed, and so we rise to the challenge, we overcome the monster, Beowulf kills Grendel and Grendel's more fearsome mother as well, Red Riding Hood kills the wolf, or Beauty finds the love within the beast and then he is beastly no more. And that is ordinary magic, human magic, the true wonder of the wonder tale.

———

I'M TRYING TO MAKE a case in favor of something that is pretty much out of fashion these days. By general consensus, we live in an age of nonfiction. Any publisher, any bookseller, will tell you that. What's more, fiction itself seems to have turned away from fiction. I'm speaking now of serious fiction, not the other kind. In the other kind of fiction, fictiveness is alive and well, it's always twilight, people are playing hunger games, and Leonardo da Vinci is just a code. Serious fiction has turned toward realism of the Elena Ferrante and Knausgaard kind, fiction that asks us to believe that it comes from a place very close to if not identical to the author's personal experience and away, so to speak, from magic. But many years ago, in a famous essay, the great Czech writer Milan Kundera proposed that the novel has two parents, Tristram Shandy and Clarissa Harlowe. From Samuel Richardson's *Clarissa* descends the great tradition of the realist novel, while from Laurence Sterne's *The Life and Opinions of Tristram Shandy, Gentleman,* comes a smaller trickle of, well, weirder books. It is the children of *Clarissa* who have filled the literary world, Kundera said, and yet, in his opinion, it was on the Shandean side—the antic, ludic, comic, eccentric side—that most new, original work remained to be done. (Ernest Hemingway famously chose a different literary parent: "All modern American literature comes from one book by Mark Twain called *Huckleberry Finn.*" That is a freer and more mythic work than *Clarissa,* but it too is a broadly realistic novel. It must also be said that in choosing *Tristram Shandy,* Kundera ignores the work to which it is deeply indebted: Cervantes's *Don Quixote.* Sterne's Uncle Toby and Corporal Trim are clearly modeled on Quixote and Sancho.)

Kundera was suggesting that the possibilities of the realist novel have been so thoroughly explored by so many authors that very little new remains to be discovered. If he's right, the realist tradition is doomed to a kind of endless repetitiveness. For innovation, for *newness*—and remember that the word "novel" contains the idea of newness—we must turn to irrealism and find new ways of approaching the truth through lies. The wonder tales of my childhood taught me not only that such approaches were possible but that they were manifold, almost infinite in their possibilities, and that they were fun. As I said, the purveyors of schlock fiction in books and in films as well have understood the power of the fantastic, but all they are able to purvey is the fantastic reduced to comic-strip two-dimensionality. For me, the fantastic has been a way of adding dimensions to the real, adding fourth, fifth, sixth, and seventh dimensions to the usual three; a way of enriching and intensifying our experience of the real, rather than escaping from it into superhero-vampire fantasyland.

The Western writers I have most admired, writers such as Italo Calvino and Günter Grass, Mikhail Bulgakov and Isaac Bashevis Singer, have all feasted richly on their various wonder-tale traditions and found ways of injecting the fabulous into the real to make it more vivid and, strangely, more truthful. Grass's co-opting of animal fables, his extensive use of talking flounders, rats, and toads, grows from his absorption in the wonder tales of Germany, as collected by the Brothers Grimm. Calvino himself collected and perhaps partially invented many Italian wonder tales in his classic work *Italian Folktales,* and all his work was steeped in the language of the Italian fable. In Bulgakov's immortal tale of the devil coming to Moscow, *The Master and Margarita,* and in the delicious Yiddish stories of Isaac Singer, with their golems and dybbuks, their possessions and hauntings, we see, as in the art of Chagall, a deep fascination with and inspiration taken from the wonder tales of the Russian, Jewish, and Slavic world. Much of the greatest work of the last hundred or so years, from the fairy tales of Hans Christian Andersen to the work of Ursula Le Guin to the midnight-black nightmares of Franz Kafka, has come from this blending of the real and the surreal, of the natural and the supranatural worlds.

Many young writers today seem to start with the mantra "write what you know" pinned to the wall behind their writing tables, and as a result, as anyone who has experienced creative-writing classes can testify, there's a lot of stuff about adolescent suburban angst. My advice would be a little different. Only write what you know if what you know is really interesting. If you live in a neighborhood like Harper Lee's or William Faulkner's, by all means feel free to tell the heated tales of your own personal Yoknapatawpha, and you'll probably find you never need to leave home at all. But unless what you know is really interesting, don't write about it. Write what you don't know. This can be done in two ways. One way is to leave home and go and find a good story somewhere else. Melville and Conrad found their stories at sea and in faraway lands, and Hemingway and Fitzgerald too had to leave home to find their voices in Spain, or the Riviera, or East and West Egg. The other solution is to remember that fiction is fictional and try to make things up. We are all dreaming creatures. Dream on paper. And if it turns out like *Twilight* or *The Hunger Games*, tear it up, and try to have a better dream.

Madame Bovary and a flying carpet are both untrue, and, what's more, they are both untrue in the same way. *Somebody made them up.* I'm in favor of continuing to make things up. Only by unleashing the fictionality of fiction, the imaginativeness of the imagination, the dream songs of our dreams, can we hope to approach the new, and to create fiction that may, once again, be more interesting than the facts.

# 2

In the novel I wrote for my then ten-year-old son, *Haroun and the Sea of Stories*, an annoyed ten-year-old boy shouts at his storyteller father, "What's the use of stories that aren't even true?" The book that followed was an attempt to answer that question, to examine why it is that we need such stories and how they fulfill us, even though we know they are made up. It's a subject I seem to have been thinking about for most of my writing life: the relationship between the world of the imagination and the so-called real world, and how we travel between the two. Five years before *Haroun*, I wrote about N. F. Simpson's play *One Way Pendulum*, one of the very few competent British contributions to the Theatre of the Absurd. In this play, a man receives by mail order a full-size replica in do-it-yourself kit form of a courtroom in the Central Criminal Court in London, known as the

Old Bailey; he assembles it in his living room and shortly afterward finds himself on trial in it. A clerk states that on a certain day the defendant, our hero, "was not in this world." "What world was he in, then?" the judge demands, and the answer comes: "It seems he has one of his own."

(Parenthetically: Those who have not read *Haroun and the Sea of Stories* will no doubt be impressed to know that it was featured on the TV series *Lost,* where it played the part of the book being read by the character Desmond on Oceanic Flight 815 during the flash-sideways timeline. I really hope some readers will understand what that sentence means, because I certainly do not. "What's the use of stories that aren't even true?" is a question that could no doubt form the basis of an interesting lecture about *Lost.*)

Even if we do not live wholly in our imaginations, we all like to make journeys therein. In Jean-Luc Godard's film *Alphaville,* the private-eye hero Lemmy Caution travels across interstellar space in his Ford Galaxy. Dorothy Gale arrives in Oz riding a whirlwind. How and why do the rest of us make the trip?

We are born wanting food, shelter, love, song, and story. Our need for the last two is not less than our need for the first three. A friend of mine, researching the horrific treatment of orphans in Ceausescu's Romania, has found that these children, given food and shelter but denied the rest, do not develop normally. Their brains do not form properly. Perhaps we, who are language animals, possess a song and story instinct; we need and move toward stories and songs not because we are taught to do so but because it is in our nature to need them. And while there are other creatures on earth who might be described as singing—I'm thinking of the trills of songbirds, the howling of wolves, the long slow song of the whale in the ocean's depths—there is nothing that swims, crawls, walks, or flies that tells stories. Man alone is the storytelling animal.

Song is the human voice used in an unnatural way—a way that not all human beings, myself included, can use it—to create the kind of meaning that beauty instills in us. Story is the unnatural means we use to talk about human life, our way of reaching the truth by making things up. And we are the only species that, from the beginning, has used stories to explain ourselves to ourselves. Sitting in Plato's cave, men told stories about the shadows on the cave wall to guess at the world outside. Unable to understand their origins, men told each other stories about sky gods and sun gods, ancestor gods and savior gods, invisible fathers and mothers who explained the great matter of our origin and offered guidance on the equally great matter of morals. In myth and legend we created our oldest wonderlands, Asgard and Valhalla, Olympus and Mount Kailash, and embedded therein our deepest thoughts about our own natures and our doubts and fears as well.

*Haroun and the Sea of Stories* is a fable about language and silence, about stories and anti-stories, written, in part, to explain to my young son the battle then swirling around his father about another novel, *The Satanic Verses.* Twenty years after *Haroun,* another son demanded, "Where's my book?" There are two answers to this question. The first answer is, "Kid, life ain't fair." It's not a nice answer, I agree. The other answer is to write the book; so I wrote *Luka and the Fire of Life,* and as a result spent much time wandering around wonderlands once again, the imaginary worlds we love to inhabit as children and as grown-ups too.

When I began work on *Luka* twenty years after *Haroun,* I thought a good deal about "Lewis Carroll," the Reverend Charles Lutwidge Dodgson, the creator of Wonderland, and I learned this from him: The best thing about his second Alice book, *Through the Looking-Glass,* is that it is not *Return to Wonderland.* Six years after publishing *Alice's Adventures in Wonderland,* he set himself the considerable challenge of creating an entirely different imaginary world, with its own internal logic.

Don't go back where you've already been. Find another reason for going somewhere else.

I decided to challenge myself to do the same thing. Commercially speaking, this may not have been the smartest move. As my son Milan advised me when he was twelve years old, "Don't write books,

Dad. Write *series*." In the age of *Harry Potter* and *Twilight*, he's obviously right.

A few words more about *Through the Looking-Glass*. By the time it was published, the first *Alice* book had become immensely popular, so the danger of publishing a sequel that disappointed the earlier work's admirers was very great; also, Alice herself—Alice Pleasance Liddell—had grown up and was no longer that child who, on July 4, 1862, on a rowing trip with her two sisters and the Reverend Dodgson, had asked for a story and been told the tale of *Alice's Adventures Under Ground*, the story that was published three years later in much expanded form as the book we now colloquially know as *Alice in Wonderland*. Many of the greatest works of children's literature were created with particular children in mind: J. M. Barrie wrote *Peter Pan* to please the Llewelyn Davies boys, A. A. Milne wrote *Winnie-the-Pooh* about his son Christopher Robin Milne's favorite toys, and Lewis Carroll wrote *Alice* for Alice. But by the time of *Through the Looking-Glass*, he had to write for the memory of Alice, that imperious little girl who seems always to be scolding people, who remains certain of the rules of life and proper behavior even in a world whose rules she cannot know.

The Alice he had created for himself, however, continued to fill his dreams: "Still she haunts me, phantomwise," he wrote, "Alice moving under skies / Never seen by waking eyes."

My task, as I wrote *Luka and the Fire of Life*, was easier. I had a new child to write for and to be guided by. And I was fortunate, I am fortunate, that I had grown up steeped in the tradition of the wonder tale, including the heroic myths of the warrior Hamza and the adventurer Hatim Tai, wanderers who married fairies, fought goblins, slew dragons, and sometimes faced enemies who flew through the air riding on giant enchanted urns. From my earliest days, I have been—and I still am—a traveler in wonderlands.

If the realist tradition has been the dominant one, it is worth spending a few moments to defend the alternative, the other great tradition. It is worth saying that fantasy is not whimsy. The fantastic is neither innocent nor escapist. The wonderland is not a place of refuge, not even necessarily an attractive or likable place. It can be—in fact, it usually is—a place of slaughter, exploitation, cruelty, and fear. Kafka's *Metamorphosis* is a tragedy. Captain Hook wants to kill Peter Pan. The witch in the Black Forest wants to cook Hansel and Gretel. The wolf actually eats Red Riding Hood's grandmother. Albus Dumbledore is murdered, and the Lord of the Rings plans the enslavement of the whole of Middle-earth. The flying carpet of King Solomon, which, according to the stories, was sixty miles long and sixty miles wide, once punished the great king for the sin of pride by beginning to shake, so that the forty thousand people upon it all tumbled to their deaths. (Not for the first time, ordinary people suffered for their rulers' sins. Wonderland can be as flawed a place as earth.)

We know, when we hear these tales, that even though they are "unreal," because carpets do not fly and witches in gingerbread houses do not exist, they are also "real," because they are about real things: love, hatred, fear, power, bravery, cowardice, death. They simply arrive at the real by a different route. They are so, even though we know that they are not so.

Before the modern literature of the fantastic, before wonderland and fairy tale and folktale, there was mythology. In the beginning, myths were religious texts. The Greek myths were originally the Greek religion. But perhaps it's only when people stopped believing in the literal truth of these myths, stopped believing in an actual Zeus hurling actual thunderbolts, that they, we, were able to start believing in them in the way in which we believe in literature—that is to say, more profoundly, the double belief/unbelief with which we approach fiction, "so and not so." And at once they began to give up their deepest meanings, meanings previously obscured by faith.

The great myths, Greek, Roman, Nordic, have survived the deaths of the religions that once sustained them because of the astonishing compression of meaning they contain. When I was writing my novel *The Ground Beneath Her Feet*, I became enthralled by the myth of Orpheus, the greatest poet who was also the greatest singer, the personage in whom song and story became one. You can recount the myth of Orpheus in a hundred words or less: his love for the nymph Eurydice, her pursuit by the beekeeper Aristaeus, the snakebite that killed her, her descent into hell, his pursuit of her beyond the doors of death, his attempt to rescue her, his being granted by the lord of the underworld—as a reward for the genius of his singing—the possibility of leading her back to life as long as he didn't look back, and his fatal backward look. And yet when you begin to delve into the story it seems almost inexhaustibly rich, for at its heart is a great triangular tension between the grandest matters of life: love, art, and death. You can turn and turn the story and the triangle tells you different things. It tells you that art, inspired by love, can have a greater power than death. It tells you, contrariwise, that death, in spite of art, can defeat the power of love. And it tells you that art alone can make possible the transaction between love and death that is at the center of all human life.

There is one story that crops up in several mythologies: the story of the moment when men have to learn to do without their gods. In Roberto Calasso's great study of Greek and Roman myth, *The Marriage of Cadmus and Harmony,* he tells us that that occasion, the nuptials of Cadmus, the inventor of the alphabet, and the nymph Harmonia, was the last time the gods descended from Olympus to join in human life. After that, we were on our own. In Nordic myth, when the World Tree, the great ash Yggdrasil, falls, the gods do battle with, destroy, and are destroyed by their appointed foes, and after that they are gone. The death of the gods demands that heroes, men, come forward to take their place. Here, in ancient Greek and Old Norse, are our oldest fables about growing up, about learning that a time must come when our parents, our teachers, our guardians, can no longer command and protect us. There is a time to leave wonderland and grow up.

THE CHILDREN OF TRISTRAM Shandy, to use Kundera's term—or the children of Quixote, or of Scheherazade—may not be as plentiful as those of Clarissa Harlowe, but you will find them in every literature, in every place, in every time. From the bedeviled Moscow of Bulgakov's *The Master and Margarita* to the dybbuk-ridden villages of Isaac Bashevis Singer; from the French Surrealists to the American Fabulists; from Jonathan Swift to Carmen Maria Machado, Karen Russell, and Helen Oyeyemi, they are everywhere, forming an alternative, joyous, carnivalesque "great tradition" to set alongside the realistic one. The best-known such writers in recent literary history were the South American practitioners of so-called magic realism. The term "magic realism" is valuable when it's used to describe the writers of the Latin American Boom: Julio Cortázar, Alejo Carpentier, Manuel Puig, Carlos Fuentes, Isabel Allende, and, of course, Gabriel García Márquez, as well as perhaps their forebears Juan Rulfo, Jorge Luis Borges, and Machado de Assis. But it's a problematic term, because when it's used, most people equate it with the fantasy fiction genre. And, as I've been trying to argue, the literature of the fantastic is not genre fiction but, in its own way, as realistic as naturalistic fiction; it just comes into the real through a different door. A naturalistic novel is entirely capable of being escapist: Read a little chick lit and you'll see what I mean.

The truth is not arrived at by purely mimetic means. An image can be captured by a camera or by a paintbrush. A painting of a starry night is no less truthful than a photograph of one; arguably, if the painter is Van Gogh, it's far more truthful, even though far less "realistic." (I say Van Gogh, you say VanGo, as if he were a competitor to U-Haul, but the Dutch, you should know, call him Van Ghogh, which sounds like a man expectorating a stream of betel juice into a Bombay gutter. Practice that.) The literature of the fantastic—the wonder tale, the fable, the folktale, the magic-realist novel—has always embodied profound truths about human beings, their finest attributes and their deepest prejudices too: about, to take just one example, women.

Some of the most brilliant practitioners and critics of the modern wonder tale, like the novelist and story writer Angela Carter and the British critic and novelist Marina Warner, have eloquently investigated the place of women in wonderland, where they are repositories of ultimate virtue (the imprisoned princess) or ultimate vice (the witch). As I personally don't have much time for princesses in need of rescuing, I will focus here on the witches. Warner points out that the iconography of the witch has always been entirely domestic. The pointed hat was common headgear in the Middle Ages, the broomstick was to be found in every household, and even the witch's supposed demonic "familiar" spirit was usually no more than a cat. The mark of the witch—the supposed third nipple or "witch's tit," upon which the devil could suck—could be found on the bodies of many women in times when moles and warts were commonplace. All that was needed, in fact, was an accusation. Point a finger and call a woman a witch and the proofs were there in almost every home.

The conventional image of the witch was that of an ugly woman, a bent and misshapen hag or crone, and this is the witch we find in the Grimm stories. But in one Grimm story at least—*Schneewittchen*, or "Snow White," with its wicked queen gazing into the magic mirror on her wall and asking her lethal question, "Who's the fairest one of all?"—we see the arrival of what will become, in Renaissance art and literature, a more prevalent motif: the beautiful witch. (In fact, the beautiful witch is found much earlier too, in Greek mythology, for example, where the sorceress Circe can be found ensnaring Odysseus and his men, turning many of his crew into pigs. Circe also traveled to India and showed up in the *Katha Sarit Sagara* of Somadeva, the same story compendium to which I referred earlier, the Kashmiri "Ocean of the Streams of Story," where she becomes a demoness whose magic flute turns men into beasts.)

This bringing together of two kinds of female power, erotic power and occult power, in the image of the beautiful witch—this replacement of the hag by the enchantress—reached its peak in the High Renaissance, when Ariosto filled his long narrative poem *Orlando Furioso* with such women, and when the artists of the period—Dosso Dossi's *Circe* comes to mind—returned over and over, one might almost say obsessively, to the theme. When I wrote my novel *The Enchantress of Florence*, I tried to look at what it might have meant for actual women to be thought capable of such double enchantment, for sex to be linked, in this way, to magic. On the one hand, it was clear, such a linkage apparently increased the power of these women. The "enchantress" in my novel, believed to be capable of working miracles, comes close to sainthood, and even the Medici pope in Rome is half persuaded of her sanctity. Also, she can make men weak at the knees with desire, on account of her exceptional physical beauty. But the suspicion of witchcraft has, as I have suggested, historically been very dangerous for women, and if the wind changes, if the public mood shifts, the same people who venerated you as a saint yesterday can come to burn you tomorrow, as the example of Saint Joan of Arc demonstrates. I too was writing about a woman walking along the knife-edge of this vulnerable power and eventually having to run for her life, and I was struck by how much of the literature of the fantastic deals with the fear of women and the veneration that is the illusory reverse of that fear.

In Sheldon Cashdan's study *The Witch Must Die,* he proposes that female characters are used in folktale as exemplars of the deadly sins: the vanity of the queen in "Snow White" ("mirror, mirror on the wall"); the envy of Cinderella, *Aschenputtel,* by her two Ugly Sisters; and the greed of the fisherman's wife in the Grimm story, culminating in her demand that she be made pope, which undoes the miracle of untold wealth granted to the fisherman by the talking flounder whose life he once spared. Everything vanishes—the palace, the jewels, the gold—and the fisherman and his wife are returned to the hovel (actually, the word used in the Grimm tale is "pisspot") in which they formerly lived.

THE WONDER TALE TELLS us truths about ourselves that are often unpalatable; it exposes bigotry, explores the libido, brings our deepest fears to light. Such stories are by no means intended simply for the amusement of children, and many of them were not originally intended for children at all. Sinbad the Sailor and Aladdin were not Disney characters when they started out on their journeys.

It is, however, a rich age in literature for children and young-hearted adults. From Sendak's place *Where the Wild Things Are* to Philip Pullman's post-religious otherworlds, from Narnia, which we reach through a wardrobe, to the strange worlds arrived at through a phantom tollbooth, from Hogwarts to Middle-earth, wonderland is alive and well. And in many of these adventures, including my own two contributions, it is children who grow into heroes, often to rescue the adult world; the children we were, the children who are still within us, the children who understand wonderland, who know the truth about stories, save the adults, who have forgotten those truths.

# PROTEUS

——

## Edward Bond and the
## Silence of Shakespeare

Now that i'm getting on a bit, i occasionally feel
like the Japanese poet-philosopher Basho, who, after many years
spent traveling in search of wisdom along the *Narrow Road to the
Deep North* in Edward Bond's play of that name, is asked what he has
learned, and replies, "I learned that there is nothing to learn in the
Deep North." Nothing to learn on the journey is the wisdom of the
journey, wisdom itself being the grand illusion.

Edward Bond was one of the great figures of the golden age of
British theater in the 1970s, his vision bleak and uncompromising but
always rich in drama. What people remember now about Edward
Bond is that he wrote a play called *Saved,* in which a baby was stoned
to death onstage, or, to be exact, actors threw stones at a pram in
which the audience was informed a baby was lying, although there
was no baby and even the stoniness of the stones is suspect, because
they were props, after all, and the fictionality of the enterprise was
clearly established by the fact that it all took place on a stage while
people, some well dressed, others not, London theatergoers being
capable of going either way, sat in cheap and expensive seats to watch
it happen, and this was not in gladiatorial Rome, after all, not even in
London back in the day when crowds would gather at what is now
Marble Arch to cheer the hangings taking place at what was then

Tyburn Tree; no, this was the Royal Court Theatre in Sloane Square, and outside the theater was "swinging London," swinging as hard as it could, swinging, as the song had it, like a pendulum do. Now, the fictionality of fiction is an important matter; it lies at the heart of the transaction, the contract, between the work and its audience, the work confessing its untruth while promising to uncover truth, the audience suspending its disbelief in what it knows is not to be believed and so discovering material that is worth believing in. This is what people do when they experience literature on a stage or in a book, but they forget they are doing it, or if they remember they don't think it's important, they think it's *natural,* even though it's the opposite, it's *unnatural,* it's an artifice, *artificial.* The act of reading or viewing is also a creative act, a participation in fiction, *clap hands if you believe in fairies,* and without it the magic doesn't work, and Tinker Bell dies. Children know this, but people grow up and forget, just as the little Darlings forgot Peter Pan.

People remember scandal, don't they, so they remember Edward Bond's stoned baby. They don't so much remember, for instance, Bond's extraordinary play *Lear,* which took on Shakespeare in a heavyweight prizefight and somehow went the distance, failed to get steamrollered, and came out of the battle with what is called a draw in England and, in an oddly sartorial image, a tie in America. People don't remember, or perhaps they do, perhaps a few people remember, Edward Bond's play *Bingo,* in which Shakespeare himself shows up, because for writers there's no escape from the fellow. (I myself have a brass door knocker in the shape of a bust of Shakespeare on my study door, so that every day when I go in to work, I can knock on my door and tell myself to come in and know that I'm entering not my domain but his, Shakespeare's, whom no door knocker can limit or contain, who leaps off the door knocker and takes possession of the room behind the door, ruling it as he rules all the rooms in literature's poor, rich house.)

Edward Bond's Shakespeare, in the play *Bingo,* which maybe people remember and maybe they don't, gets drunk with Ben Jonson,

Edward Bond's Ben Jonson, who has come up to visit Shakespeare in his mysterious Stratford retirement, to penetrate a secret as profound as the mystery of his genius—namely, the secret of his silence.

(People spend a lot of time on the wrong mystery, the un-mystery of who wrote Shakespeare's plays, Francis Bacon or Christopher Marlowe or, my personal favorite, *not William Shakespeare but another person of the same name,* but the plain truth is that obviously Shakespeare was Shakespeare. It may be unbearable that an autodidact provincial actor-cum-scribbler who couldn't spell his own name was Shakespeare, but that is who he was.)

Edward Bond understood that the silence of Shakespeare is the interesting mystery, the decision of the greatest genius in the history of English literature to walk away from that genius, at the height of his career, to give up writing and acting and theater managing and Southwark, the lowlife zone of theaters and gambling dens and whorehouses and cockfights, which he must have loved, because even after he became the most successful playwright of the age he never left it for more salubrious neighborhoods, and when he did move it wasn't very far. Then all of a sudden, sometime in 1613, he decided his work was done and dropped everything and returned to Stratford without so much as a backward look and lived on for three years of philistine but apparently contented bourgeois provincial life, life with Anne Hathaway, life and death with Anne, to whom in his will he left his second-best bed, which may not be as insulting as it sounds because, according to some scholars, in an Elizabethan bourgeois household such as Shakespeare and Anne's, the best bed was kept apart in case some mighty visitor came to stay, kept pristine and un-used in case of an earl's unexpected descent, or even a queen's or a king's, while the second-best bed was the marital bed, the bed in which they made love, Mistress Hathaway and the genius who couldn't spell his own name, writing it, on one occasion in those days before formalized orthography and spelling bees, as Chackspaw.

The silence of Shakespeare: the domesticated stilling of the song of sweet Will, the magician who, like Prospero, the magician he created, left his isle full of noises, broke his staff and abjured his art, and why? We don't know. He didn't leave us reasons. But if we trust his genius, then we can guess that the last insight of that genius was the realization that he had finished, that it was time to stop. And so he stopped, in an act of magnificent, though not sweet, will.

He left us no letters, no diaries, no first drafts, no commonplace books, no autobiography, nothing except the work, the inexhaustible work. This too was part of the genius of Shakespeare, to make sure that his silence would outlast him by destroying his stumblings, his workings-out, his hesitations and explanations, and he must have done it himself, because if you're going to destroy such materials, you have to do it yourself; don't ask anyone to do it for you after you've gone, because they won't, they'll do what Max Brod did to or for Kafka, they'll publish the stuff you wanted burned, against your express wishes they'll publish *The Trial, The Castle, Amerika,* the *Letters to Felice,* and the *Letters* to the other girl as well—*to Milena,* that was it.

But maybe Kafka knew what would happen, because he and Max had had a conversation about it, and Max Brod had told him that if named as his executor he would not destroy the unpublished work, and in spite of that, Kafka went ahead and named Brod as his executor and asked him to "burn everything," the letters to Milena and Felice, as well as *The Trial, The Castle,* and *Amerika,* asked him to do it while knowing full well he would not.

But Shakespeare was different, he wasn't like Kafka, most of whose masterworks lay unpublished until after his death; Shakespeare had said what he had to say, the poems had been written and the plays had been staged, and then having chosen silence he was determined not to speak again, not even after his death. He didn't want the half-things to be read, the wrong things, didn't want to be interpreted and explicated through the study of the workings of his mind but only through the work itself, the inexhaustible, inexplicable work. He fell silent because he had nothing to say, he burned the years that were left to him as if they were manuscripts, and he gave no sign that he minded; up there in Stratford he seemed quite content, never returning to London, never as far as we know even going to see a play, ceasing to be the person he had been, and not minding, staying, instead, with Anne. In Edward Bond's play *Bingo,* Shakespeare is visited by Ben Jonson and they go out drinking and get royally drunk and on the way home Shakespeare catches a chill and dies, but not before he has told Ben Jonson how much he envies his good reviews, not before Ben Jonson has told him how much he envies his popularity, because they are both under the curse of literature, never to be satisfied with what they have, even if they are the authors of *Volpone* and *The Alchemist, Hamlet* and *King Lear,* even if they are Jonson and Shakespeare.

Edward Bond and his Shakespeare are writers who, like Kafka, long ago entered my personal tradition, the only tradition that's worth a damn to a practicing writer being the one he forges for himself, that is not laid down by high priests of literature, not a stone-carved commandment brought down from Sinai or the Cambridge University English faculty by a Leavisite Moses but a pagan thing, a melting down of treasures, a golden calf. Or, let's say, a thing born of the happenstance of a life led in the fields of the word, born of the happy and—even better—the *useful* contaminations by others of the writer's reading mind.

I acted in a play by Jonson once, playing Pertinax Surly in an undergraduate production of *The Alchemist* performed in the cloisters of Jesus College, Cambridge, the exact spot where the first production of the play had taken place some four hundred years before, or so I was told. I acted in Jonson but he hasn't remained useful to me, whereas Shakespeare is both my door knocker and the owner of the domains to which the knock admits me, at once my Virgil opening the gates of hell and heaven, and the devil, and God, and I say this as a person who believes in neither God nor the devil, I believe only in Virgil, but I understand the nature of the contract of fiction, so I can agree to suspend disbelief in what I know is not to be believed in the hope of finding, by doing so, some truth on which I can rely, in which I can have faith.

## Howard Brenton, and Shakespeare as Proteus

As a matter of fact he's not only Edward Bond's Shakespeare; he belongs in part to another playwright, Howard Brenton. I remember a thing Brenton said long ago in a room in New College, Oxford; he said—or at least this is the way I remember it, this is the golden calf I've made from whatever it was that actually came out of Brenton's mouth—that one of the greatest gifts given by Shakespeare to writers in the English language is his incredible freedom of form, a freedom not granted to, for example, French writers by, for example, Racine, who might have been a great playwright but his forms weren't free, they were classicist and straitjacket-like and confining, he was an artist in formal attire, wearing a wig and sipping fine wine, so to speak, whereas Shakespeare wore an open shirt and sat in a tavern, spilling ale.

Take *Hamlet*, for example. It's a ghost story, to begin by stating the obvious. "I am thy father's spirit," says the dead king, whose name is also Hamlet (at least it is in Shakespeare's play, even though in Saxo Grammaticus's *The History of the Danes*, from which Shakespeare pinched the plot, the name of Hamlet's father is not Hamlet but Horwendillus, a name worth changing, I think). So *Hamlet* is about one Hamlet and the ghost of another Hamlet, a play about a son haunted by his father, written by a father haunted by the ghost of a dead son named Hamnet, all of which allows Stephen Dedalus in *Ulysses* to have some sport with the play in a well-beloved and certainly well-lubricated lecture ("Wait till I have a few pints in me first," Buck Mulligan pleads) in which he "proves by algebra that Hamlet's grandson is Shakespeare's grandfather and that he himself is the ghost of his own father." So, a ghost story, yes, but not only a ghost story, because it keeps changing form, becoming, by turns, a murder story, and a political drama about intrigues at the Danish court and the threat of invasion by Fortinbras, and a psychodrama about indecision, and a revenge tragedy, and a tragic love story, and a postmodernist play about a play, a play called *Hamlet* containing a play called *The Mousetrap*, which tells the story of a regicide just like the regicide in the story of *Hamlet* . . . but it's still a ghost story, still the story of a dead father howling for vengeance, and this is what Brenton meant, I think, by the freedom that is Shakespeare's gift to those of us who have the temerity to follow him into the English language: He meant that Shakespeare's great example gives us permission to create work that is many things at once, shape-shifting, a work that doesn't have to be either a ghost story or a love story or a cross-dressing burlesque comedy or a history play or a psychodrama but can be all those things at once, without sacrificing truth or depth or passion or shapeliness or interest, without becoming a confusing, bewildering, shallow, pointless mess. Or take *Macbeth:* the witches, Banquo's ghost, the vision of the dagger, all that hocus-pocus, all that magic, in one of the most savagely truthful plays ever written about power, a play so frightening, with such power to conjure demons, that you're not supposed to speak its name within the walls of a theater: "the Scottish Play," that realistic masterpiece about the battle for what Akira Kurosawa in his samurai movie remake called the *Throne of Blood*.

The adjective for this kind of literature is "protean."

It may be a higher-risk strategy, this protean approach to literature, but doesn't that make it more attractive rather than less? Didn't Randall Jarrell say that a novel is a long prose narrative that has something wrong with it?

(Parenthetically, I became afraid that this was another of my golden calves and Randall Jarrell didn't actually say anything of the sort, or didn't quite, just as André Malraux never said that the twenty-first century should be the age of religion—everyone says he said it, but he actually said the opposite, that it shouldn't—and just as Mae West in *She Done Him Wrong* never quite says, "Come up and see me sometime," and Ingrid Bergman in *Casablanca* never quite says, "Play it again, Sam." So I checked, and it turns out that Randall Jarrell either said what I say he said, or else, in Michael Hofmann's version in *The New York Review of Books,* he said a novel was "sixty thousand words of discursive prose with something wrong with it," or, in a recent third version, in *New York* magazine, he called it "a work in prose of a certain length that has something wrong with it," so he definitely said "something wrong with it," and definitely meant that to apply to the contents of novels. So not a golden calf, then, but something approaching a fact, although the search reminds one of the difficulties of precision, of establishing *exactly* what was said and when. Ah, but here's the original—it's in Jarrell's introduction to Christina Stead's novel *The Man Who Loved Children:* "A novel," he says, "is a prose narrative of some length that has something wrong with it." Ah, the satisfaction of being right in the first place, of offering up a quotation that has nothing wrong with it! Facts, it seems, offer us pleasures too.)

So: If a novel or indeed a play is bound to have "something wrong with it," then let it at least be a wonderful wrongness, speaking of the strangeness of the world's beauty, a wrongness that seeks to wipe from our eyes and cleanse from our ears the dull patina and muffling wax of the everyday, which makes us see reality as monochromatic and hear it as monotonous, and to reveal the rainbow music of how things really are. Let it be a play or indeed a novel containing bright moments, dark changes, living characters, sudden transformations, images of fire and ice, horrifying metamorphoses, luminous insights, comic alterations, and stories that have nothing wrong with them at all.

Knocking on my study door, telling myself to go in, I thank my two-inch brass Shakespeare for his idea of the protean. He may be just a door ornament, but he's on to something, in my view. Let us remember Proteus, the Old Man of the Sea. "Proteus, of sea-green hue, traverses the mighty main in his car drawn by fishes and a team of two-footed steeds," Virgil writes in the *Georgics*. Proteus, who knew all that had been, was now, and lay in store, was reluctant to tell anyone what he knew and assumed new forms to avoid giving up his secrets. He could turn himself into "a young man, a lion, a boar, a serpent, a bull, a stone, a tree, water, flame, or whatever he pleases." But he didn't always conceal truth; he also sometimes revealed it— for example, when he told the mortal Peleus how to capture the sea nymph Thetis, the beautiful silver-footed nereid Thetis, also a metamorph, "and though she take a hundred lying forms," Proteus advises Peleus in Ovid's *Metamorphoses*, "let her not escape you, but hold her close, whatever she may be, until she take again the form she had at first," which Peleus does and captures Thetis, and the magnificent result of their coupling is Achilles, although Thetis knows she hasn't been seduced without help—"It is not without some god's assistance that you conquer," she tells Peleus—but too late, Achilles is already on his way, thanks to the revelations of metamorphic Proteus, and it is this idea of the protean that I like, not the concealing but the revelatory. This is what Shakespeare was on about, Shakespeare who knew all that had been, was now, and lay in store, and used his metamorphic art to lay it bare, the present, future, and the past.

The point about the protean in literature, the point Shakespeare grasped and allowed all of us who follow him to grasp as well, is that *life's like that*, life itself is not one thing but many, not singular but multiform, not constant but infinitely mutable. It's a ghost story and a love story and a political saga and a family saga, it's comedy and tragedy at the same time, it's *not realistic*, not in the sense in which that word is used by those who sit in judgment over such things, not realistic in that sense at all. Family life isn't "realistic" either. We pretend it is, we all do, inventing one of the governing fictions of what gets called "reality," the fiction of Ordinary Life. We all pretend that these Ordinary Lives are the lives we "really" have, the lives we "really" lead, but we all secretly know the truth, which is that once we get through the front door of the family and close it behind us, it's mayhem in there, it isn't Ordinary at all, it's overblown and operatic and monstrous and almost too much to bear; there are mad grandfathers in there, and wicked aunts and corrupt brothers and nymphomaniac sisters, there are young men who refuse to eat their disgusting lunch and retreat instead into the trees, to remain there for the rest of their days, like the title character in Calvino's *The Baron in the Trees;* there are giant Rabelaisian families, Gargantuan, Pantagruelian, giant belchers, breakers of giant winds, and there are screaming boys of stunted growth beating on tin drums, as Oskar Matzerath does in Grass's great novel, boys who choose to remain small, dwarfed by the horror of their times, and there are mothers like Úrsula Iguarán, the matriarch of *One Hundred Years of Solitude,* the sane center of an insane world; there are untimely deaths and bizarre accidents, there's jealousy and incest and bitter lifelong hatred, injuries are inflicted from which we never recover, even when in our turn we inflict such injuries upon others, and it's noisy and inquisitive in there, inside the Family, and sometimes we flee from it, we cross continents and oceans to escape it and then, very carefully, we build a new version of it for ourselves, because the trouble with trying to escape from yourself is that you take yourself along for the ride. Oh, and there's love and care and support and tenderness also, yes, I don't forget that. Families have those things too, yes.

So this is what I like to argue when I'm sitting in an open shirt in a tavern, spilling ale: I like to argue that reality isn't realistic, and so I prefer this other kind of literature, what one might call the protean tradition, which is more realistic than realism, because it corresponds to the unrealism of the world.

## Proteus and Other Metamorphoses

The "real" is an idea of the world, a description or picture of it, just like the "unreal." You might even say it's an article of faith, like money or fairies: People have to believe in it or else it doesn't exist. If you don't believe the greenback in your pocket is worth one dollar, then it's just a scrap of paper, a dead fairy, unreal. "By the same token," as we like to say in India, if you don't believe in a given description of the world, you refuse to call it "real"; you call it, instead, a lie. The line between reality and fiction is not sharp; it's blurry and smudged. A description of the world contains facts, certainly, and facts, as we've seen, are fluttery, elusive creatures, but there are armies of fact lepidopterists chasing after them, and sometimes they do get nailed to the wall, like moths. So inside any given "reality," a given picture of the world, there will be a number of nailed-down facts—the name of the president, the age of your spouse, the place occupied by your favorite sports team in the weekly standings—but there will also, often, be nailed-down fictions—common prejudices, ignorances, mistakes, and items of state propaganda (which comes these days in a range of attractive colors)—masquerading as facts. Once, I don't have to remind anyone, it was a fact that the world was flat. Funny what one takes for granted. The world is flat, your home is your castle, God is great, your parents love you, the Red Sox will (almost) always find a way to lose, and you're not going to wake up one day to find yourself transformed into a giant dung beetle. When you live inside a picture of the world, everything in you and in the picture itself insists that this is how it is, this is the world and not something else, and there is nothing outside the frame.

Then one day the picture of the world breaks. You wake up one morning and find that you have indeed been transformed into a giant dung beetle. Or Hitler invades Poland. Or you're an advertising executive who looks like Cary Grant and you're mistaken for someone else, someone who looks like Cary Grant, and a few scenes later you're being chased by crop-duster aircraft and hanging off Mount Rushmore. Or someone must have been telling lies about you the way they did about Joseph K., because you get arrested one fine morning and nobody tells you why. Or you're a distinguished West German novelist, happily married, and one day you discover that your beloved wife of thirty years has been a Communist spy all along and the marriage was just her "front." Or you look away from your child in a supermarket, just for a few seconds, and the next minute the child is gone and with it everything you thought of as your real life. Or terrorist planes fly into the Twin Towers and your innocence dies along with your sense of safety, along with the thousands of dead. Funny what one takes for granted, until one doesn't. Or how does it feel to be Raymond Carver being told by your doctor that you have inoperable lung cancer? "I may even have thanked him," Carver writes, "habit being so strong."

As I say, it's funny what we take for granted and how solid we believe the world to be, when actually people break up and die and lose their jobs and change; they, we, never stop changing, metamorphosis begins to look like the only constant, the only real realism, but that's a problem if your idea of the real has to do with constancy and stability, if you want the world to be a cube of steel whereas in fact it's a wriggling amoeba, it's an egg frying in a pan. Go into a bar in New York, or into a pub in Manchester, England, or into a coffeehouse in Connaught Place, New Delhi, or even onto the so-called Arab Street, and what you'll hear wherever you go is disagreement. We can't even agree about the Yankees' starting rotation, how are we going to agree about the world? Here's this world we have, not flat, not anymore, we know that, but can we agree what it actually is? Round, okay, it's roundish, but beyond that? More and more it's a place where people argue, where they don't agree, where one man's liberation is another man's imperialism, where battle lines are drawn in the sand, across glaciers, through the hearts of broken cities, where a great dispute is in progress about the nature of reality, about *what is the case;* there are worlds in collision, incompatible realities fighting for the same space, and the result, often, is violence.

This is what I'm wrestling with, this great shapeless mutating blob that can't even agree with itself about what it actually is, this is what I'm trying to give shape to, and speaking for myself, speaking now not so much as a writer but as a reader, I'd rather put my trust in the writers who acknowledge the battle, who make you see that any shape they impose on the blob is only provisional, that their own picture of the world gets in the way, that it's hard to step outside the frame. Better to trust them, on the whole, than the ones who pretend that the world is as solid as a rock, even though rocks crumble, or as safe as houses, even though houses totter and explode.

In a world as unstable as this, give me literary instability every time, or at least some recognition of it, some recognition of how the world can be rocked by earthquakes, war, or chance, where there's no mistake about reality, where there's a facing up to the nature of the beast.

Proteus.

Proteus was by no means the only metamorph around in the old days, Zeus himself being partial to a spot of shape-shifting, especially when pursuing ladies—a bull for Europa, a swan for Leda, which is why his daughter Helen, Helen of Troy, was born from an egg. In India, also, metamorphosis was a well-established divine activity. The god Vishnu had ten "primary" and fourteen other incarnations or "avatars," including a fish, a giant tortoise, a boar, and the gods Rama and Krishna. In general Vishnu when metamorphosed may be said to have had a broader range of interests than Zeus; his incarnations Rama and Krishna were certainly involved in immortal love stories with Sita and Radha, but they did also have other fish to fry, both martial and philosophical. It is not stretching the point too much to say that the birth of literature, certainly the birth of the protean tradition of literature that I seek to celebrate, was a valuable side effect of the metamorphic proclivities of the gods, because without that swan there would have been no Helen and without Helen no Trojan War, my conviction being that it was Helen's war, even if the modern revisionist reading sees the conflict in terms of the power politics of the region and elevates Agamemnon's greed above the enormous sexual and erotic power of Helen of Troy. This seems to me to miss the point.

Let's be clear about this: Technically speaking, according to the facts, it was Agamemnon who sacrificed his daughter Iphigenia to the gods to persuade them to send the becalmed Greek fleet a helpful wind, it was Agamemnon who launched the thousand ships and subsequently, after long siege and great deeds by many on both sides, burned the topless towers of Ilium; but here we encounter an instructive difference between fact and truth, which is also, interestingly enough, the difference between history and literature, and the truth, the truth of literature, is that Agamemnon didn't launch those ships, Helen did, and she burned the towers too, the flames that rose over Troy being the blazing manifestations of her power, the power of the most desirable woman in the world.

Here is Helen walking below the belly of the Trojan horse and caressing it, actually caressing the wood, and the sexual heat of her caress transmits itself to the soldiers hidden inside. This is a completely surrealistic, "impossible" image, but we understand it at once because we understand what Helen is capable of—a thousand-ship-launcher can certainly turn on a wooden horse, can transmit sexual heat through wood to the soldiers hidden inside and arouse them all, one of them so powerfully that Odysseus has to kill him, actually throttle him with his bare hands, to stop him from crying out. Read that and tell me this isn't a story about a woman's power. Without Zeus's metamorphosed seduction of Helen's mother, we'd have none of this, no Homer, no *Iliad,* no *Odyssey,* and turning to the East it's the same story: Vishnu-as-Krishna is not only one of the leading players in the *Mahabharata* but also the ostensible author of the *Bhagavad Gita,* while the exploits of Vishnu-as-Rama gave us the *Ramayana* as well.

I go back to the old stories many times, I drink at those ancient unpolluted wells, in part because when one is deeply affected by the contemporary, when a good deal of one's thinking has to do with puzzling out how to fashion into coherent work one's vision of contemporary life, that giant mutating blob I mentioned, it helps to be reminded of what has endured, of what has claims to being called eternal, to sit and learn at the feet of what persists. But also there is just something joyful about, for example, discovering in the ancient Norse texts that in the beginning there was a giant cow, the cow Audumla, lying at the bottom of a bottomless chasm, the Ginnungagap, the Yawning between the lands of Muspelheim and Niflheim, the lands of fire and ice, and nourishing the giant Ymir, who suckled at her udders. While Ymir was suckling, the cow Audumla, in search of nourishment or entertainment, licked away at the salty ice at the bottom of the Ginnungagap and by her licking formed the figure of Buri, who became the grandfather of the gods Odin, Vili, and Ve, and when the gods grew up they killed Ymir the giant and used the various parts of his body to create the world, using his blood to make the sea, his bones to raise the mountains, his flesh to make the earth, and his skull for the sky. They even used the four maggots that appeared on the body of the dead giant, who took the form of four dwarfs called North, South, East, and West, giving each of them a corner of the sky to hold up, and then they made Ask and Embla, the first people, from the branches of an ash and an elm tree that grew by the sea.

It gives one a sense of historical perspective, does it not, it adds to one's understanding of the human condition, when one knows we're only here because of a hungry cow.

I have a soft spot for the polytheistic pantheons, partly because the stories are so much better in polytheism than in monotheism, partly because monotheistic deities are so, well, *inhuman*. The traditions I like are the ones in which the gods behave badly. The Greek and Roman deities are particularly good at seriously bad behavior. They are vain, thin-skinned, vengeful, partisan, lustful, drunken, jealous, bullying, cruel. Who could fail to be charmed by such a bunch, by Zeus the serial rapist, or vindictive Athena, or Dionysus the capricious drunk? What an improvement on the moral exemplars of the great monotheisms, those stern, unyielding policemen of the soul! The gods of Greece and Rome, very sensibly, are uninterested in the puritanical business of setting us an example. They do not say to us, "Do as we do," or "Think as we think." They leave us free to act and think, just as they insist on being themselves. All they require of us is that we worship them. In other words, they behave exactly like fictional characters, who may not exactly need to be worshipped but who are certainly keen on being loved, or at least becoming the subjects or objects of our fascination.

The gods were unlike fictional characters in their heyday, in the days when people actually believed in them, the days when the Greek myths were the Greek religion and the Roman myths were the Roman religion and you could have terrible things done to you for speaking the way I'm speaking now, because what is now a pleasant literary discussion would then have been the sin of blasphemy. One could wish that one or two of the current crop of monotheisms would decay to the point at which what is now considered blasphemy might turn into a pleasant literary discussion, but no such luck, or not yet. Anyway, the old Greek and Roman gods were vengeful types; they didn't need mere humans to do their dirty work, they did it themselves with considerable relish, imposing dreadful sanctions on us if we failed to worship them, or if we didn't do it often enough or well enough, or if, God forbid, we defied them: They could punish us; they could turn us into spiders like Arachne or, like Prometheus, bind us to a pillar and set a great bird to eat our liver for all eternity, the liver magically regenerating as it was consumed; they could becalm our fleets and demand that our children be sacrificed and burn our cities. Still, all that's over now, happily, and only the books remain.

Proteus.

He was a very practical god, a good god for writers to pay attention to, full of technical solutions to life's problems, and one of the things writers know is that *all literary problems are technical problems.* Aristaeus the beekeeper, the same fellow who lustfully pursued Eurydice across a field in which she was bitten by a snake and died, forcing Orpheus to follow her into the underworld, Aristaeus for whom one consequently feels a certain lack of sympathy, went to Proteus and asked him for a way of getting hold of even more bees than he already had. Proteus told him to sacrifice cattle to the gods, and when Aristaeus did so, out of their rotting corpses poured, yes, great swarms of bees. Proteus's advice, when he could be persuaded to give it, was invariably worth taking.

Poseidon tended to be the sea god who got all the headlines; people never paid much attention to Proteus then. But I'm suggesting we should start doing so now, because the idea of the protean is the foundation of what I'm calling the other great tradition, the one that isn't trapped in a mistake about the real, the mistake being to see the real as ordinary when in fact it's extraordinary, to see it as moderate when in fact it's extreme, to see it not as it is, which is to say full of wonderments, but as merely naturalistic instead. If one clings to the idea of the protean, one will avoid all these mistakes and understand further that realism in the novel is not a question of following certain rules, that it has nothing to do with naturalism or mimicry, a novel not being like a photograph but more like an oil painting, or possibly in the case of the best novels a great fresco covering the walls and ceiling of a mighty palace, and so realism in the novel isn't a question of technique; it is, in my opinion, a question of intention. That is to say, if the intention of the artist, the writer, is to make as true and honest a response to the world as he can, if it be his intention to use the best powers of language and imagination to create a vision arising out of his sense of what it is to be alive in the world, and if he be faithful to that intention, then what he makes will be a work of realism, whether it be filled with dragons and broomsticks or with kitchen sinks and offices. Van Gogh's painting of a starry night doesn't look like a photograph of a starry night or, indeed, what a starry night looks like to the naked eye, but it is a great painting of a starry night all the same, and all who look upon it understand it to be true.

And when one lives at a hinge moment in history, as we do, as Shakespeare did when he wrote his protean plays, a moment when everything is in flux, everything is changing at immense speed, when the future is up for grabs and dark storm clouds rush across the sun, and when there are plagues and dragons loose in the world, then it becomes essential to admit that the old forms will not do, the old ideas will not do, because all must be remade, all, with our best efforts, must be rethought, reimagined, and rewritten, and to do otherwise would be to fail, most lamentably to fail, in the pursuit of our art.

# HERACLITUS

---

WHEN THE CARTOONIST CHARLES M. SCHULZ ANNOUNCED that he was going to stop drawing the *Peanuts* comic strip, he received a flood of reader requests, all asking for the same thing: "Please, just once before you stop, let Charlie Brown kick the football." But Schulz set his face against his readers' wishes and followed the logic of his characters instead. If Lucy van Pelt allowed Charlie Brown to kick the football, if she didn't whip it away at the last moment from his eternally trusting, eternally betrayed feet, then she would cease to be Lucy. If Charlie Brown kicked the football, he would no longer be Charlie Brown.

For Charlie Brown, and for Lucy, their *ethos*, as Heraclitus said two and a half thousand years ago, their way of being in the world, is their *daimon*, the guiding principle that shapes their lives. Charlie Brown must eternally fume with the disappointed knowledge of his own gullible innocence, and Lucy will always delight in proving that gullibility. They can do no other. Their characters have led their author. The author, having created them, is no longer omnipotent but bound by his creations. Pinocchio is no longer a marionette; he once had strings, but now he's free. He's a real, live boy.

Have you ever read Heraclitus? Stupid question, really; it's like asking, have you ever drunk wine out of a smashed bottle, or have you ever taken a good look at a famous old painting that has unfortunately been ripped to shreds? Reading Heraclitus is like that because there's so little of him left. His great book survived the Persian, Greek, and Roman empires and was praised by Socrates and Plato and Aristotle and Marcus Aurelius, then managed to get itself lost, and all that remains of him are quotations in the works of other writers, some in the original Greek, some paraphrased or translated into Latin, just a few broken potsherds numbered from 1 to 130 like fragments in a drawer in a museum. It's as if the complete works of William Shakespeare got lost and all we had left were one hundred and thirty decontextualized lines, and we didn't know if these were his greatest hits or just words that had avoided oblivion by chance.

The fragments included in the most recent collection, appropriately called *Fragments,* obviously retain considerable power, influencing Montaigne, Nietzsche, Heidegger, and Jung; and, if we accept the argument of his latest translator, the elegant and scholarly Haxton of Syracuse—that's Brooks Haxton, poet, of Syracuse, New York—then we can agree that "an early and abiding influence on Christian thought is famously transparent in the Heraclitean language that opens the Gospel According to John: 'in the beginning was the Word.'" Heraclitus was a great fan of the Word; "All things follow from the Word," he said, and again, "For wisdom, listen / not to me but to the Word, and know that all is one." *Logos* was the word he used, a word that originally meant more than the Word, Brooks Haxton reminds us; it meant "all means of making ideas known, as well as ideas themselves, the phenomena to which ideas respond, and the rules that govern both phenomena and ideas." Or, as the evangelist John put it, writing in Greek: "The Word [*logos*] was with God, and the Word was God."

This is good news for novelists, because if the Word is with God, then what does that make us? My only difficulty is that Heraclitus comes across as something of a mixed bag, part wise man, part fortune cookie:

> "Men dig tons of earth
> to find an ounce of gold." (#8)

"Things keep their secrets." (#9)

"Wisdom is the oneness
of mind that guides
and permeates all things." (#19)

"Without the sun,
what day? What night?" (#31)

"What was scattered gathers.
What was gathered blows apart." (#40)

"An ass prefers a bed of litter to a golden
    throne." (#51)

"The way up is the way back." (#69)

"The beginning is the end." (#70)

"Goat cheese melted
in warm wine congeals
if not well stirred." (#84)

(That's a good one.)

"People need not act and speak as if they were asleep."
    (#94)

"The ape apes find most beautiful looks apish
to non-apes." (#99)

It's hard to take some of this stuff seriously, although there are
many people, wise people, who take it very seriously indeed, and to
these wise people one is tempted to say:

"Stupidity is better kept a secret
than displayed." (#109)

And yet, and yet. Heraclitus was a remarkable fellow by all accounts, the contemporary though probably not the friend of Pythagoras, Lao Tzu, Confucius, and the Buddha, and he was a genuine seeker after truth. Like the Buddha, he was born a prince, in his case in and of Ephesus, and like the Buddha, he renounced power in order to seek what he would have called wisdom (*sophos*), which the Buddha called enlightenment. And some of the fragments have plenty to say to me. For example:

"People dull their wits with gibberish and cannot use their
ears and eyes," (#4)

or:

"The eye, the ear,
the mind in action, these I value," (#13)

although obviously I'm disappointed to hear him say:

"Now that we can travel anywhere, we need no longer
take the poets
and mythmakers for sure witnesses
about disputed facts." (#14)

And then there's fragment #121, which has attained the status of one of the grand self-evident truths about life, fragment #121, which tells us, as it told Charlie Brown, that a man's *ethos* is his *daimon*, or, in plainer language, that a man's character is his fate. "Character is destiny." The key to the art of the novel in seven syllables, or so people have long believed. Captain Ahab's character, driven, obsessive, fixated on the whale to the point of selling his soul for the right to kill it—"From hell's heart I stab at thee"—makes his death inevitable. There he is at last, lashed to his prey by harpoon ropes and drowned, the two of them bound together, man and whale, inseparable in life and death. The survivor of the wreck of the *Pequod*, the one who lives to tell the tale, is the disengaged figure of Ishmael, or at least we think that's his name; "Call me Ishmael," he tells us, not "I am Ishmael" or "Ishmael is my name." Ishmael may be an alias, like the name "Alias" adopted by the character played by Bob Dylan in Sam Peckinpah's great Western *Pat Garrett and Billy the Kid.* "Call me Alias," Dylan says, playing Ishmael to Pat Garrett's Ahab (Billy the Kid being, I suppose, the hunted whale), and when Garrett asks if that's his name, he replies, with an opaque little Bob Dylan smile, "You can call me that." So, call-me-Ishmael, the outsider, the one who doesn't buy into the passion and fervor, the grand obsession, of the quest for Moby Dick, Ishmael survives, because survival is the game he's in; it's his character, so it's his fate. Ahab, because it's his fate, because it's what he wants, goes knocking on heaven's door.

Then there's character as refusal—the refusal, for example, of Bartleby, the Scrivener, who prefers not to, without ever giving a reason or even a hint of an explanation. But can Bartleby actually be called a character or is he simply that refusal, enigmatic, infuriating, important for its effect on others and not for itself? I think he can, because the refusals are not random; they cohere. Bartleby has needs. He is homeless and close to penniless and is living secretly in the scrivener's office, and when he is surprised there *en déshabillé,* he prefers not to let his employer enter until he has tidied himself. He has too a strong sense of himself as a worker, laboring assiduously at his copying but preferring not to go over his work with anyone else. His professional pride may be misplaced, but it reveals that this is a man who sets boundaries in his life. He will do this, he will not do that, and he will politely adhere to his private rules, whatever the consequences for himself. Is he, then, some sort of passive-aggressive zealot? I don't think so, because he has no ideas to impose on anyone else. In the face of poverty and even death he has chosen the path of dignity, preferring not to deviate from it, and accepts his fate. So if character is destiny, then the characteristic of acceptance is as potent as that of refusal. Bartleby both refuses and accepts. He prefers not to, but he also, silently, prefers.

I'm thinking too about another refusal, the refusal of Michael Kohlhaas the horse trader, in the great story by Heinrich von Kleist that bears his name, to accept that justice will not be done. He insists only on what the law has decreed, that the two beautiful, glossy, well-nourished horses unjustly seized from him by Junker Wenzel von Tronka and allowed to decline into "a pair of scrawny, worn-out nags" should be returned to him in the same condition they were in when they were taken, along with his other lost possessions—a neckcloth, some imperial florins, and a bundle of washing; and when his small grievance is not addressed, he embarks on a course so violent that it half-destroys his world and himself as well. His character becomes his entire community's destiny as well as his own. But when, at the story's end, and after deeds of terrible violence have been done, he gains full restitution for his losses, he accepts that justice must also be done upon him for his own deeds. Having received satisfaction, Kohlhaas is prepared to make satisfaction to the state and submits without argument to the executioner's ax. Once again, refusal goes hand in hand with acceptance.

A century and a half after it was written, *Michael Kohlhaas* inspired the American novelist E. L. Doctorow, who based the character of Coalhouse Walker in *Ragtime* on Kohlhaas—Coalhouse Walker, the dandyish African American with the fancy car that gets wrecked by racists and who, like Michael Kohlhaas, insists on restitution, insists peacefully and civilly for as long as he can, beyond the limits of most men's patience, and only turns to extreme measures when modest ones have failed. A sense of injustice will drive a man to extremes—many of the world's present discontents can be attributed to such a sense—but what makes these men special, Kohlhaas, Coalhouse, Bartleby, is their belief in civility, their refusal to step toward incivility or violence until all other avenues have been exhausted, their preference for nonviolence, even though, in two of these three examples, there is violence aplenty lurking below the surface.

The almost karmic willingness to accept what life sends is also at the heart of the nature of Mr. Leopold Bloom, Odysseus recast as modern *picaro,* as the wandering, Irish, Quixotic Jew; Mr. Leopold Bloom, who "ate with relish the inner organs of beasts and fowls," who loves his wife in spite of her infidelities with Blazes Boylan; Bloom, who, after the sojourn in nighttown, brings Stephen home in the "Ithaca" chapter of *Ulysses,* the lost son Bloom never had, who's in search of a lost mother, and afterward, in bed with Molly, speaks to her of him, presents him to her for her pleasure, allowing her to intuit what he doesn't know himself: *hes an author and going to be a university professor of Italian,* Molly ruminates about Stephen, *and Im to take lessons what is he driving at now showing him my photo* . . . meaning Bloom, what is Bloom driving at, *I wonder he didnt make him a present of it altogether and me too . . . I suppose hes 20 or more Im not too old for him if hes 23 or 24.*

How poignant it is, at the end of Bloom's long day's journey into long night, near the end of the chapter's long catechism, and just before Molly's overwhelming voice is unleashed upon us, to discover that there's a refusal in Bloom too, a refusal beneath his acceptance: He accepts her infidelity because he refuses to lose her; he enters the marital bed and finds there "the imprint of a human form, male, not his," and lying beside his sleeping wife lists to himself the names of his wife's lovers, that list of which he is not even the last term, and experiences, sequentially, "envy, jealousy, abnegation, equanimity," and yet is aroused by her, loves her in spite of what he knows, and then, in that beautiful gesture in which the cuckold's humility joins with the husband's lust, kisses "the plump mellow yellow smellow melons of her rump, on each plump melonous hemisphere, in their mellow yellow furrow, with obscure prolonged provocative melon-smellonous osculation." And as for Molly Bloom, Molly the Yes, she's nothing but character-as-destiny, is soliloquizing Molly, nothing but fate, lying on her bed, sleeping, waking, doing, and remembering; no character was ever destiny more than she, everyone's destiny as well as her guiltless, sensual own.

So: Game, set, and match to Heraclitus, you may think. Character, destiny, the one leads to the other, and there you have it, nothing more to be said. Ah, but there is, there's plenty more, because Heraclitus's dictum doesn't take into account the liquid things about life, the gaseous things, the things about people and stories and language and perception and, yes, moral values that don't stay put, that aren't dependable. James Joyce, that creator of potently destined characters, agenbitten by inwit, knew the limitations of the flesh as he knew everything else, was a master of the shifting, the mutable, and near the beginning of *Ulysses* invoked the metamorphic Old Father Ocean, Proteus: "beware," as the book warns us, "of imitations."

There is, for example, the matter of chance. In the *Mahabharata,* King Yudhisthira, an addictive gambler, loses his wealth, his kingdom, the freedom of his brothers, and even his wife in a series of throws of the dice. So in a sense his character creates his destiny, but the thought remains: What if the dice had fallen differently? Yudhisthira's character didn't account for their random fall, and the suggestion in the *Mahabharata* that his opponent, Shakuni, was a master of the game, while Yudhisthira was a novice, is unconvincing; there's really no way to be a master of the dice. An explanation of human affairs that omits the influence of the unpredictable, the chaotic, the thing for which there is no reason, will never be a full explanation. For the want of a nail, a battle can be lost. A child falls from a third-floor window and gets up, miraculously unhurt; the same child falling from the same window on another occasion would be killed. We turn right through the crowd at a certain party on a certain night and meet the man or woman who becomes our spouse. If we had turned left, we might never have met them. A house is carried away by a whirlwind with a girl inside it and, when it lands, by chance squashes a witch whose magic ruby slippers will eventually take the girl home again. But what if the witch had not been squashed?

The religious writer sees, in chance, the workings of a divine hand. In *The Bridge of San Luis Rey,* Thornton Wilder sets himself the task of understanding the meaning of the deaths of five unconnected individuals, who just happened to be crossing the bridge when it collapsed. Why these particular people and not other people? The book rather heroically refuses to accept the answer that there was no reason, that it was just bad luck, and tries to understand the purposes of God. To an extent, we all do this; we don't like the idea that our lives can be changed by the vagaries of fortune, by good or bad luck, by things beyond anyone's power to control.

Yet chance exists. A far less religious writer than Wilder, the British novelist Ian McEwan has more than once used random life-changing events as the engines of his books: the theft of the child in the supermarket at the beginning of *The Child in Time;* the image of the escaped hot-air balloon and the group of strangers again, five unconnected individuals whose lives are linked by the ballooning accident in the opening chapter of *Enduring Love.* But, lacking the religious impulse, McEwan's stories do not search for the Almighty's hidden hand, for God moving in mysterious ways, as the hymn says he does, his wonders to perform. Instead, McEwan accepts the power of the unforeseeable to change human lives and looks hard not for hidden causes but rather at the events' effects on the lives they touched, which, certainly, are lived out according to the dictates of the characters of the characters, but everybody knows—we know, the author knows, and so do the characters—that because of the intervention of luck, there is an important sense in which their characters have not forged their destinies.

Paul Auster and Jerzy Kosinski, in their very different ways, are writers who pay a lot of attention to the workings of chance. Auster, like Vyasa, the Homer figure to whom the *Mahabharata* is ascribed, uses with relish the trope of gambling to change his characters' lives. The catastrophic poker game played by the central characters, Nashe and Pozzi, against the Pennsylvania recluses Flower and Stone in *The Music of Chance* actually recalls Yudhisthira's disaster. Kosinski, in his best book, *Being There,* allows his sweet idiot, "Chauncey Gardiner," whose very name is not his name but given to him by chance, to rise from a rich man's simpleminded servant to the consort of the grand and the adviser of the mighty. (In the movie of *Being There,* Peter Sellers, in his finest role, bears an uncanny resemblance to Vice President Dick Cheney, so maybe Kosinski's novel was more prophetic than he knew.)

And in the middle 1970s a pseudonymous writer named Luke Rhinehart enjoyed an enormous commercial success with a novel called *The Dice Man,* a book about a man named Luke Rhinehart who decides to surrender all his choices to the fall of the dice—where to live, what to do, who to marry, everything. I remember the success of *The Dice Man* because at the time it happened I was sharing an apartment in Earl's Court, London, with a young publisher, Mike Franklin, whose own life had been changed by the luck of buying the rights to the book cheaply and then seeing it become a big bestseller. As a struggling young writer, I deeply resented *The Dice Man*'s success, but I remember it now as a sign that even though young writers are usually encouraged to avoid such plot motifs as random encounters and implausible coincidences, the reading public deeply believes in the power of such things to affect human lives.

The Hollywood cinema would almost cease to exist if filmmakers were forbidden to base their work on chance—the accidental spider bite that turns Peter Parker into Spider-Man, the chance discovery by the hobbit Bilbo Baggins of a mysterious ring of power (to be fair, J.R.R. Tolkien, a member of the Thornton Wilder "hidden hand" school, would have argued that the ring wanted to be found and chose Bilbo to find it: Its character was its destiny). And then there's the whole movie business of "meeting cute": Meg Ryan and Tom Hanks running into one another on the Internet, Meg Ryan and Billy Crystal colliding accidentally half a dozen times in a single movie. It seems like people in movies are never properly introduced; they prefer to dress up as women to escape a bunch of gangsters and bump into Marilyn Monroe on a train, or to bump into one another on a sinking ship, or to meet by being involved in car accidents or train accidents or airplane disasters or by being marooned on islands or forced to marry under the terms of somebody's will so that they can inherit a fortune or forced to marry on account of some fairy-tale law, or else give up being Santa Claus.

The significance in human affairs of the unpredictable—the revolution, the avalanche, the sudden illness, the stock-market collapse,

the accident—obliges us to accept that character isn't the only deter-
minant of our lives. What's more, character isn't what it was two and
a half thousand years ago. When Heraclitus made his statement
about man's *ethos* being his *daimon,* both those words, *ethos, daimon,*
expressed concepts that were seen, in his time, as stable. Character
was not mutable but fixed. The spirit that guided one's life did not
change. As Popeye the Sailor Man so succinctly put it, "I yam what I
yam and that's all what I yam." These days, however, we have a slip-
perier, more fragmented understanding of what character actually is.
We argue a good deal about how much of our behavior is externally
determined and how much comes from within. We are by no means
certain of the existence of a soul. And we know that we are very different people in different circumstances: We are one way with our
families and another way in the workplace; we are more fluid and
metamorphic than our forefathers believed they were; we know that
within the "I" there's a bustling crowd of different "I's" jostling for
space, coming to the fore, being pushed back again, growing, shrinking, even disappearing entirely while new "I's" grow. We can change,
in the course of a life, so profoundly that we no longer recognize our
younger selves. The last emperor of China, Pu Yi, began life believing
himself to be a god and ended it, under Communism, as a gardener,
claiming to be happy. Can a man change that much and be content?
Was this brainwashing or transformation? It's an open question. But
the nature of the self, and the extent to which it determines our actions, is a more problematic subject than it used to be. Character may
be destiny, but what is character?

A third answer to Heraclitus is to be found in the political sphere,
or at least in the increasing penetration of our private lives by public
affairs. The Napoleonic Wars do not feature prominently in the novels of Jane Austen. The function of soldiers in her work is to show up
at parties and look cute in uniform. But to say this is to make no
criticism of her. She is able to give a full, rounded, profound account
of her characters' lives without needing to refer to the public sphere,
which was so remote from those lives as to make almost no impact

upon them. This is no longer the case. The gap between what is private and what is public has diminished to the point at which one can almost say that it has ceased to exist.

In much of the world, the closing of this gap shapes people's lives from their early childhood. One could say that for many human beings childhood itself has been abolished, "childhood" defined as a safe, protected period during which a human being can grow, learn, develop, play, and become; in which a human being can be childlike, child*ish,* and be spared the rigors of adulthood. These days, global poverty forces children to work, in factories, in fields, on city streets. It turns children into street urchins, criminals, and whores. Meanwhile, political instability not only claims children's lives in large numbers in Sudan, in Rwanda, in India, in Iraq, but it turns them into killers too. See on TV the child soldiers of Africa toting their automatic weapons and speaking with terrifying ease about death. In a time when the external pressures upon us are so great, in Palestine, in Israel, in Afghanistan, in Iran, many artists have felt obliged to take into account the terrible truth that for a great majority of the world's population, their characters, strong or weak, have very little chance of determining their fates. Poverty is destiny, war is destiny, ancient ethnic, tribal, and religious hatreds are destiny, a bomb on a bus or in a market square is destiny, and character just has to take its place in the list. A billionaire financial speculator attacks your country's currency, and it collapses, and you lose your job; it doesn't matter who you are or how good a worker you were, you're on the street. Nor is this simply a Third World problem. On September 11, 2001, thousands of people died in America for reasons unconnected with their characters. On that horrifying day, their *ethos* was not their *daimon.*

Until the age of thirteen, when I was sent from Bombay to boarding school in faraway England, I was a much more homogeneous self than I am now. I had lived in the same house in the same city all my life, in the bosom of my family, among people whose customs I knew without having to do anything as conscious as "know" them, speaking the languages that people spoke in that city, in that country, in that time. These are the four roots of the self: language, place, community, custom. But in our age, the great age of migration, many of us have at least one of these roots pulled up. We move away from the place we know, away from the community that knows us, to a place where the customs are different and, perhaps, the most commonly spoken language is one we do not know, or if we speak it, we speak it badly and cannot express in it the subtleties of what we think and who we are. In my case, I had been brought up multilingually, so my English was fine, it was the one root still planted in the earth, but the others had all gone. In Norse mythology, the World Tree, the great ash Yggdrasil, has three roots. One falls into the Pool of Knowledge near Valhalla, the pool from which Odin drinks, but the others are slowly being destroyed, one gnawed by a monster called the Nidhogg, the other being gradually burned away by the flames of the fire region, Muspelheim. When these two roots are destroyed, the tree falls, and the Götterdämmerung begins. The migrant too is at first a tree standing without roots, trying not to fall. Migration is an existential act, stripping us of our defenses, mercilessly exposing us to a world that understands us badly, if at all: as if the earth were stripped of its atmosphere and the sun were to bear down upon it in all its pitiless force.

It's an age of migrant writers, voluntary migrants and involuntary, exiles and refugees: Tahar Ben Jelloun in France, Assia Djebar in the United States, Hanan al-Shaykh in London, the Chinese winner of the Nobel Prize, Gao Xingjian, in Paris. And even those who are able to return have sometimes faced difficulties on reentry, such as the Kenyan Ngũgĩ wa Thiong'o, a vocal opponent of the Daniel arap Moi regime, who on his return to Nairobi was badly beaten and his wife raped, with the probable connivance of the authorities. For such writers, instability is a given—instability of abode, of the future, of the family, of the self. For such writers, the lack of an automatic subject is a given too. Some, like the longtime Somali exile Nuruddin Farah, carry their homeland within them, just as Joyce carried Dublin with him, and never turn to other places or other themes. Others, like the diaspora Indian writer Bharati Mukherjee, redefine themselves according to their changed circumstances—in her case, thinking and writing as an American. Others, like myself, fall somewhere in between, sometimes looking East, sometimes West, but always with a sense of the provisionality of all truths, the mutability of all character, the uncertainty of all times and places, no matter how settled things may seem. V. S. Naipaul, the "arrived" writer of *The Enigma of Arrival*, labors mightily to bring his new world to life, describing it into being, hedgerow by hedgerow, lane by lane, and if the effort exhausts him, so that the book loses narrative momentum, then it is a comprehensible exhaustion.

A migrant writer like myself can only envy deeply rooted writers like William Faulkner or Eudora Welty, who can take their patch of the earth as a given and mine it for a lifetime. The migrant has no ground to stand on until he invents it. This too increases his sense of the precariousness of all things and leads him toward a literature of precariousness, in which neither destiny nor character can be taken for granted, nor can their relationship. Perhaps this is why I respond so strongly to novels like *The Confidence-Man* by Herman Melville, with its elusive, slippery, changeable protagonist, or to other protean fictions such as Philip Roth's novel *The Plot Against America*, whose alternative history of an America in which the Nazi sympathizer and anti-Semite Charles A. Lindbergh defeats Roosevelt for the presidency in the middle of World War II reminds us of what Jorge Luis Borges knew, that history is a garden of forking paths, and that although things did go one way they might have gone another and who would we be then, how differently might we have thought or acted, might not our destinies have shaped our characters rather than the other way around?

American literature, as befits the literature of a land built by migration, knows a good deal about the protean shape-shifting processes by which migrant selves, and migrant communities, remake themselves and are remade, and it's no accident that so many of its preeminent masterpieces—*The Great Gatsby*, for example—deal with the comedy and tragedy of the reinvented self. American literature is being reinvented nowadays by writers whose stories come from everywhere; many of today's younger writers (younger, I mean, than me) are embracing and enlarging America's protean horizons: Yaa Gyasi, Esi Edugyan, Edwidge Danticat, Ocean Vuong, Viet Thanh Nguyen, Laila Lalami, Maaza Mengiste, lots of them.

Vladimir Nabokov tells us not to identify with characters in novels but rather pay attention to the author as he strives to create his work of art. Unfortunately, he is also the creator of Humbert Humbert, for whom you can't help feeling, even though he's a pedophile, and Lolita, for whom you can't help caring in spite of her essential banality, and Lolita's mother, Charlotte Haze, for whom you want to weep; so I don't believe he wholly believed that himself. At the heart of the novel is and always will be the human figure, which is to say human character, and the nature of the novel is to show the human figure in motion through time, space, and happenstance, and if we don't care about the character, we rarely care about the novel; it's as simple as that. But human beings aren't the whole story—in fact, often they aren't even the heroes of the stories they're in; they're bit-part players in their own lives. Even the most potent of fictional characters has to face up at some point to the sheer strangeness of the world.

Character can shape destiny powerfully and must be allowed to do so in the novel whenever it can, but the surreal too is a part of the real; the surreal is the strangeness of the world made visible. Heraclitus, who taught us that a man's *ethos* is his *daimon,* also wrote:

> "Pythagoras may well have been
> the deepest in his learning of all men. And still he
> claimed to recollect details of former lives,
> being in one a cucumber and one time a sardine." (#17)

I'm with Pythagoras on this. I want the story of the whole Pythagoras, the square on his hypotenuse as well as the sum of the squares on his other two sides, and I wouldn't feel I knew Pythagoras properly if I didn't also know about those secret, earlier lives spent far away from mathematics as a cucumber, or sardine.

# ANOTHER WRITER'S BEGINNINGS

––––––

(This essay is a somewhat expanded version of the inaugural
Eudora Welty Lecture, given in the National Cathedral,
Washington, D.C., on October 20, 2016.)

I HAVE LONG ADMIRED THE WORK OF EUDORA WELTY AND AM
privileged to be asked to follow in the footsteps of her classic *One Writer's Beginnings* to talk about my own start in the writing game. I'm lucky enough to have met Eudora, just once, in London in 1982. Her novel *Losing Battles* had just been published in the UK by the feminist house Virago, twelve years after its first appearance in the United States. I had been asked to review it, had found it hilarious and brilliant, and had said so in print, and so, when Eudora showed up in London, I was invited by Virago's formidable leader, Carmen Callil, to a small lunch for her at a restaurant in Covent Garden. I'm not exactly sure who I was expecting to meet, but I suspect I thought she might be a little old provincial lady from the South. She was nothing of the sort. She was surprisingly tall and immensely sophisticated and regaled us for two hours with stories of Paris and photography, both passions of hers. As the lunch drew to a close, I realized that I had been so swept away by her anecdotes that I hadn't asked her anything about writing in general or her writing in particular. She was perhaps seventy-two years old then, an age that seemed impossibly distant to my thirty-four-year-old self (I'm older than seventy-two now). I thought that I must ask her something, as I

might never meet her again. (As a matter of fact, I never did meet her again, so my sense of urgency was retrospectively justified.) I couldn't think of a proper question, and so, in a sort of blurt, I uttered the words: "William Faulkner!"

She turned and looked at me benevolently. "Yes, dear," she said. "What about him?"

What about him indeed, I thought, panicking a little. "On the whole," I ended up asking, "would you say that he has been a help or a hindrance to you?"

"Well, dear, neither one," she replied. "It's like having a big mountain in the neighborhood. It's very nice to know it's there, but it doesn't help you do your work."

This was a fine reply, but I dared to ask one question more. "So do you not think of Faulkner as one of the writers who are closest to you?"

"Oh, no, dear," she replied, affecting shock. "I'm from Jackson. He's from Oxford. It's miles away."

I CONFESS I HAVE always envied writers like Welty and Faulkner for the depth of their roots, for their ability to mine a tiny piece of the earth for a lifetime of masterpieces. My own life has been more peripatetic than theirs, and perhaps as a result my literary beginnings were slow and filled with error. It took me a long time to find my way.

I grew up in Bombay, India, the son of parents who didn't read many novels, though my father knew a good deal of Urdu poetry and when among friends in the evening would recite with gusto the verses of Hafiz, Ghalib, and Faiz. Both my parents were excellent storytellers, however. This is what I said about them in my memoir, *Joseph Anton*, which, I should warn you, is written in the third person, for reasons too complicated to explain:

When he was a small boy his father at bedtime told him the great wonder tales of the East, told them and retold them and remade them and reinvented them in his own way. . . . To grow up steeped in these tellings was to learn two unforgettable lessons: first, that stories were not true (there were no "real" genies in bottles or flying carpets or wonderful lamps), but by being untrue they could make him feel and know truths that the truth could not tell him, and second, that they all belonged to him, just as they belonged to his father, Anis, and to everyone else, they were all his, as they were his father's, bright stories and dark stories, sacred stories and profane, his to alter and renew and discard and pick up again as and when he pleased, his to laugh at and rejoice in and live in and with and by, to give the stories life by loving them and to be given life by them in return. The story was his birthright, and nobody could take it away.

His mother, Negin, had stories for him too. Negin Rushdie had been born Zohra Butt. When she married Anis she changed not just her surname but her given name as well, reinventing herself for him, leaving behind the Zohra he didn't want to think about, who had once been deeply in love with another man. Whether she was Zohra or Negin in her heart of hearts her son never knew, for she never spoke to him about the man she left behind, choosing, instead, to spill everyone's secrets except her own. She was a gossip of world class, and sitting on her bed pressing her feet the way she liked him to, he, her eldest child and only son, drank in the delicious and sometimes salacious local news she carried in her head, the gigantic branching interwoven forests of whispering family trees she bore within her, hung with the juicy forbidden fruit of scandal. And these secrets too, he came to feel, belonged to him, for once a secret had been told it no longer belonged to her who told it but to him who received it. If you did not want a secret to get out there was only one rule: *Tell it to nobody.* This rule, too, would be useful to him in later life. In that later life, when he had become a writer, his mother said to him, "I'm going to stop telling you these things, because you put them in your books and then I get into trouble." Which was true, and perhaps she would have been well advised to stop, but gossip was her addiction, and she could not, any more than her husband, his father, could give up drink.

So that was one kind of beginning, a boy at his parents' feet, listening, learning. Both my parents told me that when their friends asked me what I wanted to be when I grew up, I would say that I wanted to be a writer. I have no memory of this myself, but my parents told me I said it, and so it must be true. I've wondered what my six- or seven-year-old self might have meant by this strange remark and have concluded that what he was really saying was that he loved being a reader and dreamed about becoming a part of the world he loved, the world of books. But wanting to be a writer and being a writer are not the same thing, and, in my case, the journey from wanting to being was not an easy one.

There are writers who, like the goddess Athena, spring fully formed from the head of Zeus and rocket into the literary sky. Ian McEwan and Zadie Smith are examples of this impressive precocity. My way was slower, and the road was full of potholes.

I read a lot, and not always wisely, smuggling comic books into my bedroom and believing that my parents didn't know. Superman and Batman, Wonder Woman and Aquaman, entered my life at an early age, and to this day I can tell a Joker from a Riddler and I know the difference between green and red kryptonite. Also, from the paperback lending library at the wonderfully named Scandal Point near our house, I was able to borrow, for pocket money, many alliteratively titled volumes (*The Case of the Drowning Duck, The Case of the Lucky Legs*) by Erle Stanley Gardner, detailing the exploits of the great defense lawyer Perry Mason and the many defeats of his hapless adversary, the prosecutor Hamilton Burger, named after fast food but slow of mind and phrase. One of the enduring mysteries of these murder mysteries was exactly how, after so many defeats, Ham Burger managed to keep his job. Somebody told me and I have no idea if it was true that Erle Stanley Gardner had three Airstream trailers on his lawn, with a secretary in each one, and spent his days dictating three separate Perry Mason stories to his three assistants, and had a fertile enough imagination to keep all three ladies fully employed. Now that, I thought, was a literary goal worth aspiring to.

At the foot of the little hill in the Breach Candy district of Bombay where I grew up, there was a magical bookstore called Reader's Paradise, in which I spent many of the happiest hours of my childhood. The English children's books I found there, the ones that made it all the way to India, included *Alice's Adventures in Wonderland* and *Through the Looking-Glass*, which made so deep an impression on me that to this day I am able to recite the whole of "Jabberwocky" and "The Walrus and the Carpenter." They did not include *Winnie-the-Pooh*, which was a loss. There was a series of books collectively known, after its first volume, as *Swallows and Amazons*, about two families of children having adventures in small sailboats on an unnamed lake in the Lake District of Britain. These books fascinated me, as *Huckleberry Finn* also had, because of the great degree of personal liberty enjoyed by the children, who seemed free to wander the region with only the faintest scintilla of adult supervision. To that young boy in Bombay, such wild liberty seemed more fantastic than anything Alice found down the rabbit hole, and England came to seem like an alluring place.

My maternal grandparents lived in the university town of Aligarh, south of Delhi. My grandfather Dr. Ataullah Butt—"Ataullah" is the name Shakespeare Anglicized as "Othello"—was a familiar figure in Aligarh, bicycling through the streets of the town as he went about his rounds, much as my later fictionalized version of him, Dr. Aziz, cycled through the streets of a different town, Agra, in *Midnight's Children*. He was also connected to the university, and so I would sit on the back of his bike and he would take his bookish grandson to the university library to choose whatever books I pleased. Then as now, perhaps the two most popular English authors in India were Agatha Christie and P. G. Wodehouse, and I would clamber around the gloomy book stacks and bring down piles of Hercule Poirot and Miss Marple mysteries, and tales of Bertie Wooster and Jeeves, and

of the Earl of Emsworth and his beloved pig, the Empress of Blandings. These too were among my earliest and most formative literary
influences.

My grandfather influenced me in another way as well. He was a
religious man, had performed the *haj* to the holy places of Islam, and
dutifully said his prayers five times a day, seven days a week. But he
also struck my younger self as one of the most open-minded men I
had ever met, and he considered no subject off-limits or too scandalous to debate. You could tell him, "Grandfather, I don't believe in
God," and he would pat the seat next to him and say, "Come and sit
down here and tell me how you arrived at such a damn fool notion as
that." In this way he gave me the gift of free thinking, perhaps the
greatest gift of all.

(Many years later I discovered an awful truth about my grandfather, which obliged me to discard the above affectionate portrait of
him. He misbehaved with young girls, including, to my certain
knowledge, at least one of his own grandchildren. He never misbehaved with me, but, then, I wasn't a young girl. The discovery of his
pedophilia has had a devastating effect on me, forcing me to rewrite
the entire story of my family. But that is a subject for another place.
I have explored it in my novel *Quichotte*.)

I must have been about ten years old when I first saw the film of
*The Wizard of Oz*, and it made such a deep impression on me that I
went home and wrote a story—my first, I think—called "Over the
Rainbow," about a boy like myself in a city like Bombay who finds,
one day, not the end of the rainbow but the beginning; a broad high
rainbow arcing up and away from him from the sidewalk where he
stands, with useful steps cut into it, allowing him to climb up and
over. On the rainbow he meets various fantastic creatures whose
identities escape me, perhaps mercifully, except that I do recall a talking pianola. When my father read the story, he took it away and got
his secretary to type it up and then said he would look after it so that
it didn't get lost, because children were not to be trusted; and then he
lost it, which proves one of the strong messages of the story, which is

that grown-ups are the ones you can't rely on, Aunt Em and Uncle Henry can't protect Toto from Miss Gulch, and even the Wizard—"pay no attention to that man behind the curtain"—is a fraud.

One other childhood literary memory still irks me, even more than my father's misplacement of my first work of fiction. Perhaps as a result of reading Edward Lear, I became a fan of the limerick form. My personal favorite was the meta-limerick about the old man of Japan.

> There was an old man of Japan
> Who could never get limericks to scan.
> When they asked him why
> He replied with a sigh,
> "Well, you see, it's because I always try and put as many
>     words into the last line as I possibly can."

The day came in English class at my school, the Cathedral School in Bombay, when we were asked by the teacher to compose as many limericks as we could during a period of twenty minutes. I was overjoyed and made up, if memory serves, well over a dozen, while my classmates struggled to produce even one or two. I remember only one.

> To a very old man was once said,
> "I bet you can't stand on your head."
> When he said, "Yes, I can,"
> They replied, "Prove it, man,"
> So he did it, and promptly fell dead.

A little macabre, a little derivative of Lewis Carroll's "You Are Old, Father William," I admit, but, in my defense, I was only twelve years old, and it scans. At the end of the lesson I proudly handed in my work and was at once accused of cheating. It was impossible that I could have written so many. I must have copied them. The obvious injustice of this remark still rankles. Copied them from where? How could I have known we would be set this test? It made me furiously want to prove that I was actually not bad at this writing thing. I'm still trying to prove it, I suppose.

From these various small acorns, a tree would eventually grow. It began, however, with an uprooting. In January 1961 I left Bombay and went to board at Rugby School in England. I should emphasize that this was my choice. My mother didn't want me to go and my father left the final decision to me. What made that thirteen-year-old boy leave home? I was very happy in Bombay, and at school, and among my friends. Yet something drove me away across the world. I still wonder at that. Was it some hitherto unsuspected spirit of adventure? (I was a notoriously "good" and quiet child, unlike my naughtier and more enjoyable sisters.) Was it a dream of being like those unsupervised Swallows and Amazons or of lighting out for the territory like Huck Finn? I had read English boarding school stories too, most frequently the frankly awful Billy Bunter series about a much put-upon fat boy at a school called Greyfriars. There was one Indian boy at Greyfriars, an aristocratic fellow named Hurree Jamset Ram Singh, who spoke oddly. Instead of saying, for example, that he was thirsty, he might say, "The thirstfulness is terrific." If he was angry, the wrathfulness was terrific, and so on. He was popular, and maybe I thought I would be too. Instead, I encountered racism and learned for the first time what it was to be someone else's Other, judged not by my character, my selfhood, but by my ethnicity. It was a radical awakening. The almost-eighteen-year-old who left Rugby was still fairly conservative. In that sense, he was an unremarkable product of an English boarding school education. But about racism, he already knew everything. In the four months or so between school and college, I wrote a long text called "Terminal Report," a thinly fictionalized account of my final months at Rugby School, in which my experience of racial prejudice featured strongly. This text too has been lost, this time by me, which proves that children can be as careless as their parents. I know, from what little of it I remember, that it was pretty poor stuff, but it was a document of that moment, and as such I am sad about its loss.

I had been so unhappy at Rugby that even though I had already won a place at Cambridge University, I asked my parents to allow me to refuse it and go to college nearer home. My father persuaded me to go, and I'm glad he did, because my Cambridge experience was the opposite of my Rugby years. It healed the wounds of school and showed me an England in which I might be able to live. These were the years in which I woke up into something like my adult self.

At Cambridge I discovered a tolerant Britain that erased my memories of another, racist one. I also discovered internationalism, and Vietnam protests, and feminism, and civil rights, and flower power, and girls. I discovered the writing of Jorge Luis Borges and James Joyce, both of whom blew open little windows in my mind. From the study of history I learned that the past is contested territory and that reality is not a given but a thing we make. I learned from one of my professors, Arthur Hibbert, that "you should never write history until you can hear the people speak." All of these were good lessons for the aspiring novelist that I was beginning to dare to admit to myself I might be.

However, I spent more of my spare time at university involved with student theater, as an actor, not a writer, and took part in productions of plays by Bertolt Brecht, Ben Jonson, Eugène Ionesco, and others. I did do some writing for the student newspaper, *Varsity*. My last assignment was to write a piece about a spate of thefts from students' rooms across the university. In good New Journalism style, I decided the thing to do was to "be the thief," to visit a series of "staircases" in various colleges to see how many students left their rooms unlocked, to go inside and list what I might have stolen if I had actually been the burglar. One room I entered contained a large amount of expensive audio equipment and other valuable stuff. I duly reported that this was the room of the editor of *Varsity* himself. To his credit he did not censor the piece, and ran it. However, I was never asked to write for the paper again.

It was at Cambridge, during the final year of my degree in history, that I studied the early history of Islam and first heard about the so-called incident of the satanic verses, a well-documented episode in which, it would appear, the religion first flirted with recognizing three popular Meccan winged goddesses and afterward rejected them—a story of the temptation of a prophet by compromise that seemed to me to echo many stories of the temptations of prophets to be found in the Bible. When I first heard the story, I thought, like the budding writer I hoped I was, "Good story." That was in 1968. Twenty years later, with the publication of *The Satanic Verses*, I found out just how good a story it was.

By the time I left Cambridge, I knew that my little boy self had been right. I wanted to be a writer. I also wanted to be an actor, but after a few efforts in plays on the then very active Fringe of London theater, including one mercifully unrecorded performance as an agony aunt in a long black dress with a long blond wig and a black Zapata mustache, I understood that I would be wise not to go further down that path. Writing was what I most deeply desired, and writing, from that time on, it would be. My father didn't like it. Writing wasn't a job, it was a hobby. Working with him in his textile factory was a job. But, I said, I wanted to be a writer. What, after all that money spent on my fancy foreign education? After my mother had to put up with my absence for much of the previous eight years? I wanted to go back to England and write?

A piteous cry, entirely involuntary, burst out of my father, expressing what he most profoundly thought. "What," he cried, "will I tell my friends?"

(I did not come from literary stock. My father had a library, but it was musty; the books rarely left their places on the shelves. It was said that he had purchased it by the yard from its original owner, a story I would like to disbelieve but have never completely managed to dismiss. I was always a big reader, but there was little on my father's shelves that enticed me. There wasn't much fiction. There was, I recall, *The Tribe That Lost Its Head* by Nicholas Monsarrat, and there was a memoir, *The Egg and I*, by someone called Betty MacDonald, both collected, in abbreviated form, as Reader's Digest Condensed Books. There were a couple of Russian novels, even though I never heard my father discuss Russian literature, but as the novels were

*Mother* by Maxim Gorky and *Resurrection* by Tolstoy, I don't blame him for being put off. Elsewhere on the shelves were better-thumbed books, with titles like *Ripley's Believe It or Not!* and *Little Known Facts About Well Known People.* Immanuel Velikovsky's crackpot pseudo-science was there—*Worlds in Collision* and *Ages in Chaos,* expanding on Velikovsky's crazy theories of how interplanetary events shaped human history. This was the "cosmic catastrophism" that prefigured so much subsequent mumbo-jumbo, from Erich von Däniken's *Chariots of the Gods* to Dan Brown and his *Da Vinci Code,* a book so badly written, so badly imagined, so badly plotted, that it makes other bad books look good. There were dull brick-like books analyz-ing current affairs, written by John Gunther and Chester Bowles. There was a four-volume set of Winston Churchill's *A History of the English-Speaking Peoples.* Winston Churchill, I was reminded more than once, had mysteriously won the Nobel Prize in Literature; I continued to be resistant to his prose. And then, in twice as many volumes as the Churchill, and in the irresistibly bizarre version made by Richard Burton, illustrated by exotically Orientalist monochrome plates featuring luscious harem damsels, dashing sheikhs, thieves, magic carpets, magic lamps, and the Roc bearing Sinbad the Sailor away to its giant nest, there were *The Arabian Nights.* I wrestled my way through my father's moth-eaten volumes, fascinated by Burton's long, sexually obsessed footnotes, and fell in love.)

To be fair to my father, once he understood that I was serious about becoming a writer, he supported my decision, bought me a plane ticket back to London, and put some money in my pocket to get me started. Now that I'm a parent too, I know how hard this must have been for him and my mother. I never lived at home again and saw them only rarely, when I crossed the world or they did. And I was their eldest child and only son. But, through all the long years of dif-ficulty that followed, they never once said, "Give it up and come home." It was what I wanted, and so they loved me enough to want it too. I'm glad they lived long enough to see that it wasn't a com-pletely stupid idea.

Why come back to London? In part because in those days in

South Asia it was very hard to lead a literary life. You either had to be personally wealthy, or be broke and live with your parents, or you had to get a full-time job doing something else and write at the weekends. And the absence of a literary milieu felt important because it meant there was no informed opinion to test one's early work against, to improve and harden it by subjecting it to good criticism. None of this is true anymore, but it was then. And there was one more thing. By 1968, when I graduated, my parents had moved from my beloved hometown of Bombay to Karachi, in Pakistan, which I immediately disliked. If Bombay was no longer available to me, and if the choice was between London and Karachi, which it was, then I chose London.

So now I was twenty-one years old in London, sharing a house with four friends in the west of the city, on Acfold Road near the New King's Road, which was the utterly untrendy extension of the mega-groovy King's Road itself. My room was in the attic. To get into it I had to climb a wooden ladder and go through a hatch. I could pull the ladder up after me and close the hatch and then I was in my private universe and could not be disturbed. I was living inside a wooden pyramid with a sisal rug on the floor, a mattress on the rug, and a worktable, a chair, and a lamp. It was the perfect author's garret.

Like many young men I swung in those days between cockiness and panic, between spells of rudderless bewilderment and states of grace in which I was sure that the world was just about to open up for me like a flower. All I had to do was to take up my net, like a Nabokovian butterfly collector, and capture the elusive stories that were fluttering around somewhere inside me. The stories proved difficult to pin down, however, and much of what I did in my high aerie was a form of written-down daydreaming, summaries of stories I might write or, even worse, accounts of books I imagined I had already written, a whole daydream oeuvre summarized from a vantage point far in the future. I wrote myself glowing reviews for this as-yet-uncreated body of work and allowed myself a kind of pretend pride in my make-believe achievements. These self-glorifying prose fantasies usually embarrassed me into throwing them away moments after they appeared on the page. They offered a fleeting, onanistic comfort, usually followed by a pang of shame. I tapped away day after day but failed to hide from myself the uncomfortable truth, which was that my work had not begun, and I had no idea how to do it. I sat long hours in my wooden pyramid, as unproductively and vulnerably entombed as a mummy without a sarcophagus. I emerged for several days a week to earn money as an advertising copywriter and found that I was able, with a degree of competence, to write about unit trusts, dog food, potato chips, cigarettes, and perfume. My own work remained obstinately absent.

In the end, some words did come. I had an idea for a novel about an Eastern country in which a military man and a billionaire conspired to make a coup and to use, as a figurehead, a religious leader, a *pir* or holy man, whom they believed they could easily control. But the holy man, when he became leader, proved uncontrollable and swallowed up the world, including the people who had brought him to the fore. If I had had the intelligence to tell this story clearly and plainly, it might have proved to be serviceable, perhaps even prophetic of an age in which religious tyrants have behaved in exactly this way. Unfortunately, I was overly interested in experimental writing, and the text I produced, titled *The Book of the Peer,* was by universal consensus unreadable and unpublishable. Rebuffed, downcast, I proceeded to write something even less attractive, a script for television in which the two thieves on Golgotha, waiting for the soon-to-be-crucified Christ, engage in a form of nihilist banter that recalled the absurdist plays of Ionesco and Beckett I had admired at college. Vladimir and Estragon on their crosses, waiting for a Godot who did, finally, come. The play, I am embarrassed to admit, was titled *Crosstalk.*

To become a writer, one must first understand oneself, and it's harder to reach that understanding when your self is spread across the world. Throughout the first half of the 1970s I floundered because I had not worked myself out. I wrote yet another unpublishable novel-length text, called *The Antagonist,* a work overly influenced by Thomas Pynchon, by whom I was much affected in those days, which in the end I decided not to show anybody, and then a short, strained effort at political satire called *Madame Rama,* aimed at Indira Gandhi. In retrospect, both these pieces of juvenilia were false starts in the process that would eventually lead me to *Midnight's Children. Midnight's Children* took on Indira Gandhi too. And in *The Antagonist* there was a secondary character named Saleem Sinai, who had been born at the exact moment of Indian independence, midnight, August 14–15, 1947. I just hadn't understood then what to do with him.

After four unpublished texts, my first published novel, *Grimus,* to my mind very clearly reveals that the author hasn't fully worked himself out, hasn't fully understood what are his books to write, his books that are not echoes of other people's books and in which his reality, which is nobody else's reality, can be expressed. When I look at it now, it feels somehow fitful. A paragraph sparks into life, then a page feels awkwardly amateurish. There are people who like this book, I should say, but in general it had a bumpy ride on publication. For this rough treatment, I am retrospectively grateful, because it forced me to look at my writing with an unsparing eye and work out what, in my own opinion, not that of the critics, I was doing wrong. And it was during this period of savage introspection that my writing career finally began.

As I approached my thirtieth birthday I was still earning a living as a part-time advertising copywriter, and my greatest achievements were slogans such as the bubble-words I came up with to sell Aero chocolate bars ("the bubbliest milk chocolate you can buy"): *Adorabubble, Delectabubble, Irresistibubble.* An ad on the side of a bus could read: *Transportabubble.* A trade advertisement: *Profitabubble.* A sign in a shop window: *Availabubble here.* Success! The campaign ran for years, continuing long after I left ad-land. Also thanks to my advertising work, I had visited America for the first time, sent on an expenses-paid trip to San Francisco and L.A. and Las Vegas and Washington and New York by the United States Information Service so that I could go home and write an advertising campaign, "The Great American Adventure," encouraging people in Britain to take their vacations in America. (The photographs for this campaign were the best thing about it. The photographer was the great Elliott Erwitt.)

These were slim pickings for a would-be novelist, but the work was well paid and the agency people wanted me to commit myself to a full-time career, offering me startling financial inducements to do so. My confidence was low, and the dangled temptation of the ad-agency salary was hard to refuse. But somehow I found the strength to resist. As I look back now at my frustrated, unachieved younger self, that refusal is the thing of which I'm proudest. "Imagine how badly you'll feel," a voice whispered in my head, "if when you're fifty or fifty-five" (I couldn't imagine being older than that) "you have to tell yourself that you gave up your dream after one unsuccessful publication." So I resisted the blandishments of the enemies of promise. The sirens of ad-land sang sweetly and seductively, but I thought of Odysseus lashing himself to the mast of his ship, and somehow stayed on course.

I decided to give writing one last try.

I used the seven-hundred-pound advance I received for *Grimus* to travel around India as cheaply as possible for as long as I could make the money last, and on that journey of fifteen-hour bus rides and humble hostelries, *Midnight's Children* was born. It was the year that India became a nuclear power and Margaret Thatcher was elected leader of the Conservative Party and Sheikh Mujib, the founder of Bangladesh, was murdered; when the Baader-Meinhof gang was on trial in Stuttgart and Bill Clinton married Hillary Rodham and the last Americans were evacuated from Saigon and Generalissimo Franco died. In Cambodia it was the Khmer Rouge's bloody Year Zero. E. L. Doctorow published *Ragtime* that year, and David Mamet wrote *American Buffalo*, and Eugenio Montale won the Nobel Prize. And just after my return from India, Mrs. Indira Gandhi was convicted of election fraud, and one week after my twenty-eighth birthday she declared a state of emergency and assumed tyrannical powers. It was the beginning of a long period of darkness that would not end until 1977. I understood almost at once that Mrs. G. had somehow become central to my still-tentative literary plans.

At first, however, I had decided simply to write a novel of childhood, arising from my memories of my own childhood in Bombay. I spent long hours and days digging out childhood memories from the attics in my mind, where they lay gathering dust. I remembered an old clock tower around which we played, and, as well as Reader's Paradise, the candy store Bombelli's and its fabled three-foot box labeled *One Yard of Chocolates*. I remembered my anger at the whites-only swimming pool at the bottom of the hill, and the day when my best friend lost control of his bicycle and smashed into a wall and lost his front teeth. I remembered the school bullies and the day the taxi driver's son died during class. I remembered my tomboyish sister beating up a boy who had been teasing me, and I remembered his father coming to complain to my father, "Your daughter just beat up my son," and my father's amused laughter in response: "I wouldn't say that too loudly if I were you." I remembered the footbridge near Chowpatty Beach that bore, on one side, the advertising slogan *Esso puts a tiger in your tank* and, on the other side, a public-service warning, *Drive like hell and you will get there*. I remembered songs and the movies containing the songs. A world came flooding back and I knew it was the birth of a book. Traveling in India, both to old haunts and to new places I thought I might want to write about, I felt a second healing as important as Cambridge's healing of the wounds inflicted at boarding school. This second healing was the healing of the rift within myself, which had begun to separate me from my past. I would write my book, I told myself, to reclaim that past. Bombay is a city that stands in large part upon land reclaimed from the sea. My book would stand on literary land rescued from the tides of forgetting. I am this world, the book would say, and this world is me.

Now, having drunk deeply from the well of India, I conceived a more ambitious plan. I would write, I told myself, the most ambitious, challenging book I could dream of. Hollywood or bust. If I was to fail as a writer, I would prefer to go down in flames rather than as the author of a timid little failure. The question of high ambition is complex, raising as it does issues of ego and other unartistic factors. But what I meant was that I wanted to take the greatest artistic risk I could imagine. I had very little thought of money—in fact I doubted I'd ever make any—and fame, such a big subject nowadays, literally did not cross my mind. I simply wanted to set the literary bar as high as I possibly could. "For all serious daring starts from within" is the last line of *One Writer's Beginnings*, and that spirit of serious daring was what, after long years of confusion, I finally found the courage to embrace.

And I remembered Saleem Sinai, born at the midnight moment of Indian independence, who lay unborn in my abandoned draft of *The Antagonist*. As I now placed Saleem at the center of my new scheme, I understood that his time of birth would oblige me immensely to increase the size of my canvas. If he and India were to be paired, I would need to tell the story of both twins. It was no longer a simple novel of childhood. History rushed in. Then Saleem, ever a striver for meaning, brought the two strands together, suggesting to me that the whole of modern Indian history happened as it did because of him; that history, the life of his nation-twin, was somehow *all his fault.* With that immodest proposal the novel's tone of voice, comically assertive, unrelentingly garrulous, and with, I hope, a growing pathos in its narrator's increasingly tragic overclaiming, came into being. I even made the boy and the country identical twins. When the sadistic geography teacher Emil Zagallo, giving the boys a lesson in "human geography," compares Saleem's nose to the Deccan peninsula, the cruelty of his joke is also, obviously, mine.

For a while, however, I didn't understand that Saleem needed to speak. He didn't want his story told. He wanted to tell it himself. I began to write the book in the third person, and to my growing frustration it felt somehow inert. I knew, I was sure, that there was a host of good stories waiting to be told, but the writing was falling short of what the stories needed. Then one day, as an experiment, I let Saleem begin to narrate the novel himself. I have always thought of that day as the day I became a writer, because what came out of me, somehow, was what I at once recognized as the best page I had ever written, in a voice that was not my own and yet gave me voice. As Saleem Sinai poured out of me onto the page, I understood that he was my salvation and that the best and only thing I could do was to let him rip, to let that omnivorous spirit loose on the page, and to hang on to his coattails as he ran.

I was broke, and the novel would be long in the writing. I was forced back into the world of advertising on a part-time basis to pay the rent. I worked as a copywriter two or three days a week. On Friday nights I would come home to Kentish Town in North London, then a somewhat down-at-heel neighborhood, now extensively gentrified, like a sort of British Williamsburg, and I would ritually take a long hot bath to wash the week's commerce away and would emerge as a novelist, or so I told myself. The folks at the agency didn't understand why I wouldn't accept a full-time job and went on dangling substantial sums of money under my nose. I went on refusing them.

It took me five years to write *Midnight's Children*, because I was teaching myself how to write it as I wrote it. I was a member of the first generation of free Indian children to be born in over two centuries, infused with the spirit of new liberty but carrying with us also the knowledge of blood, of the great massacres of Muslims by Hindus and Hindus by Muslims that attended the moment of freedom. A transitional generation is exceptional, it is neither of the past nor wholly of the future, and it was my gift as a writer to have that unique moment as my birthright. I had to learn how to write about that, how to allow public events and private lives to flow in and around one another, how to avoid being merely topical but demonstrate, at the same time, how history shapes us all, and to ask the great question: Are we masters or victims of our times? Do we make history or does it unmake us? And can we, by our own choices and actions, shape and change our world?

Parenthetically: I was enough of a child of the sixties to answer that last question in the affirmative. The sixties were foolish in many ways, but to be young then was to be convinced that, yes, the world needed changing and, yes, we could do it. I have carried that spirit of possibility with me long enough to see it reborn in the yes-we-can spirit that brought Barack Obama to the White House and in the new young activism of the Trump era that is determined to shape the future and believes it has the power to do so.

Not only were the times interesting, my family was too. I had an uncle who wrote for the movies and was married to a glamorous wife, one of two thespian sisters who were my most enjoyably racy relatives. I had another uncle who was a military man, starting off as aide-de-camp to Field Marshal Auchinleck, the last commander of the British Army in India, and ending up as a general in the Pakistan army, friend of the military dictator Ayub Khan and, to my considerable embarrassment, the founder and first head of the notorious Pakistani secret service, the Inter-Services Intelligence agency or ISI, the same ISI that, much later, would supervise the safe havens in Pakistan occupied by the Taliban's Mullah Omar and Osama bin Laden. That was long after my uncle died, but he was the creator of the system that made such things possible, even normal, in Pakistan.

However, as I wrote, I was also learning something important. Fiction is not autobiography. The family in the novel has quite a lot in common with my actual family. Saleem's grandfather is a doctor; so was mine. He too has an uncle in the movies and another uncle who is a general. His sister Jamila, known as the Brass Monkey, is a tomboy just as my sister was. I had a Christian ayah from South India and so does Saleem. And so on. But as I began to create these characters on the page, I found it difficult to bring them to life. As long as they were merely imitations of real life, they had no fictional life. And so I began to push the characters away from the real people, to make them unlike their models, and at once they stirred, and stood up, and lived. So, the Christian ayah, working for a time as a nurse, commits the crime from which the story of the novel is born, whereas my actual ayah was the most law-abiding of people. And the sister in the novel becomes a wonderful singer, whereas, as anyone who knows my family will tell you, until the arrival of my niece the concert pianist, not a single one of us could sing at all. And the movie-world uncle's story darkens toward tragedy, and his fate is utterly unlike my actual uncle's. And the grandfather in the novel becomes deeply involved with the politics of the independence movement, unlike my grandfather, who was resolutely nonpolitical. And the military uncle is pushed toward comic-satirical caricature. By the time the book was done, the characters had left their models behind and become simply themselves.

I read somewhere that when Gabriel García Márquez finished working on his masterpiece, *One Hundred Years of Solitude*, he and his wife, Mercedes, took it to be mailed, and all the way from their home to the post office she was thinking, Suppose it's no good. When I finished *Midnight's Children*, I thought, As far as I can tell, this is a good book; but after the long years of un-success I was utterly lacking in confidence in my own judgment, and I genuinely had no idea if anyone in the world would agree with me. If nobody agrees with me, I told myself, then maybe I don't know what a good book is, and I should stop trying to write one. Everything was riding on the book's reception. Hollywood or bust.

Fortunately, it wasn't bust, and I finally had an answer to my father's question, "What will I tell my friends?"

WHEN I WAS A child in Bombay, I had a recurring flying dream, a version of which I would later give to a character in my novel *Two Years Eight Months and Twenty-Eight Nights*. I would dream that I was in my own bed in my own room and when I opened my eyes in the dream I could simply float upward, shedding my covering bedsheets, and fly around the bedroom without any effort at all. It was easy, and so after a while I would fly toward the open window and go through it into the world. At once I would begin, very slowly, to lose height, not vertiginously or frighteningly, but perceptibly. As I have mentioned, our house in Bombay stood on the top of a little hill, and it became clear to me that a moment would come at which I would be too low down to be able to fly back into my bedroom and I would inevitably drop lower and lower toward the busy main road at the base of the hill, a road full of pedestrians, cyclists, scooter riders, and motorists, none of whom would care that there was a fallen angel in their midst. Somewhere around here I would wake up. The dream was a nightmare.

The dream of becoming a writer is a little like that childhood dream. To achieve your dream you leave your safe place, in which you feel confident and protected, and you fly out into the world and you begin to lose height. If you are unlucky you land, as flightless as a dodo, in a crowd of unsympathetic strangers, and your dream turns out to be a nightmare. But if you're lucky and determined, the dream recurs, and gradually you discover you don't need the protection of your bedroom to stay up in the air and you can fly out through the window without feeling endangered. You no longer lose height or control. You navigate through the bright and buoyant air. Maybe you soar. But once you have found your wings, however long it takes, however many times you have failed before you found them, once you have found your wings, you fly.

# PART
# TWO

# PHILIP ROTH

---

(The Philip Roth Lecture, delivered at
Newark Public Library on September 27, 2018.)

THE LAST TIME I HEARD FROM PHILIP ROTH WAS IN OCTOBER
2017. "Because I am a son of Newark," his email read, "the Newark
Public Library has recently instituted a lecture series in my name. . . .
It's only 12 minutes to Newark by train and not much more by car.
This library and its branches were a great stimulant to me as a boy,
and I'd be delighted if you'd come sometime in the latter half of September 2018 and talk about the present American moment, which is
so exuberantly made manifest in your new book. Yours, Philip."

Now, if Philip Roth writes to you and asks you to deliver the
Philip Roth Lecture, the correct answer to that question is "yes." So
I accepted immediately, and was also, I confess, surprised and flat-
tered to know that Philip had read and liked my novel *The Golden
House.* You don't expect your literary heroes to read your work. I also
agreed to talk, as he proposed, about this present American moment,
which I will get around to doing. But after he died (I believe that
Philip would have disliked "passed away" or "left us"; this was not a
writer to whom one looked for euphemisms!) I felt that the first
Philip Roth Lecture after Philip Roth's death should properly take,
as its subject, Philip Roth himself, a writer through whose writing
many American moments, past and present, can be explored and understood and whose work, to use his phrase, has been a "great stimu-

lant" to me, and many writers of my generation and the generations following mine.

To my regret, I didn't know Philip as well as I would have liked, in spite of my great admiration for his work and the happy coincidence of our being represented by the same literary agency, the Wylie Agency. We did however meet several times over a long period. My most vivid memory is of a conversation in London in the mid-1980s, at a dinner in the house in Chelsea where he was living with Claire Bloom. He spoke of his desire to return to America because of his growing dislike of British anti-Semitism, and the irritation caused by the accompanying British refusal to admit that there was such a thing as British anti-Semitism, and the desire of some British people to explain to Philip that he had probably made some sort of cultural misunderstanding. I have been thinking again about what Philip perceived all those years ago, because the British Labour Party has been for many years in the midst of a controversy about the widespread anti-Semitism within its ranks, a problem whose existence the party leadership has appeared to minimize or even deny until quite recently. Not for the first time, Philip Roth was a long way ahead of the curve.

I told him that evening about my only personal experience of anti-Semitism. One summer when I was young, before I had published anything, and when I was not even slightly fashionable, I was somehow invited to a fashionable rooftop party in London, at which I was introduced to a designer of extremely fashionable hats, whose work, I was told, was often featured in *Vogue*. He was quite uninterested in meeting me, was curt to the point of discourtesy, and quickly went off in search of more-fashionable party guests. A few minutes later, however, he came back toward me at some speed, his whole body contorted into a shape designed to convey embarrassment and regret, and offered the following apology. "I'm so sorry," he said, "you probably thought I was very rude to you just now, and actually, I probably was very rude, but you see, it's because they told me you were Jewish." The explanation was offered in tones that suggested I would immediately understand and forgive. I have never wanted so much to be able to say that I was in fact Jewish. When I recounted this incident to Philip, he said with great emphasis, "Exactly. That's it, exactly." So for that moment we were just a couple of Jews having dinner together in London. It's a proud memory.

I still have the battered Corgi paperback edition of *Portnoy's Complaint* that I read in 1971, when I turned twenty-four years old. This was before I had ever set foot in the United States, a magic land that I knew only through its literature and its movies. America for me then was *Bonnie and Clyde, The Graduate, In Cold Blood, Rosemary's Baby, Bullitt, Easy Rider, Midnight Cowboy, M\*A\*S\*H, Love Story, Klute, Carnal Knowledge,* and *The Last Picture Show.* In literature, it was *Native Son* and *Invisible Man* and *Augie March.* It was Pynchon and Vonnegut and Morrison and Updike's *Rabbit* and Cheever's "Swimmer" and Joseph Heller's Yossarian and Nabokov's *Lolita.* My knowledge of Jewish American life too came exclusively from books, from Bellow and Malamud and Singer. This is how America is to those of us looking at her from outside: simultaneously very well known indeed and totally unknown. It is both the embodiment of power and the many-sided expression of liberty, both Uncle Sam and Emma Lazarus, both "The Star-Spangled Banner" and "Blue Suede Shoes" or Louis Armstrong singing "What a Wonderful World." When as strangers we first set foot on New York streets, we think we recognize everything because we have seen it many times, filmed and photographed and televised and painted, and yet we don't know our way around and easily get lost. We carry in our heads the music of America, but we don't know the lives of the people from whom that music came, and, if we are bookish people, we carry the written words too, without really knowing anything of the lived experiences from which those words arose. Without ever having seen the Windy City I memorized the opening lines of *Augie March,* "I am an American, Chicago born—Chicago, that somber city—and go at things as I have taught myself, free-style, and will make the record in my own way . . ." and the equally celebrated last lines, "Why, I am a sort of Columbus of those near-at-hand and believe you can come to them in this immediate *terra incognita* that spreads out in every gaze. I may well be a flop at this line of endeavor. Columbus too thought he was a flop, probably, when they sent him back in chains. Which didn't prove there was no America." I was looking for help, for words that would open doors for me into the unknown lands that would, I hoped, spread out in my own gaze, and these words, these images, these sounds, were what I clung to. Maybe they would show me how to do what I wanted to do.

Into this imaginary, imagined America, *Portnoy's Complaint* dropped like a bomb. "Whacking Off"? "Cunt Crazy"? I'd never read anything like it. I can remember being genuinely astounded, not only by the subject matter but also by the rhapsodic glee with which it was treated, the unashamed nakedness of the language, the almost fanatical frankness of the prose. I grew up in India, where people weren't even allowed to kiss onscreen in the movies, and public displays of affection were frowned upon in real life, and where the ancient sexuality of Tantric art had long ago been replaced by an easily shocked prudery of which I too was partly guilty. In my own writing I've often been reluctant to be explicit about the details of human sexual activity, believing that these things are best done offstage, so to speak, but there are scenes in which, looking back, I can easily discern the influence of Mr. Roth, about whom Jacqueline Susann—of all people, Jacqueline Susann!—said to Johnny Carson, "I'd like to meet him, but I wouldn't want to shake his hand."

In *Midnight's Children* there's a moment in which the narrator's mother, fondly remembering her long-lost first husband, pleasures herself in the bathroom, not knowing that her son the voyeur is hiding out in the family washing chest, watching her. This scene may be Philip Roth's fault. In general, however, my narrators, unlike Alexander Portnoy, have found sex tough to write about. In *The Moor's Last Sigh*, the narrator tries to describe his parents making love for the first time. "He came to her as a man goes to his doom, trembling but resolute, and it is around here that my words run out, so you will not learn from me the bloody details of what happened when she, and then he, and then they, and after that she, and at which he, and in response to that she, and with that, and in addition, and for a while, and then for a long time, and quietly, and noisily, and at the end of their endurance, and at last, and after that, until . . . phew! Boy! Over and done with!" This passage does owe to Roth my realization that if you are going to write about sex, make it funny. Elsewhere in that passage, I confess, I was given courage by my readings of Roth to be a little more shocking and, what's more, to conflate sex and religion. "Did you ever see your father's cock, your mother's cunt? Yes or no, doesn't matter, the point is these are mythical locations, surrounded by taboo, put off thy shoes for it is holy ground, as the Voice said on Mount Sinai, and if Abraham Zogoiby was playing the part of Moses then Aurora my mother sure as eggs was the Burning Bush." Thank you, Philip. Taboos, he taught me, are there to be broken. This lesson has, on occasion, gotten me into trouble.

During the biggest time of trouble, the furor that followed the publication of *The Satanic Verses,* I thought of Roth many times. I remembered that after the publication of *Goodbye, Columbus* he was accused by some Jews of anti-Semitism, and after the publication of *Portnoy* a Kabbalah scholar (Gershom Scholem) called the novel "worse than the notorious *Protocols of the Learned Elders of Zion.*" I also recalled that one of the ways in which his radical text was attacked was by accusing it of being unreadably bad writing. "The cruelest thing anyone can do with *Portnoy's Complaint,*" Irving Howe wrote, "is read it twice." That form of attack was one with which I also became familiar and that stung more than the assault of the ayatollah. It was comforting to know that Philip Roth had come through the same fire.

In spite of Irving Howe, I have now read *Portnoy's Complaint* twice. When I first read it, at age twenty-three, I was less than a decade older than Alexander Portnoy, and the anguish of male adolescence was still a living memory. What then struck me most forcibly was that this utterly unknown world, the world of a Jewish boyhood in Newark, felt so familiar to this Bombay boy. The overwhelming family above all. My own mother was quite unlike Sophie Portnoy, but many of my friends' mothers—Hindu, Christian, Parsi—would have fit right in to Roth's Newark. It was strange, and delightful, to find in this writing from far away so much that gave me the pleasure of instant recognition.

Reading the book again at seventy-one, that recognition-pleasure is still there, even though Roth's evocation of adolescence now seems to me like a message from a distant planet. What is most striking, however, is the sheer relentlessness of the text. If one were to be critical of it, one would say that it is all on the same note. But that note, that supercharged shriek of need, pain, and desire, that voice of which Roth said that, for the first time, he "let it rip," had never been heard before and still, all these years later, retains all its power. Yes, it's shocking, but also, yes, it still knocks you off your feet. To find this kind of speech today, we have to listen to stand-up comedians. Maybe Dave Chappelle is Alexander Portnoy's African American child.

To reread *Portnoy* and *Goodbye, Columbus* is also to encounter the earliest versions of what one might call the Rothian Beloved: Brenda Patimkin, Bubbles Girardi, the much-fantasized-about blond *shiksa* Alex Portnoy names Thereal McCoy, and most significantly Mary Jane Reed, a.k.a. the Monkey, whose sexual appetites match Alex's own. The Rothian Beloved has come in for a good deal of criticism over the years, but the rediscovery of these first examples of the breed made me see, firstly, with what affection they are drawn, and secondly, that Roth's male voices are quite obviously and deliberately unreliable narrators of his women. That is to say, we can see through Alex Portnoy's tirade and understand that his creator sees his women with more profundity and passion than Alex does. One finishes *Portnoy* feeling a genuine affection for Alex, born of the knowledge that he represents a deep truth about young boys and men, but we come away with an equally deep affection for, and understanding of, the Monkey.

Humor is what makes the book work. Without humor, Alex Portnoy and the novel itself would be unbearable. But there's humor in every line, and so instead of finding him, and it, unbearable, we love him. After half a century, his power is undimmed.

HERE IS WHAT PHILIP Roth wrote in *The New Yorker* about rereading Saul Bellow's *Augie March,* which was published fifteen years
before *Portnoy's Complaint* and undoubtedly helped to show Roth the
way to his own work. "The transformation of the novelist who published *Dangling Man* in 1944 and *The Victim* in 1947 into the novelist
who published *The Adventures of Augie March* in 1953 is revolutionary.
Bellow overthrows everything.... In *Augie March,* a very grand, assertive, freewheeling conception of both the novel and the world the
novel represents breaks loose from all sorts of self-imposed strictures,
the beginner's principles of composition are subverted, and ... the
writer is himself 'hipped on superabundance.'... There is the narcis-
sistic enthusiasm for life in all its hybrid forms propelling Augie
March, and there is an inexhaustible passion for the teemingness of
dazzling specifics driving Saul Bellow." If one substitutes Alexander
Portnoy for Augie March, *Letting Go* and *When She Was Good* for
*Dangling Man* and *The Victim,* and Philip Roth for Saul Bellow in
this passage, we have a near perfect description of the revolutionary
genius of *Portnoy's Complaint* and its extraordinary impact, especially
coming after the two more conventional novels that preceded it. The
device of making the entire text a record of Alex's session or sessions
with his analyst set Roth free. "The theater of the analyst's office," he
once said to David Remnick, "says the rule here is that there are no
rules, the rule here is no inhibitions, the rule here is no restraint, the
rule here is no decorum."

Roth and Bellow, Bellow and Roth. The two writers are forever
yoked together, at least in the minds of writers of my generation. To
give, again, the view from elsewhere: For Martin Amis, Ian McEwan,
and myself, these were the two American writers who not only
showed us America most clearly, most brilliantly—who took the
American Jewish novel and transformed it into something pretty
close to the Great American Novel—but who also helped us to see
more clearly how to make the worlds we were trying to make.

I was thinking a good deal about language, trying to find an English that didn't sound like it belonged to the English, that could incorporate and represent the polyglot hubbub of the Indian street, and in Roth and Bellow I heard the energy I was striving for. I saw too a willingness to use untranslated words from another language. Reading Roth, I wondered, do all Americans know what it means to be given a *zetz* in the *kishkes*? Because I had to look it up. I guessed from context that a *zetz* was painful and that the *kishkes* were vulnerable, but the exact details eluded me. And yet here they were, Yiddish words in an English text, unapologetically offered. This was the way we spoke English in Bombay, sprinkling it with Hindi, Urdu, Marathi, or Gujarati words. It was also the way we spoke Hindi, Urdu, Marathi, and Gujarati, sprinkling those languages with English words where they seemed appropriate. Also, Indian English was not very like the Queen's English. Like the Irish, West Indians, Australians, and Americans, Indians had reshaped English to suit themselves. The Indian English word for the accused person in a court case is the "undertrial," because, you see, he is under trial. Your boss is your "incharge," so Martians landing in Bombay would have to request, "Take me to your incharge." When the police kill somebody in a shootout, he is said to have died in a police "encounter." And sexual harassment, I'm sorry to report, is "Eve teasing." I read *Augie March* and *Portnoy* and understood that I could use "my" English, just as these two masterworks used "theirs." And if I wanted to drop in words from other languages—*rutputty, khalaas, shanti*—that was okay, as long as I made their meanings clear from context, so the Anglophone reader would understand, or guess, that *rutputty* meant something like "ramshackle," *khalaas* meant, approximately, "finished" or "done for," and *shanti* meant "peace." English, I understood, could be chutnified. That was a moment of real liberation.

I was also thinking about form. I have long believed that there are only two kinds of really good novel. One is what I call the "everything novel," what Henry James called the "loose baggy monster," the novel that tries to include as much of life as possible. The other is the "almost nothing novel," the novel that, so to speak, plucks a single thin narrative strand from the head of the goddess and turns it in the light to reveal truth. Jane Austen, W. G. Sebald, and, in his very different way, in the short-story form, Raymond Carver are writers of this kind. The interesting thing about Bellow and Roth is that they have been both kinds of writer at different points in their career. Bellow started small (*Dangling Man*) then did the big, world-swallowing baggy monsters *Augie March, Herzog, Henderson the Rain King, Humboldt's Gift,* and then in later life went small again (*The Bellarosa Connection, A Theft, Ravelstein*). In Roth's case, the big, all-encompassing books came in a late, brilliant surge—*Sabbath's Theater, American Pastoral, I Married a Communist, The Human Stain*—which revealed him to be at least the equal of Bellow's "grand, assertive, freewheeling conception of both the novel and the world the novel represents."

I'll have more to say about those books in a moment, but I want to look at Roth's "middle period" first, the period of his many alter egos: David Kepesh, Peter Tarnopol, and preeminently Nathan Zuckerman, who first walked onstage in *The Ghost Writer* and then essentially, like Kaufman and Hart's *Man Who Came to Dinner,* never left. Again, there's a Bellow comparison. Moses Herzog in *Herzog* and Charlie Citrine in *Humboldt's Gift* are Bellow's stand-ins. Charlie is a sort of disciple of the poet Von Humboldt Fleisher, just as Bellow was a sort of disciple of the model for Humboldt, Delmore Schwartz. And the story of *Herzog,* in which Moses loses his wife to his friend, mirrors events in Bellow's life during his years at Bard. (In the novel, the traitorous friend has become a one-legged man. Such are the privileges and revenges of fiction.) But perhaps nobody has explored more nuances of the literary alter ego as thoroughly as Philip Roth.

We know, or we ought to know, that autobiographically based fiction is not reliable as autobiography, that Stephen Dedalus is and is not James Joyce; that "Marcel," the narrator of *À La Recherche du Temps Perdu,* is and is not Proust; that Nathan Zuckerman's controversial novel *Carnovsky* is and is not *Portnoy's Complaint.* But, because we live in an autobiographically obsessed age, there's a tendency simply to equate the alter ego with the author. Nobody has done more both to encourage, to play with, and also finally to demolish that idea of equivalence than Roth. Somewhere in one of Hemingway's bullfighting texts he writes that the greatest bullfighters work closest to the bull. Roth, by allowing Zuckerman to stand as close to the bull as it's possible to stand and yet to pirouette so expertly that he is never impaled on the horns, is the unquestioned master of that sport. If Zuckerman and Kepesh and Tarnopol begin, come to life, at a point pretty adjacent to their creator, by the time he's done with them they have moved into independent lives of their own, and that journey, from personal origins to fictional autonomy, may be called the act of creation.

Roth explores with subtlety the ambiguities of this kind of writing. In *The Counterlife*, the anger of Nathan Zuckerman's dentist brother, Henry, at Zuckerman's fictional portrait of him and of their family strikes a chord in the heart of any writer who has worked this close to the bull. When I read *The Counterlife*, I was in the middle of writing the novel that became *The Satanic Verses*, and perhaps a little affected by my reading of Roth's book, I decided to use some very personal material, my father's death, to create the scene near the end of the book in which Saladin Chamcha is present at his father's deathbed. When the novel was finished, that scene caused some distress to my sister Sameen, because, she argued, I had left her out of my depiction of the moment, which was as important to her as it was to me. "You didn't do that for him," she said, "I did that. He didn't say that to you, he said it to me." I could only reply that she wasn't a character in the novel, an answer that didn't really appease her. At that moment I understood exactly how Henry Zuckerman felt. Having a writer in the family is perhaps always a disaster for the family, especially when his alter ego is as ornery as Nathan Zuckerman. In Roth's partly nonfictional book *The Facts*—its very title just one of Roth's ways of messing with our heads—he allows Zuckerman to comment on his portrait of his "real" family. Zuckerman tells him that he has made himself and his family too nice. "Don't publish," he advises. In *The Facts*, he suggests, Roth is not telling the truth, or not nearly as well as his alter ego Zuckerman tells it in the novels.

In the end, this inward-looking, self-referential, mirror-image approach was bound to run out of steam, and it's plain that Roth knew that. *Operation Shylock* is his transitional book: on the one hand, perhaps the most extreme example of mirror-image writing yet, in which Philip Roth, emerging from a Halcion-induced breakdown, seemingly the same breakdown referred to in *The Facts*, discovers that there's an impostor Philip Roth in Israel attending the trial of John Demjanjuk from Cleveland, who may also be—who probably is—Ivan the Terrible of the Nazi death camps, and that this fake Roth is promoting ideas the real Roth dislikes, notably "Diasporism," which proposes that Jews should exit Israel and return to Europe, before the Arabs launch a second Holocaust. Europe, the fake Roth is telling people in Israel, is "the most authentic Jewish homeland there has ever been." On the other hand, while the Rothian game of mirrors continues in this novel, the subject matter has changed. We see Roth beginning to look outward as well as inward, to take the world as his subject instead of, or at least as well as, himself, and to begin the grand project of tackling, in his fiction, the great matters of his time, in this case, Israel. This turning outward will be the key to his late-period literary golden age and the answer to the problem that faces Nathan Zuckerman: the loss, the exhaustion, of his subject.

Zuckerman had lost his subject. His health, his hair, and his subject. Just as well he couldn't find a posture for writing. What he'd made his fiction from was gone—his birthplace the burned-out landscape of a racial war and the people who'd been giants to him dead. The great Jewish struggle was with the Arab states; here it was over, the Jersey side of the Hudson, his West Bank, occupied now by an alien tribe. No new Newark was going to spring up again for Zuckerman, not like the first one: no fathers like those pioneering Jewish fathers bursting with taboos, no sons like their sons boiling with temptations, no loyalties, no ambitions, no rebellions, no capitulations, no clashes quite so conclusive again. Never again to feel such tender emotion and such a desire to escape. Without a father and a mother and a homeland, he was no longer a novelist. No longer a son, no longer a writer. Everything that galvanized him had been extinguished, leaving nothing unmistakably his and nobody else's to claim, exploit, enlarge, and reconstruct.

In this passage from *Zuckerman Bound* I feel my deepest point of identification with Philip Roth. I too know something about what it is to lose a place, a past, and to be unable to reclaim it because it's no longer there to reclaim; something about the feeling of having, all of a sudden, no ground beneath one's feet, no solid ground for the wheels of art to grip, and the things that made one want to write in the first place being used up, and a second act being hard to find; and something too about finding that second act not in oneself but in the world in which, having no alternative, one has lived. "There are no second acts in American lives," Fitzgerald famously said, but the late grandeur of Philip Roth disproves the assertion, because Roth, if not Nathan Zuckerman, found his new subject by looking away from his origins and taking a good hard look at the present, in which, having no alternative, he found himself.

The prologue to the great trilogy is a novel that many people think may be Roth's finest, the rambunctious, astonishing *Sabbath's Theater*, for which an alternative title might have been *Alexander Portnoy Grows Up*. The aging puppeteer Mickey Sabbath delivers himself, as young Alex did, of what one of the other characters calls "a remarkable panegyric for obscenity." Like young Portnoy, old Sabbath is aroused not a little sleazily by sex objects—not a piece of liver this time, or his "fat elder sister's brassière," but underthings stolen from the dresser of a teenage girl, or a phone sex tape, or the blouse concealing a student's breast. He, or his author, also possesses the astonishing, driving narrative force with which Portnoy and Roth burst upon the scene so long ago. He is outrageous, and sometimes close to unbearable, but what we have here is the mature Roth, not the youthful one-note monologuist—what we have here is *Great Expectations*, not *David Copperfield*. Mickey Sabbath and the novel that bears his name both turn out to be moving and profound. Mickey Sabbath remembering his beloved older brother who died in the Second World War; Mickey's memories of his childhood on the Jersey Shore; Mickey in the cemetery where his family lies, picking out his own grave; perhaps above all, Mickey bidding farewell to his lover Drenka . . . These great scenes show that Roth has moved past Zuckerman and now his subject is as much other people as himself. Of course, there is a little of Portnoy in Sabbath, and the moment in which, as an act of love, the puppeteer urinates on Drenka's grave, and is then arrested for doing so by her son the policeman, is a moment of which Alex Portnoy would have been proud.

Of the trilogy of masterpieces that followed *Sabbath's Theater*—*The Human Stain, American Pastoral,* and *I Married a Communist*—so much has been written and so much deserved praise bestowed that I will not add more than a few contextualizing molehills to that mountain. Suffice to say that Nathan Zuckerman shows up in all three novels, but now he's telling other people's stories, not his own, and the people whose stories he tells—Coleman Silk, Swede and Merry Levov, and Iron Rinn—also take Roth's work into the dark heart of America as it was during the course of his lifetime, and that time finds many echoes in our own.

*I Married a Communist* deals with McCarthyism, and at an American moment when powerful fingers are being pointed at so many good men and women, notably journalists, when good men and women are being defamed as "enemies of the people," the destructive force of red-scare politics can easily be read as a metaphor for the present.

*The Human Stain* takes up the subject of crossing the color line, of passing for white, which has been a subject for American writers from Mark Twain's *Tragedy of Pudd'nhead Wilson* through Nella Larsen's *Passing,* Langston Hughes's stories "Passing" and "Who's Passing for Who?" and Fannie Hurst's *Imitation of Life,* about a light-skinned black girl named Peola, whose name Toni Morrison echoes in the character of "Pecola," the black girl driven insane by her unattainable dreams of white beauty, in *The Bluest Eye. Imitation of Life* was filmed, the story much transformed but still concerning the subject of passing, by Douglas Sirk in 1959, starring Lana Turner and Susan Kohner as "Sarah Jane," the renamed Peola.

Philip Roth's Coleman Silk, the powerful academic living his life as a Jewish American, echoes the real-life case of Anatole Broyard, who, as Henry Louis Gates has said, "was born black and became white." Broyard was successful, sexually attractive, and often actually anti-black, attacking James Baldwin's *If Beale Street Could Talk* thus: "If I have to read one more description of the garbage piled up in the streets of Harlem, I may just throw protocol to the winds and ask whose garbage is it?" Henry Louis Gates also quotes an associate of Broyard's, Evelyn Thornton, who remembered Broyard's reaction to being asked for money by a drunken black man. He remarked in anger, "I look around New York, and I think to myself, If there were no blacks in New York, would it really be any loss?" (In *The Human Stain*, Roth's Coleman Silk is also accused of anti-black racial prejudice.) These dark choices, real and fictional, transformed by Roth into art, gave him his point of entry into the subject of race in America, a subject still at the very center of the American story.

And if *The Human Stain* took on race, then *American Pastoral* faced up to the consequences in America of the Vietnam War and the rise, driven in part by the anti-war movement, of an American radicalism that took the form of violent, even murderous domestic terrorism. Today, when most terrorist acts in America are carried out by heavily armed white people, Roth's portrait of the terrorist Merry Levov has more resonance than ever. *American Pastoral,* perhaps Roth's most "public fiction," includes consideration of the bombings carried out by the so-called Weathermen or Weather Underground, as well as the 1967 Newark riots, the Black Panthers, the trial of Angela Davis, the Watergate affair, and Deep Throat (both the then-anonymous source for Woodward and Bernstein, subsequently identified as the FBI's associate director Mark Felt, and the porno movie starring Linda Lovelace). Once again, one can't help hearing contemporary echoes. Now that the present administration speaks so often about the alleged attempts by the "deep state" to undermine the government, the story of "Deep Throat," a man at the heart of the deep state who did just that during the Nixon presidency, reminds us that there may be times when loyalty to the country takes precedence over loyalty to the presidency.

These books transformed my thinking about Philip Roth. Until I read them, I confess that in the Roth–Bellow debate I had placed Bellow just a little above Roth, just one step above him on the highest rungs of the ladder—thinking Bellow's greatest books to be a little more ambitious, more world-swallowing, bigger. The trilogy silenced that line of argument forever. I have always believed that we live at a time when public events impinge so directly on our private lives that literature now needs to show how that works, that novels can no longer be accounts of wholly private lives, as *Madame Bovary* was, or *Pride and Prejudice*. In my own work I have often tried to find the points of intersection where the private conversation within me engages with the public conversation all around me, and to see Philip Roth writing in that way was and is exhilarating and inspiring.

This is the Philip Roth who, in *The Plot Against America*, ended up as a kind of prophet, a Cassandra for our age, warning us what was to come, and, like Cassandra, not being taken seriously. When I first read *The Plot Against America*, with its highly imagined alternative-history account of the rise to the presidency of the celebrity aviator Charles Lindbergh, a populist demagogue, a radical isolationist, a racist, and an anti-Semite, a man who found it easy to make an accommodation with Adolf Hitler and who revealed, in his electoral triumph, the dark underbelly of American prejudice, I remember thinking that I didn't buy it, that it was too extreme, that, in short, it couldn't happen here. But here we stand, with a celebrity president who is a populist demagogue, an isolationist who is putting up tariff barriers against most of the world, a man whose cultural targets (LeBron James, Don Lemon, Maxine Waters) are very frequently people of color, and whose administration has unleashed, in its political base, a tide of racism; a man who has found it easy to cozy up to the murderous tyrant Vladimir Putin, and whose followers, some of them seen wearing T-shirts reading *I'd rather be a Russian than a Democrat*, are indeed revealing to us how dark and swollen the underbelly of American prejudice (and stupidity) still is. To use R. D. Laing's description of schizophrenia, America has become a deeply "divided self," and Roth, a writer fascinated, from *Portnoy* onward, by psychoanalysis, offered us, in this book, the shrewdest of analyses of our divided reality. This is Philip Roth's accidental fate: to begin as a literary revolutionary and to end up, after a long, strange, relentlessly interesting journey, as a political prophet. One can only bow one's head before such a career, while expressing deep regret that, in this prophetic work from fourteen years ago, he turned out to be right on the money and that he's no longer around to help us work out where we go from here.

# KURT VONNEGUT AND
## *SLAUGHTERHOUSE-FIVE*

———

I FIRST READ *SLAUGHTERHOUSE-FIVE* IN 1972, THREE YEARS
after it was published, and three years before I published my own first
novel. I was twenty-five years old. 1972 was the year of the Paris Peace
Accords, which were supposed to end the war in Vietnam, though
the final, ignominious American withdrawal—the helicopters airlift-
ing people from the roof of the American embassy in Saigon—would
not take place until three years later.

I mention Vietnam because, although *Slaughterhouse-Five* is a
book about World War II, Vietnam is also a presence in its pages,
and people's feelings about that later war have a good deal to do with
the novel's huge success. Eight years earlier, in 1961, Joseph Heller
had published *Catch-22*, and that was the year that President Kennedy began the escalation of the United States's involvement in the
conflict in Vietnam. *Catch-22*, like *Slaughterhouse-Five*, was a novel
about World War II that caught the imagination of readers who were
thinking a lot about another war. In those days I was living in Britain,
which did not send soldiers to fight in Indochina but whose government did support the American war effort, and so, when I was at
university, and afterward, I too was involved with thinking about and
protesting against that war. I did not read *Catch-22* in 1961, because I
was only fourteen years old. As a matter of fact, I read both
*Slaughterhouse-Five* and *Catch-22* in the same year, eleven years later,
and the two books together had a great effect on my young mind.

It hadn't occurred to me until I read them that anti-war novels could be funny as well as serious. *Catch-22* is crazy-funny, slapstick-funny. It sees war as insane and the desire to escape combat as the only sane position. Its tone of voice is deadpan farce. *Slaughterhouse-Five* is different. There is much comedy in it, as there was in everything Kurt Vonnegut wrote, but it does not see war as farcical. It sees war as a tragedy so great that perhaps only the mask of comedy allows one to look it in the eye. Vonnegut is a sad-faced comedian. If Joseph Heller was Charlie Chaplin, then Kurt Vonnegut was Buster Keaton. His predominant tone of voice is melancholy, the tone of voice of a man who has been present at a great horror and lived to tell the tale. The two books do, however, have this in common: They are both portraits of a world that has lost its mind, in which children are sent out to do men's work and die.

As a prisoner of war, aged twenty-two—which is to say, three years younger than I was when I read his story—Vonnegut was in the famously beautiful city of Dresden, locked up with other Americans in *Schlachthof-Fünf,* where pigs had been slaughtered before the war, and was therefore an accidental witness to one of the greatest slaughters of human beings in history, the firebombing of Dresden, which flattened the whole city. The firebombing took place between February 13 and 15 of 1945.

Vonnegut tells us in his novel that more than 135,000 people died in Dresden during that attack. By comparison, over 70,000 people died as a result of the dropping of the atom bomb called Little Boy on Hiroshima later that same year, on August 6. Somewhere around 60,000 people died as a result of the bomb named Fat Man dropped on Nagasaki three days later. The firebombing of Dresden, Vonnegut claimed, was a horror approximately equal to the horrors of Hiroshima and Nagasaki combined.

His figure for deaths in Dresden has not proved to be reliable. The numbers killed there are now estimated at somewhere over 20,000, maybe as many as 25,000. Which is not Hiroshima plus Nagasaki but is terrible enough.

So it goes.

I had not remembered, until I reread *Slaughterhouse-Five* recently, that that famous phrase, "so it goes," is used only and always as a comment on death. Sometimes a phrase from a novel or play or film can catch the imagination so powerfully that it lifts off from the page and acquires an independent life of its own. Something of this sort has happened to the phrase "so it goes." The trouble is that when this kind of liftoff happens to a phrase, its original context is lost. I suspect that many people who have not read Kurt Vonnegut are familiar with "so it goes," but they, and also, I suspect, many people who *have* read Kurt Vonnegut, think of the phrase as a kind of resigned commentary on life. Life rarely turns out in the way the living hope for, and "so it goes" has become one of the ways in which we verbally shrug our shoulders and accept what life gives us. But that is not its purpose in *Slaughterhouse-Five*. "So it goes" is not a way of accepting life but of facing death. It occurs in the text every single time someone dies, and only when someone dies.

It is also deeply ironic. Beneath the apparent resignation is a sadness for which there are no words. This is the manner of the entire novel, and it has led to the novel being, in many cases, misunderstood. I am not suggesting that *Slaughterhouse-Five* has been poorly treated. Its reception was largely positive; it has sold an enormous number of copies; the Modern Library ranked it eighteenth on its list of the hundred best English-language novels of the twentieth century; and it is also on a similar list issued by *Time* magazine. However, there are those who have accused it of the sin of "quietism," of a resigned acceptance, even, according to Anthony Burgess, an "evasion" of the worst things in the world. One of the reasons for this is the phrase "so it goes," and it is clear to me from these critiques that the British novelist Julian Barnes was right when he wrote in his book *A History of the World in 10½ Chapters* that "the definition of irony is what people miss."

Kurt Vonnegut is a deeply ironic writer who has sometimes been read as if he is not. The misreading goes beyond "so it goes" and has a good deal to do with the inhabitants of the planet of Tralfamadore. As it happens, I am a great fan of Tralfamadorians, who look like toilet plungers, beginning with their mechanical emissary Salo, who, in an earlier Vonnegut novel, *The Sirens of Titan*, was marooned on Titan, a moon of the planet Saturn, needing a replacement part for his spaceship. And now comes the classic Vonnegut subject of free will, expressed as a comic science-fiction device. We learn in *The Sirens of Titan* that the whole of human history has been manipulated by Tralfamadorians to persuade the human race to build large messages to their emissary Salo and to get our primitive ancestors to develop a civilization capable of building the spare part. Stonehenge and the Great Wall of China were some of the messages from Tralfamadore. Stonehenge read, "Replacement part being rushed with all possible speed." The Great Wall of China said, "Be patient. We haven't forgotten you." The Kremlin meant, "You will be on your way before you know it." And the Palace of the League of Nations in Geneva, Switzerland, meant, "Pack up your things and be ready to leave on short notice."

Tralfamadorians, we learn in *Slaughterhouse-Five*, perceive time differently. They see that the past, present, and future all exist simultaneously and forever and are simply there, fixed, eternal. When the main character of the novel, Billy Pilgrim, who is kidnapped and taken to Tralfamadore, "comes unstuck in time" and begins to experience chronology the way Tralfamadorians do, he understands why his captors find comical the notion of free will.

It seems obvious at least to this reader that there is a mischievous ironic intelligence at work here, that there is no reason for us to assume that the rejection of free will by aliens resembling toilet plungers is a rejection also made by their creator. It is perfectly possible, perhaps even sensible, to read Billy Pilgrim's entire Tralfamadorian experience as a fantastic traumatic disorder brought about by his wartime experiences—as "not real." Vonnegut leaves that question open, as a good writer should. That openness is the space in which the reader is allowed to make up his or her own mind.

To read Vonnegut is to know that he was repeatedly drawn to the investigation of free will, of what it might be and how it might or might not function, and that he came at the subject from many different angles. Many of his ruminations were presented in the form of works by his fictional alter ego, Kilgore Trout.

I love Kilgore Trout as deeply as I love the inhabitants of the planet Tralfamadore. I even own a copy of Kilgore Trout's novel *Venus on the Half-Shell,* in which the writer Philip José Farmer took a Trout story written by Vonnegut and expanded it to novel length. *Venus on the Half-Shell* is about the accidental destruction of the earth by incompetent universal bureaucrats and the attempt by the sole surviving human being to seek answers to the so-called Ultimate Question. In this way Kilgore Trout inspired Douglas Adams's celebrated series *The Hitchhiker's Guide to the Galaxy,* in which, you may recall, the earth was demolished by Vogons to make room for an interstellar bypass, and the sole surviving human, Arthur Dent, went in search of answers. Finally, the supercomputer Deep Thought revealed that the answer to life, the universe, and everything was, and is, "42." The problem remains, what is the question?

In Vonnegut's novel *Breakfast of Champions* we learn about another Kilgore Trout story, *Now It Can Be Told,* written in the form of a letter from God addressed to the reader of the story. God explains that the whole of life itself has been a long experiment. The nature of the experiment was this: to introduce into an otherwise wholly deterministic universe one single person who is granted free will, to see what use he makes of it, in a reality in which every other living thing was, is, and always will be a programmed machine. Everyone in the whole of history has been a robot, and the single individual with free will's mother and father and everyone he knows are also robots, and so, by the way, is Sammy Davis, Jr. The individual with free will, God explains, is YOU, the reader of the story, and to be frank the experiment hasn't worked out that well, and so God would like to offer you an apology. The end.

It's worth adding one further detail. Throughout the many works by Kurt Vonnegut in which Kilgore Trout appears, he is consistently described by everyone else as the worst writer in the world, whose books are utter failures, and who is completely and even contemptuously ignored. We are asked simultaneously to see him as a genius and a fool. This is not accidental. His creator, Kurt Vonnegut, was at once the most intellectual of playful fantasists and the most playfully fantastic of intellectuals. He had a horror of people who took things too seriously and was simultaneously obsessed with the consideration of the most serious things, things both philosophical (like free will) and lethal (like the firebombing of Dresden). This is the paradox out of which his dark ironies grow. Nobody who futzed around so often and in so many ways with the idea of free will, or who cared so profoundly about the dead, could be described as a fatalist, or quietist, or resigned. His books argue about ideas of freedom and mourn the dead, from their first pages to their last.

Around the same time that I first read *Slaughterhouse-Five* and *Catch-22*, I also read another novel about a similar subject. That novel was *War and Peace,* which is longer than Heller's book and Vonnegut's book combined and isn't funny at all. On that first reading of Tolstoy's masterpiece, my twenty-five-year-old self thought, in summary: loved peace, hated war. I was absorbed by the stories of Natasha Rostova, Prince Andrei, and Pierre Bezukhov and found the extremely long descriptions of fighting, especially of the battle of Borodino, pretty boring, to be frank. When I reread *War and Peace* perhaps thirty years later, I discovered that I now felt exactly the opposite. The description of men at war, I thought, had never been bettered, and the greatness of the novel was to be found in those descriptions and not in the somewhat more conventional stories of the leading characters. Loved war, hated peace.

Rereading *Slaughterhouse-Five,* I also found my valuation of the text changing. That younger self was strongly drawn to fantasy and science fiction, and sought out magazines called things like *Galaxy* and *Astounding* and *Amazing,* and was drawn to the work not only of the crossover giants like Kurt Vonnegut and Ray Bradbury and Isaac Asimov and Ursula K. Le Guin and Arthur C. Clarke—as well as Mary Shelley and Virginia Woolf, whose *Frankenstein* and *Orlando* are honorary members of the canon—but also of the hardcore genre masters, James Blish, Frederik Pohl and C. M. Kornbluth, Clifford

D. Simak, Katherine MacLean, Zenna Henderson, and L. Sprague de Camp. That young man, faced with Vonnegut's masterpiece, responded most strongly to the sci-fi aspects of the book. To read it again has been to discover the humane beauty of the non-sci-fi parts, which make up most of the book.

The truth is that *Slaughterhouse-Five* is a great realist novel. Its first sentence is "All this happened, more or less." In that nonfictional first chapter Vonnegut tells us how hard the book was to write, how hard it was for him to deal with war. He tells us that his characters were real people, though he has changed all the names. "One guy I knew really was shot in Dresden for taking a teapot that wasn't his. Another guy I knew really did threaten to have his personal enemies killed by hired gunmen after the war." And later, when his characters, the ones with the changed names, arrive at *Schlachthof-Fünf*, Slaughterhouse-Five, whose name he has not changed, he reminds us that he's there with them, suffering right along with them.

> Billy looked inside the latrine. The wailing was coming from in there. . . . An American near Billy wailed that he had excreted everything but his brains. Moments later he said, "There they go, there they go." He meant his brains.
>
> That was I. That was me. That was the author of this book.

At one point Vonnegut quotes a conversation he had with a filmmaker called Harrison Starr, who would achieve a kind of modest renown as the executive producer of Michelangelo Antonioni's movie about American hippies, *Zabriskie Point*, which was a huge commercial flop.

> [Harrison Starr] raised his eyebrows and inquired, "Is it an anti-war book?"
>
> "Yes," I said. "I guess."
>
> "You know what I say to people when I hear they're writing anti-war books?"

"No. What *do* you say, Harrison Starr?"

"I say, 'Why don't you write an anti-*glacier* book instead?'"

What he meant, of course, was that there would always be wars, that they were as easy to stop as glaciers. I believe that, too.

Vonnegut's novel is about that, about the inevitability of human violence, and about what it does to the not-particularly-violent human beings who get caught up in it. He knows that most human beings are not particularly violent. Or not more violent than children are. Give a child a machine gun and he may well use it. Which does not mean that children are particularly violent.

World War II, as Vonnegut reminds us, was a children's crusade.

Billy Pilgrim is an adult to whom Vonnegut gives the innocence of a child. He is not particularly violent. He does nothing awful in the war or in his prewar or postwar life, or in his life on the planet Tralfamadore. He seems deranged and is mostly thought of as crazy, or as a near-simpleton. But he has a characteristic in common with many of Vonnegut's characters throughout his career, and it is this characteristic that allows us to care for him and therefore to feel the horror that he feels.

Billy Pilgrim is lovable.

If he were not lovable, the book would be unbearable. One of the great questions that faces all writers who have to deal with atrocity is: Is it possible to do it? Are there things so powerful, so dreadful, that they are beyond the power of literature to describe? Every writer who faced the challenge of writing about World War II—and the Vietnam War, in fact—has had to think about that question. All of them decided they needed to come at the atrocity at an angle, so to speak, not to face it head-on, because to do that would be unbearable.

Günter Grass, in *The Tin Drum*, used surrealism as his angle of entry. His character Oskar Matzerath, who stops growing because he can't face the adult reality of his time, is one kind of fabulist being that allows the author to enter the horror. And little Oskar with his tin drum, drumming the beats of history, is, like Billy Pilgrim who has come unstuck in time, lovable. He is also, as the first sentence of *The Tin Drum* tells us, an inmate in a lunatic asylum. From opposite sides, German and American, these two deranged child-men give us our finest portraits of the great derangement of their time. Kurt Vonnegut, like Grass, combines the surrealism that has become the reality of his characters' time with a detached, almost stunned tenderness that makes the reader feel fondly toward them, even as they stumble incompetently through life.

It may be impossible to stop wars, just as it's impossible to stop glaciers, but it's still worth finding the form and the language that reminds us what they are. It's worth calling them by their true names. That is what realism is.

*Slaughterhouse-Five* is also a novel humane enough to allow, at the end of the horror that is its subject, for the possibility of hope. Its final passage describes the end of the war and the liberation of the prisoners, who include Billy Pilgrim and Vonnegut himself. "And somewhere in there was springtime," Vonnegut writes, and in the last moment of the book, birds, once again, begin to sing. This cheerfulness in spite of everything is Vonnegut's characteristic note. It may be, as I've suggested, a cheerfulness beneath which much pain is hidden. But it is cheerfulness nonetheless. Vonnegut's prose, even when dealing with the dreadful, whistles a happy tune.

More than fifty years after its first publication, seventy-four years after Kurt Vonnegut was inside Slaughterhouse-Five during the firebombing of Dresden, what does his great novel have to say to us?

It doesn't tell us how to stop wars.

It tells us that wars are hell, but we knew that already.

It tells us that most human beings are not so bad, except for the ones who are, and that's valuable information. It tells us that human nature is the one great constant of life on earth, and it beautifully and truthfully shows us human nature neither at its best nor at its worst but how it mostly is, most of the time, even when the times are terrible.

It doesn't tell us how to get to the planet Tralfamadore, but it does tell us how to communicate with its inhabitants. All we have to do is build something big, like the pyramids or the Great Wall of China. Maybe the wall that some individual whom I will not name is planning to build between the United States and Mexico will be read as an urgent message on Tralfamadore. The person who wants to build the wall will not know what the message means. He is a pawn, being manipulated by a power greater than his own to send the message in this time of great emergency.

I hope the message reads, "Help."

# SAMUEL BECKETT'S
# NOVELS

———

IN MY EYES SAMUEL BECKETT HAS ALWAYS BEEN A NOVEL-
ist first and playwright later, though I concede that this opinion may
simply be a consequence of my own Beckettian chronology. I read
Beckett's novels before I saw any of his plays, so that when I did encounter *Godot*'s existentialist tramps Didi and Gogo I saw them
through the glass, so to speak, of their prose sidekicks and therefore
at once divined that the Godot they were waiting for was death,
death being the great bugaboo facing so many of the novels' characters, with life's last twitches, its last grins and belches and its desper-
ate, crucified crosstalk, doing service in place of plots.

When I was a college student, browsing in bookstores was meat
and drink to me. I never studied English literature but, loving books,
plunged into libraries and bookshops like a starving man, gobbling
up whatever came to hand. I went on long idiosyncratic reading jags,
experimenting with literature's mind-altering effects at a time when
many of my contemporaries were fumbling with other, less verbal
keys to perception's doors. For a time I devoured science fiction, and
then one day, as if someone had pulled out a plug, lost interest, and
stopped. Then came an addiction to American literature (not only
the canonical Huck Finns and white whales but also the weirder
creations of Pynchon, John Gardner, John Hawkes). Then came
Borges, whose *Fictions* shifted something important in my head and
made me want to read everything else published in austere paperback
editions by the publisher John Calder. In thrall to the Calder im-

print's mandarin tastes, I discovered Alain Robbe-Grillet's *Jealousy* and after it many more *nouveau romanciers,* and so, one summer's day, I came, as was only right, by way of France to Beckett. I first picked up a copy of *Molloy,* and afterward the other two volumes of the Trilogy, *Malone Dies* and *The Unnamable,* in Bowes & Bowes, a Cambridge bookstore at the northern end of King's Parade, my favored browserie, its name lacking only a pair of "r"s (which I, with playful orthographic generosity, mentally added) to be an anagram of Browse & Browse.

It was 1966 and I was not quite nineteen years old and at that time death and I were no better than nodding acquaintances. That is to say, I had on occasion seen death from a distance but we had not yet been properly introduced. There had been a day at the Cathedral School in Bombay *circa* 1958 when all the classroom doors and windows opening onto the quadrangle were shut and locked so that we could not see the vehicle that entered through the back gate to remove the dead body of a child of my own age whose name was Jimmy King. There was a day at King's College, Cambridge, when word spread quickly of the death by drug overdose, death by *bad acid,* of one of my fellow freshmen, but I saw nothing of this ending for myself. In my family life also, death was still an abstraction. My maternal grandparents were still alive. My father's father had died before I was born, and he was no more than a photograph to me. My father's mother, ailing badly, came to stay when I was perhaps three years old and suffered me to play doctor, toy stethoscope and all, rising from her sickbed to hobble painfully, at my injudicious bidding, back and forth across her curtained bedroom, but then she left us and went home to Old Delhi, and when she died there soon afterward it was an invisible, elsewhere thing that a child could easily learn to disregard; it was not much worse than waving goodbye to us at Bombay Central station and puffing away into the evening on the mail train.

Death was, as you might say, still a word in a book to me. I had not at that time washed my father's short, heavy corpse or murmured a farewell to the openmouthed body of the first woman I ever loved or wept tears of rage when I was denied by circumstance the right to stand beside my mother's grave. Consequently, I still felt immortal, and immortals deal differently with the subject of mortality, knowing themselves to be immune from that strange incurable affliction. Thus, when as a young man I first faced these texts that deal so intensely with the matter of our common ending, which Henry James had called the Distinguished Thing but which, in Beckett, is always grubbily undistinguished, a bleak pratfalling business made up of flatulence, impotence, and humiliation, I experienced the books, their ferocious hurling at death of immense slabs of undifferentiated prose, as essentially fabulous, fantastic tales told by the voices of antic ghosts. I experienced them, in sum, as comedies, and so they are, they are comedies, but not of the sort I then imagined them to be. They are darker and, yes, even heroic; for all that comedy scoffs at heroes, pulls down their drawers and pushes custard pie into their faces, still there remains, in the comedy of these broken, scrabbling personages, a stale whiff of odorous heroism. Some of this I when green in judgment only half perceived or neglected entirely to grasp. However, in failing to respond glumly to an oeuvre that wears glumness like a favorite unwashed shirt, I got something half right, at least.

To revisit these books is to have to answer, promptly and up front, the question of difficulty, for there is no getting around it, these are difficult books. A headache after reading would not, or not in all cases, be an inappropriate response, though it should be added in fairness that there are headaches that feel worthwhile, headaches given up in return for something of value gained, and the Beckettian headache is a pounding of this satisfactory stripe. For example, from *The Unnamable*, this: "Perhaps they are somewhere there, the words that count, in what has just been said, the words it behoved to say, they need not be more than a few. They say they, speaking of them, to make me think it is I who am speaking. Or I say they, speaking of God knows what, to make me think it is not I who am speaking. Or rather there is silence," and so on, you see what I mean, the pounding begins, but also an awareness of beauty, of a thing being said that is said with difficulty because it is not an easy thing to say, and the saying of a difficult thing is not without importance, we are too much in love, more than half in love, in our pampered days, with ease.

These are books in which direct speech is denuded of the distinction of quotation marks, in which paragraphing feels like a luxury the author could ill afford, in which a sentence may be three pages long or even longer, so that when other, briefer sentences reveal their author's familiarity with pithiness, the reader is or may be moved to irritation or at least sighing, why couldn't he do that more often, the cry rises, why does the man torment us so, why these dark interminable labyrinthine tunnels of words down which he makes us go. And yet, and yet. There is the beauty at the tunnel's end. I can't go on, the reader cries, I'll go on.

The answer to the question of difficulty is surrender. Give in to the text and it opens up, a rare if shabby flower. Stop asking for what is not there and you start to see what is. "It is in the tranquillity of decomposition that I remember the long confused emotion which was my life," Molloy writes, "and that I judge it, as it is said that God will judge me, and with no less impertinence." A writer, Samuel Beckett not Molloy, or Beckett as Molloy, or Beckett reaching through Molloy for something that is neither Beckett nor Molloy, attempts the impossible: *viz.*, to write of death, of the end of ends, the ending that ends the future as well as all the other tenses, the past imperfect, the present subjunctive, the present indicative, the pluperfect, and to do so using the tool not of prophecy but of memory. To remember not only what has happened, the long confused emotion, but also what has not happened, the thing of which no human being has a living memory—because the thing itself is memory's end—is to assert life's primacy over death, for memory is the tool by which the living know and forget and understand and misunderstand themselves, so what tool could be better to wield, like a weapon, against death, knowing it will be inadequate, knowing the inexorability, knowing and not giving in, or not yet, not quite yet, not before a few more words have been spoken, not until memory has spoken, as the artist, Beckett as much as Nabokov, requires and commands.

This is why it is possible to assert, and I assert it here, I summon all my assertive powers to make the assertion, that these books, whose ostensible subject is death, are in fact books about life, the lifelong battle of life against its shadow, life shown near the battle's end, bearing its lifetime of scars, but life, nevertheless, remembered, putrid, unimportant life, than which nothing matters more. Life as paradox, each statement contradicted by the next, life as contradiction, life canceling itself out. Molloy, Malone, the Unnamable, face death. But they are living beings. "Throes are the only trouble," Malone warns himself, "I must be on my guard against throes." But even as the danger of throes increases, he finds he still has stories to tell, "one about a man, another about a woman, a third about a thing and finally one about an animal," knowing that they are all a part of his own story. "What tedium," he cries, "I wonder if I am not talking yet again about myself," and he is, of course, and a good thing too, using his half-story of Saposcat who metamorphs into Macmann, and his other half-stories, to shore up life's last dike, until he can shore it up no more, until the "gurgles of outflow," which we will all hear in the end, as memory knows. Death strips life down to its essence before it takes that essence away, and these books mimic death and strip away everything that is not essential. Words are essential and so a few words remain, and stories cannot entirely be dispensed with; they are begun and changed and discarded but never entirely disposed of, because in stories resides life, while it resides, until the last eviction. So: some words, some fragments of stories, which retain in spite of their apparent perfunctoriness an unexpected ability to charm, not merely to pass the time but to enliven it, and beyond the words and stories are things, crutches, for example, or bicycles, and beyond the things are other people, a son, a lustful woman, a man in pursuit of another man, not finding the other but losing himself instead, a man with, it must be said, an umbrella. "I have lost my stick," Malone says. "That is the outstanding event of the day." In these days, Beckett's happy days, breathing is an outstanding event, and thought as well, and at the last or near the last there is the I that gives up imagining, the nameless, unnamed, unnamable I, "all these Murphys, Molloys and

Malones do not fool me," it says. "They have made me waste my time, suffer for nothing, speak of them when, in order to stop speaking, I should have spoken of me and of me alone," it says, the I who is the author and also the not-author, who is Beckett and Unnamable, or Beckett as Unnamable, or Beckett through the Unnamable reaching for something beyond, something that is neither Beckett nor Unnamable. "There is no one here but me," it says, "I, of whom I know nothing."

And this finally is the great subject of this great writer, the I of whom he knows nothing, the I that lies beyond Malone's hat, or Molloy's greatcoat, or Murphy's suit, though it has at times worn all three, the I that cares nothing for chophouses or alehouses though it has frequented such places at times. "Perhaps that's what I am, the thing that divides the world in two, on the one side the outside, on the other the inside, that can be as thin as foil, I'm neither one side nor the other, I'm in the middle, I'm the partition."

It is the thing that speaks. A man speaking English beautifully chooses to speak in French, which he speaks with greater difficulty, so that he is obliged to choose his words carefully, forced to give up fluency and to find the hard words that come with difficulty, and then after all that finding he puts it all back into English, a new English containing all the difficulty of the French, of the coining of thought in a second language, a new English with the power to change English forever. This is Samuel Beckett. This is his great work. It is the thing that speaks.

Surrender.

# CERVANTES AND
# SHAKESPEARE

————

In 2015 I was asked to write an introduction to a collection of
stories, *Lunatics, Lovers and Poets*, in which six English-
language writers wrote texts inspired by Cervantes, and six
Spanish-language writers wrote texts inspired by Shakespeare,
to commemorate the double anniversary of the two giants.
This is that introduction. And a personal note: My rereading of
*Don Quixote*, in the brilliant Edith Grossman translation—so
much more vivid than the old J. M. Cohen version, which I
first read back in the 1970s—became the starting point, the first
inspiration, for the novel that became *Quichotte*.

As WE HONOR THE FOUR HUNDREDTH ANNIVERSARIES OF THE
deaths of William Shakespeare and Miguel de Cervantes Saavedra,
it may be worth noting that while it's generally accepted that the two
giants died on the same date, April 23, 1616, it actually wasn't the
same day. By 1616 Spain had moved on to using the Gregorian calendar, while England still used the Julian and was eleven days behind.
(England clung to the old Julian dating system until 1752, and when
the change finally came, there were riots and, it's said, mobs in the
streets shouting, "Give us back our eleven days!") Both the coincidence of the dates and the difference in the calendars would, one
suspects, have delighted the playful, erudite sensibilities of the two
fathers of modern literature.

We don't know if they were aware of each other, but we do know that *Don Quixote* was translated into English during Shakespeare's lifetime, and we also know that there's a lost play attributed at least in part to Shakespeare, perhaps Shakespeare in collaboration with John Fletcher: *Cardenio*, which is also the name of one of the most prominent secondary characters in *Don Quixote*. The story of Cardenio is one of star-crossed lovers, a theme that might have attracted the author of *Much Ado About Nothing* and *A Midsummer Night's Dream*. So it's possible that Shakespeare had read, and been inspired by, Cervantes. However, there's nothing to suggest that Cervantes was familiar with Shakespeare's poetry or plays. Nevertheless, they had a good deal in common, beginning right here in the what-we-don't-know zone, because they are both men of mystery; there are missing years in the record and, apart from *Cardenio*, many missing documents. Neither man left behind much personal material. Very little in the way of letters, work diaries, abandoned drafts; just the colossal, completed oeuvres. "The rest is silence."

Consequently, both men have been prey to the kind of idiot minds that seek to dispute their authorship. A cursory Internet search "reveals," for example, that not only did Francis Bacon write Shakespeare's works, "he wrote 'Don Quixote' as well." And Cervantes faced a challenge to his authorship in his own lifetime, when a certain pseudonymous Alonso Fernández de Avellaneda, whose identity is also uncertain, published his fake sequel to *Don Quixote* and goaded Cervantes into writing the real Book Two, whose characters are aware of the plagiarist Avellaneda and hold him in much contempt.

Cervantes and Shakespeare almost certainly never met, but the closer you look at the pages they left behind, the more echoes you hear. The first, and to my mind the most valuable, shared idea is the belief that a work of literature doesn't have to be simply comic, or tragic, or romantic, or political/historical: that, if properly conceived, it can be many things at the same time. They are both protean, shape-shifting writers, and they are both self-conscious, modern in a way that most of the modern masters would recognize, the one creating plays that are highly aware of their theatricality, of being staged, the other creating fiction that is acutely conscious of its fictive nature, even to the point of inventing an imaginary narrator, Cide Hamete Benengeli—a narrator, interestingly, with Arab antecedents.

And they are both as fond of, and as adept at, lowlife as they are of high ideas, and their galleries of rascals, whores, cutpurses, and drunks would be at home in the same taverns. This earthiness is what reveals them both to be realists in the grand manner, even when they are posing as fantasists, and so, again, we who come after can learn from them both that magic is pointless except when in the service of realism—was there ever a more realist magician than Prospero?—and realism can do with the injection of a healthy dose of the fabulist. Finally, though they both use tropes that originate in folktale, myth, and fable, they refuse to moralize, and in this above all else they are more modern than many who followed them. They do not tell us what to think or feel, but they show us how to do so.

Of the two, Cervantes was the man of action, fighting in battles, being seriously wounded, losing the use of his left hand, being en-slaved by the corsairs of Algiers for five years until his family raised the money for his ransom. Shakespeare had no such dramas in his personal experience; yet of the two he seems to have been the writer more interested in war and soldiering. *Othello, Macbeth, Lear* are all tales of men at war (within themselves, yes, but on the field of battle too). Cervantes used his painful experiences—for example in the "Captive's Tale" in *Quixote* and in a couple of plays—but the battle on which Don Quixote embarks is—to use modern words—absurdist and existential rather than "real." Strangely, the Spanish warrior wrote of the comic futility of going into battle and created the great iconic figure of the warrior as fool (one thinks of Heller's *Catch-22* or Vonnegut's *Slaughterhouse-Five* for more recent explorations of this theme), while the imagination of the English poet–dramatist plunged (like Tolstoy, like Mailer) headlong toward war.

In their differences, they embody very contemporary opposites, just as, in their similarities, they agree on a great deal that is still use-ful to their inheritors. Above all, they are inexhaustible, and, end-lessly revisited, they have something new to say to us each time we pay them a call.

# GABO AND I

W HEN I PUBLISHED MY FIRST AND NOW JUSTLY OBSCURE
novel *Grimus,* a friend of mine said to me, "You've obviously been
deeply influenced by Gabriel García Márquez." The year was 1975
and I was twenty-seven years old and I had never heard that name
before. The English edition of *One Hundred Years of Solitude*—
translated by Gregory Rabassa—had been published five years earlier, three years after the original Spanish edition, but it had not
crossed my path. "Who is Gabriel García Márquez?" I asked my
friend, and he looked at me with a mixture of disbelief, pity, and contempt. "He is the author of a book you are going to go out and buy
right now," he told me. "Today, this afternoon, at once." He told me
the book's title and I replied dubiously, "Really? *One hundred* years?
Of *solitude*? That's a good book?" "Don't be a moron," my friend said,
only he used a ruder word. "Just go and get it."

For some reason I meekly did as he said. In a London bookstore
I found a Penguin Modern Classics paperback edition with its gray
jacket and, on the cover, a detail from J. C. Orozco's mural *The Misery
of the Peasants.* This was dispiriting. Not only was I going to have to
sit through an entire century of solitude, but in that interminable
isolation I would have to be told about miserable peasants. I opened
the book right there in the bookstore, frankly expecting to encounter
an insufferable tedium, and for the first time I saw, and seemed to
hear, these now world-famous words:

Many years later, as he faced the firing squad, Colonel Aureliano Buendía was to remember that distant afternoon when his father took him to discover ice. At that time Macondo was a village of twenty adobe houses, built on the bank of a river of clear water that ran along a bed of polished stones, which were white and enormous, like prehistoric eggs. The world was so recent that many things lacked names, and in order to indicate them it was necessary to point.

I wrote the date on which I bought the book on the first page below the author's biodata, and so I know for sure that this happened on March 13, 1975, the same month in which my first novel was published. I still have that copy, though I have since bought many others, to keep and to give away, because what happened to me that day is what happened to millions of people when they read those words. I fell deeply in love, and that love has lasted now for over forty years, without diminishing. These peasants were anything but miserable, and the title on the jacket, which had at first seemed so forbidding to me, now seemed like a promise of long delight, a promise that the pages that followed would amply fulfill.

I knew almost nothing about the Latin American literary world I had entered, nor of the reality from which it sprang. At the moment of that first encounter, I didn't care. I responded with the simple openness, the happy innocence, of the reader appalled and illumined by the beauty and comedy of the text:

The children would remember for the rest of their lives the august solemnity with which their father, devastated by his prolonged vigil and by the wrath of his imagination, revealed his discovery to them:

"The earth is round, like an orange."

Úrsula lost her patience. "If you have to go crazy, please go crazy all by yourself!" she shouted. "But don't try to put your gypsy ideas into the heads of the children."

The comedy of the moment prefigures what will become a trademark of the novel's brand of magic realism, which was present even in the famous first sentence about the miracle of the ice. In Macondo it is the world of technology and science that feels "marvelous," that is to say, unreal, while the village realities of superstition and faith seem "natural" and therefore true. An ice machine is magical. The discoveries of science are crazinesses. The scholar–gypsy Melquíades—whose mother tongue, we learn almost at the very end of the novel, was Sanskrit, a revelation that contains, perhaps, the author's homage to the wonder tales of the East—is received in Macondo as a kind of ragged sorcerer–king, able to transcend most earthly norms, death included. And the arrival of the first railway train drives at least one woman mad with fear. "It's coming," she cries. "Something frightful, like a kitchen dragging a village behind it."

Nor is this vision of technology as essentially surreal limited to the village. In *The Autumn of the Patriarch,* the power of American knowhow results in the literal loss of the Caribbean. After the dictator, the patriarch, sells the Caribbean to the Americans, the American ambassador's nautical engineers "carried it off in numbered pieces to plant it far from the hurricanes in the blood-red dawns of Arizona, they took it away with everything it had inside general sir, with the reflection of our cities, our timid drowned people, our demented dragons."

By contrast, when the pure and saintly Remedios the Beauty achieves transcendence so that one day when the women are folding sheets she rises up into the sky and presumably floats all the way up to heaven, nobody in Macondo turns a hair. Even the matriarch Úrsula, whose practicality and good sense anchor the Buendía dynasty and the novel itself, even Úrsula accepts the miraculous nature of the event, and so Remedios is lost, without argument, "in the upper atmosphere where not even the highest-flying birds of memory could reach her." "Outsiders," we are told, disbelieved the tale of levitation, but in Macondo, "most people believed in the miracle and they even lighted candles and celebrated novenas."

What we have here is something extraordinary: the creation, by a reversal of the expectations of the modern world, of a tone of voice that nobody in the long history of literature had quite found before. It owes something to many people, of course; no writer is entirely *sui generis*. Even Shakespeare got Lear and Macbeth from *Holinshed's Chronicles*, and who knows what he owed to Thomas Kyd's lost *Hamlet*, which came before his own? So also in García Márquez we see traces of the great writers from whom he learned; we see Faulkner's Yoknapatawpha somewhere in the neighborhood of Macondo, and Juan Rulfo's Comala is in the near vicinity also; and the town loomed over by Kafka's Castle is there too, as also is Kafka's use of metamorphosis, which in his turn Kafka derived from Ovid's *Metamorphoses* and Apuleius's *Golden Ass*. We can see traces of Machado de Assis's *Brás Cubas* and *Dom Casmurro* in the many José Arcadios and Aurelianos (and Arcadios and Aureliano Josés) of the Buendía dynasty. Machado's "anti-melancholy plaster" could easily have migrated into Úrsula Iguarán's medicine cabinet, and Brás Cubas's useful trick of narrating his story from beyond the grave by a process too complex and tedious to describe could have been learned from Melquíades. Or the other way around.

Parenthetically: The golden-hearted and melancholy whore is one of the most beloved and recurring character types of Latin American literature. If I may be permitted to introduce one discordant note, I am reminded that Angela Carter—a great admirer of García Márquez—used to say, wistfully but sharply, that she wished that just one of García Márquez's glorious prostitutes was shrewish by temperament and looked like a walleyed goat.

It is in the nature of literary criticism to seek to place a great writer in the context of his own literature, in the context of the times in which he lived and worked, and in the case of the greatest, in the context of world literature too; and in a minute I want to discuss the links between magic realism and other literature from other lands that also moves beyond the borders of naturalism. But to do this is not to diminish the singularity of the artist. And the singularity of García Márquez lies, I believe, in the precise note he strikes, a note somewhere on the scale between sweetness and bitterness, between a gentle acceptance of one's fate and an anger about it; "the wrath of his imagination" from which note proceeds the music of solitude, of human beings locked, alone, in destinies they cannot escape, moving toward deaths foretold. The power of this music, with its unique tone, has proved both great and enduring, its influence widely pervasive. I've quoted before, but I'll quote here again, the joke Carlos Fuentes once made to me. "I have the feeling," Fuentes said, "that writers in Latin America can't use the word 'solitude' anymore, because they worry that people will think it's a reference to Gabo. And I'm afraid," he added, mischievously, "that soon we will not be able to use the phrase 'one hundred years' either."

I'm reminded of something García Márquez's fellow Nobel laureate, the great German writer Heinrich Böll, once said about humor. The Latin word *humor*, Böll explained, means "dampness," and he recommended a way of writing—a way of *seeing*—that used a human eye "that normally is not quite wet and not quite dry, but damp," which is to say, *humorous*. Böll was describing the manner in which he and his postwar German contemporaries were trying to rebuild German literature from the rubble left behind by Nazism, but the "eye" of which he speaks, neither sentimentally wet nor cynically dry, but *damp*, has something to do with García Márquez's way of seeing as well.

AT THE TIME OF that long-ago first reading of *One Hundred Years of Solitude*, I responded to its story as pure story, to its characters simply as characters in a book. My interest in the world from which it sprang came later. We live in one of the great ages of literary translation, thanks to which the world's literatures arrive in our backyard, speaking our languages, giving us the feeling that they belong to us too, and not only to the soil from which they grew. Any discussion of the global impact of the writing of Gabriel García Márquez must also include a salute to his translators.

I remember meeting, once, long ago, the translator Gregory Rabassa, who told me that García Márquez had once said, publicly, that he considered Rabassa's English version to be superior to the Spanish original. This is probably not the case, but the generosity of the remark touched the great translator deeply and he told the story (probably not for the first or last time) with immense pride. It is a great translation, which gives the reader the impression of perfect transparency. It makes one feel one is experiencing the full beauty of the original. Rabassa's version of *The Autumn of the Patriarch*, a work whose immensely complex and convoluted sentences make it an even greater challenge than the limpid clarity and straight-faced comedy of *One Hundred Years*, is perhaps an even greater achievement.

To see how translation can either illuminate or damage the original text, one need only compare the recent, largely dreadful retranslations of the work of Borges to the previous versions. To take just one example: Borges's famous story *Funes el Memorioso* uses, in its title, a word ("memorioso") that the author made up and that was perfectly rendered in the English version as "Funes the Memorious"— "memorious" being an invention that exactly captured the feeling of Borges's original. In the new translation the title has been changed to "Funes, His Memory," which does dreadful damage to the original text. The retranslation of Günter Grass's masterpiece, *The Tin Drum*, is similarly leaden-footed when compared to Ralph Manheim's marvelous original. I hope nobody is planning to retranslate any of the books of García Márquez. They will have an army of disgruntled readers to contend with if they do.

It is tempting to see the worlds of translated literatures as parallel worlds to our own, as magic realms of otherness in which the self can wander, and I suspect that for many non–Latin American readers of García Márquez, this "wonderland illusion" may be a part of the initial appeal. What happened to me was a little different. For me, that first reading of *One Hundred Years of Solitude* opened the door to Latin American literature, and, thanks to one bookstore and one publisher, I plunged in.

The publisher was Avon Books, which in the 1970s issued a remarkable series of the best Latin American books: Mario Vargas Llosa's *The Green House*, Julio Cortázar's *Rayuela* (*Hopscotch*), Jorge

Amado's *Dona Flor and Her Two Husbands,* Alejo Carpentier's *Explosion in a Cathedral,* Manuel Puig's *Betrayed by Rita Hayworth,* and many more. The series was not widely available in London. However, a small independent store in North London, Compendium Books in Chalk Farm, not far from Camden Lock, where you could find all manner of otherworldly stuff—science-fiction and occultist texts, books that taught you numerology and explored black magic, novels such as the paranoid fantasy *Illuminatus! Trilogy,* and art books about the mysticism of the spiral—also specialized in interesting imported editions, and there was just about the whole of the Avon list for me to explore. By the time I had devoured those books, I began to understand that the "realism" part of magic realism was as important as the "magic." I saw that these books were this way because the world the writers lived in was this way as well. And so I began to understand how great my own affinity was, not only to the books, but to the then-never-visited countries from which they had traveled to the post-hippie eccentricity of that long-gone bookstore near Camden Lock.

We live in an age of invented, alternate worlds. Tolkien's Middle-earth, Rowling's Hogwarts, the dystopic universes of the Hunger Games, the places where vampires and zombies prowl, these places are having their day. Yet in spite of the vogue for straightforward fantasy fiction, in the finest of literature's fictional microcosms there is more truth than fantasy. In William Faulkner's Yoknapatawpha, R. K. Narayan's Malgudi, and, yes, the Macondo of Gabriel García Márquez, imagination is used to enrich reality, not to escape from it; the wonderful has deep roots in the real and for that reason is able to use the surreal to create metaphors and images of the real that come to feel more real than reality, more truthful than the truth.

This is the trouble with the term "magic realism"—that when people say or hear it they are really hearing or saying only half of it, "magic," without paying attention to the other half, "realism." But if magic realism were just magic, it wouldn't matter. It would be mere whimsy—writing in which, because anything can happen, nothing has affect. It's because the magic in magic realism has deep roots in the real, because it grows out of the real and illuminates it in beautiful and unexpected ways, that it works.

Consider the following:

As soon as José Arcadio closed the bedroom door the sound of a pistol shot echoed through the house. A trickle of blood came out under the door, crossed the living room, went out into the street, continued on in a straight line across the uneven terraces, went down steps and climbed over curbs, passed along the Street of the Turks, turned a corner to the right and another to the left, made a right angle at the Buendía house, went in under the closed door, crossed through the parlor, hugging the walls so as not to stain the rugs . . . and came out in the kitchen, where Úrsula was getting ready to crack thirty-six eggs to make bread.

"Holy Mother of God!" Úrsula shouted.

In this famous passage from *One Hundred Years of Solitude,* something utterly fantastic is happening. A dead man's blood acquires a purpose, almost a life of its own, and moves methodically through the streets of Macondo until it comes to rest at his mother's feet. The blood's behavior is "impossible," yet the passage reads as truthful, the journey of the blood feels like the journey of the news of his death from the room where he shot himself to his mother's kitchen, and its arrival at the feet of the matriarch Úrsula Iguarán reads as high tragedy: A mother learns that her son is dead. José Arcadio's lifeblood can and must go on living until it can bring Úrsula the sad news. The real, by the addition of the magical, actually gains in dramatic and emotional force. It becomes more real, not less.

"Less is more," we are taught. But sometimes, in these books, more is more. García Márquez has a deep fondness for hyperbole, as can be seen from the passage I just quoted. "Thirty-six eggs to make bread." That's a lot of eggs. The same sort of numerical inflation is present in the celebrated description of Colonel Aureliano Buendía: "Colonel Aureliano Buendía organized thirty-two armed uprisings and he lost them all. He had seventeen male children by seventeen different women and they were exterminated one after the other on a single night before the oldest one had reached the age of thirty-five. He survived fourteen attempts on his life, seventy-three ambushes, and a firing squad. He lived through a dose of strychnine in his coffee that was enough to kill a horse." Most literary characters would be content with one or maybe two uprisings, a smaller family, fewer wives, not quite as many assassination attempts, and a more moderate dose of poison to swallow. The characters of García Márquez have to work harder, fight more frequently, marry more often, sire more children, survive more murder attempts, ambushes, and firing squads, and drink more strychnine than ordinary folk. It must be exhausting for them.

Reading the works of García Márquez and the other writers I discovered at Compendium Books, I found myself thinking, in response to almost every page, how much of their worlds I recognized from my own experience in India and Pakistan. In both places, Latin America and South Asia, there was and still is a conflict between the city and the village, and there are similarly profound gulfs between rich and poor, powerful and powerless, the great and the small. Both are places with powerful colonial histories—different colonialists, same results—and in both places religion is of great importance, and God is alive, and so, unfortunately, are the godly.

I knew García Márquez's colonels and generals, or at least their Indian and Pakistani counterparts; his bishops were my mullahs; his market streets were my bazaars. His world felt to me like mine, translated into Spanish. It's little wonder I fell in love with it not for its magic, though, as a writer reared on the fabulous "wonder tales" of the East, that was appealing too, but for its realism. Long before I ever visited Latin America, its writers had made me feel that it would be familiar. And when at last I did go to Nicaragua, Mexico, Colombia, Argentina, Chile, Peru, and Brazil I thought, What do you know, these places are exactly as crazy as their writers told me they were, and they are crazy in the same way as my places are. The same tropical vegetation, the same garish billboards and storefronts, the sidewalk life, the rich tradition of oral storytelling, the excess, the odors, the sensuality, the heat. Driving in Managua on my first-ever day in the region, I found myself thinking, I know this place. And that was partly because of García Márquez and his colleagues, and partly because our worlds were, are, genuinely alike.

García Márquez himself always asserted the realism of his work rather than its fabulism. "I invent nothing," García Márquez once told the BBC about his literary style. "People always praise my imagination, but I believe I am a terrible realist. Everything I invent was already there in reality."

The writer Daniel Alarcón once told the BBC, "A couple of years ago when I was in Cartagena I was in a cab and the cabbie was like, 'This is Gabo's house,' and he added, 'Here in the Caribbean we all have great stories. Gabo is just a good typist.'"

WE DO NOT LIVE in magical times. The world is dark and literature responds to it with dystopias. Many of the most highly praised new fictions are remarkable for their bleakness. There is, it seems, little joy to be found. In literature as in all things, fashion exists, and the current fashion is for a kind of writing that is almost the antithesis of García Márquez. The vogue term for this new kind of work is "autofiction," a literature that shies away from everything invented, that trusts only the deeply autobiographical, the nakedly personal.

Nonfiction outsells fiction in the bookstores and so fiction becomes nonfictional as well. It seems that for many readers the imagination is a thing that must not be trusted, and so they turn toward the work of the Belgian novelist Amélie Nothomb, the pseudonymous Italian Elena Ferrante, and the Norwegian Karl Ove Knausgaard, the second author to call his book *Min Kamp,* which is to say, *Mein Kampf.*

It is not my purpose in any way to criticize these writers. I appreciate their talent and it is plain that they have captured the rapt attention of many readers in many countries. And in many ways it is a great thing to have become unfashionable. It removes the work from the glare of the world's attention and allows it simply to be there, greeting what readers do come, and waiting for the great wheel to turn, as it must, as it always does.

There's no doubt that in Latin America and beyond, the grand moment of magic realism has passed, and the new writers want to do almost anything but that kind of work. The most highly regarded writer of the generation after García Márquez, the late Roberto Bolaño, notoriously declared that magic realism "stinks," and jeered at García Márquez's fame, calling him "a man terribly pleased to have hobnobbed with so many presidents and archbishops." It was a childish outburst, but it showed that for many Latin American writers the presence of the great colossus in their midst had become more than a little burdensome. With García Márquez's death, that burden has been lifted, and it becomes possible to appreciate the oeuvre not as the phenomenon it was but simply as work.

It needs to be said, clearly, that while literary fashions come and go—and "autofiction" with its rejection of the fictional may well be no more than a current fashion—what in Latin America became known as magic realism is not a passing fad. It is a recent manifestation of a tradition that manifests itself in every language in every age and that is at least the equal of the realist tradition. Kafka's giant insect in *The Metamorphosis*, Bulgakov's devil making mayhem in the Moscow of *The Master and Margarita*, and Charles Dickens too flow alongside García Márquez. The Circumlocution Office in *Bleak House*—a government department whose entire purpose is to do nothing—and the endless trial, *Jarndyce v. Jarndyce*, in the same novel, are images that any self-respecting magic realist would be proud to have created. On my first readings of García Márquez, the name that most often came to mind was that of Luis Buñuel, a surrealist whose masterpieces, such as *The Exterminating Angel*, come closer to the unique tone of García Márquez than anyone else's. García Márquez knew very well that he belonged to a far-flung literary family. The American novelist William Kennedy, author of *Ironweed*, quotes him saying, "In Mexico, surrealism runs through the streets." And again: "The Latin American reality is totally Rabelaisian."

The Buendía dynasty, and the patriarch, and the innocent Eréndira, and the sad colonel to whom nobody writes belong to this tradition, which includes many of the most durable works ever created, including now the work of Gabriel García Márquez, which will continue to endure, while fashions come and go.

I NEVER MET HIM, and I greatly regret that, but we did have one long conversation. I was in Mexico City at a friend's house and Carlos Fuentes came to dinner. I told him I'd been disappointed to learn that García Márquez was out of town, in Cuba, visiting his friend Fidel. Fuentes said something like, "It's ridiculous that you two have never met," and shortly afterward he left the room for a few minutes, returning to summon me into another room, where he handed me a telephone receiver. "There's somebody you have to talk to," he said, and left me alone with Gabo's voice in my ear.

The conversation began awkwardly. He claimed not to know any English, but it quickly became clear that he knew plenty but preferred not to speak it. My Spanish is very poor. I don't speak it at all, but I understand a little. And we both had some French. So we proceeded trilingually and things got better. In fact, in my memory of the conversation, there is no language problem. In my memory we are just talking to each other and understanding one another perfectly. It was quite a long conversation. We covered a lot of ground. I remember telling him that I'd read about his grandmother's stories and their importance in helping him to formulate his own, and I told him about the family stories my mother told me and their importance in my work. He was very kind about my writing. We talked about the differences between us, the difference between Macondo and Bombay, the village and the city. I told him that I had written about the *Chronicle of a Death Foretold* and also about his nonfiction work *Clandestine in Chile*, in which he told the story of the filmmaker Miguel Littín making his secret film under the nose, the very dangerous nose, of the tyrant Pinochet, and I noted that he responded with more enthusiasm to my interest in his journalism than in my review of his fiction. Once a journalist, always a journalist. He was interested in my own foray into reportage, my little book about Nicaragua during the Contra War. I told him the story of a dinner at the home of Daniel Ortega with almost all the Sandinista leadership present, during which I had been reluctant to produce a tape recorder, knowing it would change the nature of the dinner table conversation. Instead, I pretended to have a stomach upset and retreated every ten or fifteen minutes to the toilet, where I scribbled furiously in the notebook in my pocket, writing down dialogue and other observations. He found that amusing and he told me, "You see, you are a reporter too."

Many years later, when I became president of PEN America, I tried many times to get him to come to New York as our guest, and he always replied politely, and declined. It was New York's loss, and mine.

I never met Borges either, but in my early twenties I saw him lecture in London, and much later, in Buenos Aires, thanks to the kindness of his widow, María Kodama, I met his library, which was almost as good. And though I never met García Márquez, I have the memory of our conversation, and I have, we all have, his books, and they are more than enough.

The occasion of the arrival of his archive at the Ransom Center in Austin, Texas, is perhaps comparable to that fictional American acquisition of the Caribbean, which, in *The Autumn of the Patriarch*, was carried off to Arizona. And now the great sea of his writing has been transplanted too, not to Arizona but to Texas. There is irony in this, which he would undoubtedly have appreciated. Here he is now. He has been carried off in numbered pieces. Yet he is also everywhere, he is still in Colombia, still in Mexico.

Everywhere.

# HAROLD PINTER
## (1930–2008)

IN 1993, AT THE ALMEIDA THEATRE IN LONDON, DAVID Leveaux directed a revival of Harold Pinter's play *No Man's Land,* in which Paul Eddington—famous as the minister "Jim Hacker" in the TV sitcom *Yes Minister*—and Harold himself took the leading roles originally played by John Gielgud and Ralph Richardson in the play's first production in 1975. Leveaux once told me that during rehearsals Paul Eddington expressed puzzlement and asked Harold for help in understanding a certain moment of the play, what was his character after at that point, where should he go with it, what was he trying to achieve. Harold took the script from Paul Eddington's hand, had a look at it, and handed it back, saying, "The author's intentions are not clear from the text." Some time later I asked Harold if he had really done that. "Yes," Harold replied. "Yes, as a matter of fact, I may have done that." But why, I asked. Wouldn't it have been easier just to answer Paul Eddington's question? "I wrote that play almost twenty-five [expletive deleted] years ago," Harold said. "How the [expletive deleted] would I know?"

The story demonstrates Pinter's legendary intransigence and his dislike of being asked to explain his work. For him, the strength of a work of art lay in its resistance to the idea of "meaning," or at least in the reduction of meaning to a plain verbal explanation of what a scene, or a play, or a poem, or a novel, was "about." (Asked, on another occasion, what *The Birthday Party* was about, he replied, according to legend, "It's about a man sitting in a room, and then two other men come in.") But it also reveals his honesty—if he had forgotten the writing of a decades-old passage, he wasn't going to make up a spurious explanation of it. Harold Pinter was an unrelentingly honest artist and man.

(Harold always favored the concrete and tangible over the abstract and theoretical. Soon after we first met he asked me about my writing. He was generous, but he also mentioned its "shapelessness." I was very much in awe of him at the time but nevertheless mumbled a defensive little something about how, under the surface, there was what I may have called "deep structure." Harold unleashed his celebrated and terrifying glittering smile and repeated, "Deep structure. Now, what would that be?" I found myself seized by panic and gabbled some stuff about being interested in the Wagnerian idea of the leitmotif, in the way the repeated use of an image in different contexts—a silver spittoon, the shape of a hand with a pointing finger, the sound of a ticking clock—can lead to interesting accumulations of meaning. But I soon dried up. I heard myself sounding like a theorist, not a novelist. I learned something from Harold's savage smile and afterward tried not to use that kind of lit-crit language anymore.)

Like all of us, he liked to have his work liked. Every so often he would fax his friends new poems, and we knew that we had to reply pretty darn quickly or else risk the feared Wrath of Pinter. He once sent us a poem about a famous English cricketer called Len Hutton. This was the poem. The whole poem.

> I saw Len Hutton in his prime,
> Another time,
> Another time.

According to a much-relished piece of gossip, his close friend the playwright Simon Gray did not respond punctually, and finally Harold called him.

"Simon, you haven't told me what you think of my new poem yet."

"I'm sorry, Harold," said Gray, "I haven't had time to finish it."

Harold was extremely amused, and Simon was spared the feared wrath of Pinter. This Wrath often led to the phenomenon of "being Pintered," when some poor friend or enemy felt the lash of Harold's mighty tongue. I am happy to say that I was never Pintered. The closest I came to it was when Harold directed a production of David Mamet's play *Oleanna* at the Royal Court Theatre in London—also in 1993, the year of his performance in the revival of *No Man's Land* at the Almeida—and after I went to see it I failed sufficiently to praise his work and started talking to his wife, Antonia Fraser, about something else. Out of the corner of my eye I saw Harold beginning to melt down, and, fearing a full-fledged China Syndrome calamity, I hurriedly turned back toward him.

"Harold, did I forget to say that your production of *Oleanna* was absolutely fucking marvelous?"

"Yes," he said. "Yes, as a matter of fact, you did forget to say that."

"Harold," I said, "your production of *Oleanna* was absolutely fucking marvelous."

"Well, that's more like it," he replied, and grinned his lethal grin.

There was a great anger in Harold Pinter, and he thought of it as a fault and often apologized for it. I do not think of it as a fault but, rather, as the wellspring of his art, and of his political passion as well. It was, one might say, a public anger, born of his fury at all that is wrong, cynical, amoral, corrupt, bullying, and ugly in human affairs; and beneath that it was an existential anger, a rage against the prison of human life, against the traps we build for ourselves, from which we can never escape. The violence that bubbles below the surface of all his plays, and the almost savage precision of the text's surface, is what gives Pinter's work its essential quality; that, and the magnificent blackness of his comedy. The menace of Harold's smile, the most dangerous smile in literature, can be seen in every sentence he ever wrote, every scene he brought to life.

When I first met Harold Pinter in the early 1980s, his work had only just begun to move toward direct political expression. I wasn't sure if this was a good thing. So powerful was my memory of Harold playing the part of Goldberg in the 1968 British television production of *The Birthday Party,* so great was my admiration for the elliptical force of that play and, in fact, of *No Man's Land* (I had been lucky enough to see the original Gielgud–Richardson production), that I worried that direct political engagement might be too explicit a path for Pinter's somber genius. Others agreed, and the early reception of the "political plays"—*One for the Road, Mountain Language,* and *Party Time*—was a little perplexed. Time has shown these three short plays to be masterpieces, so, as usual, Harold knew better than us all.

In the 1980s Harold threw himself into political engagement with all his energy. In 1985, on a PEN International trip, he and Arthur Miller protested at a reception at the American embassy in Ankara about the torture of imprisoned Turkish writers; they were asked to leave. Afterward, Harold described being thrown out of the American embassy with Arthur Miller as "one of the proudest moments in my life." He became involved in the Nicaraguan cause during the Contra War, and later in the Kurdish cause, and offered an increasingly trenchant critique of American foreign policy, especially during the years of the George W. Bush administration. He used his Nobel lecture to speak with equal eloquence about both sides of his work, the art and the politics, and by the end of his life the two had become inseparable. The lecture was entitled "Art, Truth and Politics," and in that title we can see the bridge that joined the artist and the political activist. The bridge was his hatred of the lie and his determination to uncover and express as much as he could of what he saw as the truth.

Outside his dramatic work, Harold Pinter did not resist explaining what he meant. This is how he began his Nobel Prize lecture:

In 1958 I wrote the following: "There are no hard distinctions between what is real and what is unreal, nor between what is true and what is false. A thing is not necessarily either true or false; it can be both true and false." I believe that these assertions still make sense and do still apply to the exploration of reality through art. So as a writer I stand by them, but as a citizen I cannot. As a citizen I must ask: What is true? What is false?

Because of what he felt he needed to do as a citizen, Pinter became a clear-spoken, passionate opponent of bigotry, prejudice, censorship, and the abuse of power by the powerful. In *Mountain Language* and *Party Time,* he succeeded in giving his arguments proper dramatic form. And certainly those of us who were lucky enough to have known him knew, during the eighties and nineties, that simply to mention the words "Latin America" would provoke a Pinterian harangue. There were, consequently, times when we avoided mentioning those words, and also the words "United States."

But it was always language that Pinter scrutinized most closely. He spoke, memorably, of discerning "a disease at the very center of language, so that language becomes a permanent masquerade, a tapestry of lies. The ruthless and cynical mutilation and degradation of human beings, both in spirit and body . . . these actions are justified by rhetorical gambits, sterile terminology and concepts of power which stink. Are we ever going to look at the language we use, I wonder? Is it within our capabilities to do so? . . . Does reality essentially remain outside language, separate, obdurate, alien, not susceptible to description? Is an accurate and vital correspondence between what is and our perception of it impossible? Or is it that we are obliged to use language only in order to obscure and distort reality—to distort what is—to distort what happens—because we fear it? I believe it's because of the way we use language that we have got ourselves into this terrible trap, where words like freedom, democracy, and Christian values are still used to justify barbaric and shameful policies and acts."

HAROLD PINTER WAS MY FRIEND, and a great and loyal ally. On February 6, 1990, just less than a year after the Khomeini *fatwa* against *The Satanic Verses,* I had been asked to deliver the annual Herbert Read Lecture at the Institute of Contemporary Arts in London. To my immense frustration, however, the British police refused to guarantee security at the event and so I was unable to go. I called Harold and asked him if he would deliver the lecture for me, and he agreed at once, without an instant's hesitation, at a time when many others might have discovered unbreakable appointments elsewhere. For that act of principle and courage, and for many, many other such public acts; for the private gift of his friendship to myself and my family; and above all, for his genius, I thank him, and, like all those who loved him, I still miss him every day.

THESE ARE SOME ADDITIONAL WORDS *taken from my acceptance speech when I was awarded the PEN Pinter Prize in October 2014:*

A part of the reason for my own resistance to excessive textual explication is what happened in the aftermath of the publication of *The Satanic Verses* in the autumn of 1988. In those days the book's opponents set out with remarkable success to prescribe the book's meaning to their followers, and for many people, to this day, that prescription still works and tells them exactly why the novel is, so to speak, sick. At the very beginning I hoped the obviously distorted and biased nature of these prescriptions would become self-evident, and the book itself would provide its own best defense. I also hoped that my own track record, the things I'd written, the work I'd done, the person I had been, would be my best defense against the demonization of my character and motives that was taking place. But those were thoughts from before the time in which we all became too frightened of religion in general and one particular religion in particular—religion redefined as the capacity of religionists to commit earthly violence in the name of their unearthly sky god.

These days, what ought to be self-evident has begun to look like self-indulgence, and the narrow pseudo-explications of religion, couched in the new—or actually very old—vocabulary of blasphemy and offense, have increasingly begun to set the agenda. I felt obliged for a long time to fight back against the creation of that false version of *The Satanic Verses* by offering counter-explanations of my own. I loathed doing it and often felt that by offering the almost line-by-line defense that seemed necessary I was damaging the kind of open, private reading of my novel for which, like every writer, I had hoped.

And I was forced to ask myself a tough question. If I believed, as I did, that the reader completed the book, and that all those versions of the book, the book in the minds of each of its readers, were valid versions and, in fact, the versions for whose creation I had hoped, then were not the versions that angered people as authentic as the versions in the minds of the book's more sympathetic readers? Did not my own idea of the nature of the literary experience undermine my defense of my book? The only answer I have found is that a distinction has to be made between judgment and response. People are entitled to judge a book as kindly or as harshly as they choose, but when they respond to it with violence or the threat of violence, the subject changes, and the question becomes: How do we face down such threats? We have all been wrestling with the answer to that question on many fronts ever since.

Harold's Nobel Prize jeremiad was primarily aimed at the distortions of language by secular powers, and the world's most powerful superpower in particular, but everything he speaks of holds true of the uglinesses being perpetrated all over the world in the name of this or that faith. It's fair to say that more than one religion deserves scrutiny. Christian extremists in the United States today attack women's liberties and gay rights in language they claim comes from God. Hindu extremists in India today are launching an assault on free expression and trying to rewrite history, literally, proposing the alteration of school textbooks to serve their narrow saffron dogmatism. But the overwhelming weight of the present-day problem lies in the world of Islam, and much of it has its roots in the ideological language of blood and war emanating from the Salafist movement within the religion, globally backed by Saudi Arabia.

This is Ed Husain, a British advocate of a modern and pluralist Islam, writing in *The New York Times:*

> Let's be clear: Al Qaeda, the Islamic State in Iraq and Syria, Boko Haram, al-Shabab and others are all violent Sunni Salafi groupings. For five decades, Saudi Arabia has been the official sponsor of Sunni Salafism across the globe. Most Sunni Mus-

lims around the world, approximately 90 percent of the Muslim population, are not Salafis. Salafism is seen as too rigid, too literalist, too detached from mainstream Islam.... Salafi adherents and other fundamentalists represent 3 percent of the world's Muslims.

To that Sunni 3 percent, we can perhaps add a further percentage of extremist Shias sponsored by the Iranian revolution, whose ideologue Ali Shariati, adapting Marxist language, called the Khomeini revolution a "revolt against history." In this sense Shia and Sunni extremists are the same. Modernity itself is the enemy, modernity with its language of liberty, for women as well as men, with its insistence on legitimacy in government rather than tyranny, and with its strong inclination toward secularism and away from religion. This, the language of the modern world, has been targeted by the deformed medievalist language of fanaticism, backed up by modern weaponry.

This language is being heard, more and more, in mosques and on social media, and for some young men its appeal is so great that it persuades hundreds, perhaps thousands, of British Muslims to join the decapitating barbarians of ISIS (worryingly, far more British Muslims join the jihadists than enlist in the British armed forces). On some of these social networking sites a Saudi opinion poll is now circulating showing that 92 percent of respondents agree that ISIS "conforms to the values of Islam and Islamic law." If accurate, this kind of information makes Ed Husain's 3 percent look a little over-optimistic. Even if one discounts this as a rogue poll, it's hard not to conclude that hate-filled religious rhetoric, pouring from the mouths of ruthless fanatics into the ears of angry young men, has become the most dangerous new weapon in the world today.

A word I dislike, "Islamophobia," has been coined to discredit those who point at these excesses, by labeling them as bigots. But in the first place, if I don't like your ideas, it must be acceptable for me to say so, just as it is acceptable for you to say that you don't like mine. Ideas cannot be ring-fenced just because they claim to have this or that fictional sky god on their side. And in the second place, it's important to remember that most of those who suffer under the yoke of the new Islamic fanaticism are other Muslims. The Taliban oppressed the people of Afghanistan and are on the verge of returning to do so again; the ayatollahs continue to oppress the people of Iran; the people who died in the Iraq War are almost all Muslims, killed by other Muslims in the name of their own religion, re-described in sectarian terms to permit their murder. It is right to feel phobia toward such matters. As several commentators have said, what is being killed in Iraq is not just human beings but a whole culture. To feel aversion toward such a force is not bigotry. It is the only possible response to the horror of events.

Like Harold Pinter, I greatly prefer the artist's language of ambiguity and indirection, which allows a work to have many readings. But also, following Harold's lead, I can't, as a citizen, avoid speaking of the horror of the world in this new age of religious mayhem, and of the language that conjures it up and justifies it, so that young men, including young Britons, are led toward acts of extreme bestiality and believe themselves to be fighting a just war.

The work of PEN in this dark time has never been more important. Journalists around the world have never been more in danger. In the conflicts in Iraq and Syria they are considered to be legitimate targets. The beheading of James Foley by a British jihadi shocked us all, but Mr. Foley was not the first casualty of that war. According to the Syrian Journalists Association, over 150 journalists have been killed in Syria during the civil war there, and the Committee to Protect Journalists says that over 190 more have died in Iraq since 1992. In Putin's Russia, the journalistic body count has also entered three figures. Everywhere from Eritrea to China, writers and reporters are being detained without charge, disappeared, and sometimes even killed.

I myself, when I needed help, received the strong support of PEN in Britain, in the United States, and elsewhere, and was immensely grateful for it. Harold Pinter himself led a delegation to Downing Street asking that I be protected. It was Harold and Antonia who allowed me to use their home as a place to meet my young son. It was

Harold who spoke to Václav Havel on my behalf and enlisted his support. And when the British government was refusing to meet or have any contact with me in the months after the *fatwa*, it was Harold who called William Waldegrave, then a junior minister in the Foreign Office, to insist successfully that I be spoken to. No writer in trouble could wish for a better ally.

I have tried since then to follow Harold's example and do what I can to help PEN help others. The work is important and PEN has proved itself, time and again, an effective advocacy organization. An example of this is the PEN/Barbara Goldsmith (now the PEN/Barbey) Freedom to Write Award, given annually since 1987 by PEN American Center to highlight the case of particular writers in trouble. Four of the honored writers had been released by the time they received their award. Of the thirty-eight who were in prison when honored, no fewer than thirty-five have since been released. That is a track record to be proud of. We will continue with the work of defending the written word and those who risk everything to tell the truth.

I am proud to receive an award named for Harold Pinter, a great writer, great citizen, and a great friend in need.

# INTRODUCTION TO
# *THE PARIS REVIEW*
# *INTERVIEWS, VOL. IV*

———

I ONCE ASKED A MAKER OF FINE GOLD JEWELRY WHY SHE only worked in such an expensive material, and she replied that the point about gold was its malleability: You can do anything with gold, you can twist it and turn it and it will take whatever shape you want it to take. I thought then, and think now, that English is the gold of languages—that, unlike some other languages I could name, its syntactical freedom and its elasticity allow you to make of it what you will, and that this is why, as it has spread across the world, it has made so many successful local metamorphoses—into Irish English, West Indian English, Australian English, Indian English, and the many varieties of American English. I was happy to see that, in the *Paris Review* interview reprinted in this volume, Maya Angelou feels the same way, speaking of "how beautiful, how pliable the language is, how it will lend itself. If you pull it, it says, okay."

Foolishly, perhaps, I have long assumed that English possesses this quality to a greater degree than any other language, and so it is salutary to be reminded by David Grossman that other writers in other languages feel the same way. "Hebrew," Grossman says, "is a flexible language and it surrenders enthusiastically to all kinds of wordplay. You can talk in slang about the Bible and you can speak biblically about everyday life. You can invent words that people can easily understand, because almost every word has a root, and people know the derivation or can usually figure it out. It is a very sexy language. It is gigantic, heroic, and glorious, but at the same time it has large gaps that yearn to be filled by writers." Oh, okay, I find myself conceding, just a touch grumpily; okay, so maybe among languages there's more than one variety of gold.

This is one of the reasons why the *Paris Review* interviews are so terrific. They don't just entertain you, they make you think, and they even make you rethink what you think you know. Like many writers (and would-be writers, and readers too) I've been a fan of the "Art of Fiction" series for as long as I can remember. I've pulled my old copies of the magazine off their shelf and have them beside me as I write.

In the summer of 1981, when I was writing the first draft of *Shame,* I was greatly inspired by Donald Barthelme in his *Paris Review* interview, in particular his comments about his use of fantastic effects. To give a woman golden buttocks in a story was "a way of allowing you to see buttocks." And: "If I didn't have roaches as big as ironing boards in the story I couldn't show Cortés and Montezuma holding hands, it would be merely sentimental. You look around for offsetting material, things that tell the reader that although X is happening, X is to be regarded in the light of Y." How very *useful* that was to me then and, indeed, how useful it still is!

The "Art of Fiction" interviews satisfy our deep and abiding inquisitiveness about the writing life. Like most writers, I am interested in other writers, both as a reader and as a nosy parker. I want to know their work, but I also want to know where it came from, and how. Perhaps the only writer I can think of who denies feeling like this is V. S. Naipaul. I was once present at the Hay-on-Wye literary festival when Naipaul was being interviewed onstage by the American writer and editor Bill Buford. He replied to Buford's question about the writers he read with a majestic dismissal: "I'm not a reader, I'm a writer." Yet here he is in these pages, offering up one of his many published accounts of his own literary origins, and his writing process too, presumably because he is willing to go along with the idea that, while he himself is uninterested in reading or learning about other writers, those other writers—and readers too—might be interested in learning about *him.* But then, as he tells us, there are many excellent reasons why we might wish to learn about him. "It is immensely hard to be the first to write about anything. It is always easy afterward to copy," he says, speaking of *Miguel Street,* and of *In a Free State* he is happy to tell us that "it is very well made."

It is at moments like these that the "Art of Fiction" interviews are most revealing, showing us, perhaps, more of the author than even the author knows. The great P. G. Wodehouse's well-known sunniness of spirit acquires an almost shockingly innocent quality when he talks about his wartime broadcasts from Nazi-occupied Paris—broadcasts that led many to denounce him as a traitor, and that, as he himself says, "altered his whole life," leading him to spend the rest of it in the United States and never go home again. It has always felt painful to me that this most English of English writers, creator of the fantasy England of Jeeves, Bertie Wooster, the Drones Club, Blandings Castle, and the imperishable pig the Empress of Blandings, should have spent so long in exile. But Wodehouse sounds perfectly happy about the whole thing. Does he resent the way he was treated by the English? "Oh, no, no, no. Nothing of that sort. The whole thing seems to have blown over now." And how about his American exile? "I'd much sooner live here than in England, I think. I can't think of any place in England I prefer to this. I used to like London, but I don't think I'd like it now.... I'm rather blessed in a way. I really don't worry about anything much. I can adjust myself to things pretty well." Oh, so that's all right, then.

In these pages Jack Kerouac comes over exactly as he should, at once vivid and muddy, full of Kerouacity. Here he is, explaining his own name: "Now, *kairn.* K (or C) AIRN. What is a cairn? It's a heap of stones. Now *Cornwall,* cairnwall. Now, right, *kern,* also KERN, means the same thing as *cairn.* Kern. Cairn. *Ouac* means 'language of.' So, *Kernouac* means the language of Cornwall. *Kerr,* which is like Deborah Kerr. *Ouack* means language of water. Because *Kerr, Carr,* etc., means water. And *cairn* means heap of stones. There is no language in a heap of stones. Kerouac. *Ker* (water), *ouac* (language of). And it's related to the old Irish name, Kerwick, which is a corruption. And it's a Cornish name, which in itself means cairnish. And according to Sherlock Holmes, it's all Persian." It's a sign of the skill with which these interviews are conducted and afterward edited—a process in which the interviewees are closely involved—that the writers come out sounding so honestly and (for the most part) undefendedly like themselves.

And there's disagreement too. William Styron accepts the influence of Faulkner, among others, and praises him, but with some reservations. "I'm all for the complexity of Faulkner, but not for the confusion. . . . As for *The Sound and the Fury*, I think it succeeds in spite of itself. Faulkner often simply stays too damn intense for too long a time." Maya Angelou, though, is politely but firmly unimpressed by both Faulkner and Styron. She is asked, "What do you think of white writers who have written of the black experience—Faulkner's *The Sound and the Fury* or William Styron's *Confessions of Nat Turner*?" And she replies, "Well, sometimes I am disappointed—more often than not." Literature, we are reminded, is disputed territory. Nowadays, with the rise of a brilliant new generation of African American writers of fiction, memoir, and poetry—Jesmyn Ward, Colson Whitehead, Mitchell S. Jackson, Safiya Sinclair, Natasha Trethewey, Tracy K. Smith, to name only a few—it's still possible, even right, to argue that anybody can write about anything, that nobody owns any subject, but in the face of all this brilliance, it feels redundant to do so. These authors have so powerfully laid claim to their subject that it would be a rash colleague who sought to intrude.

Two of the writers collected in this volume are friends of mine: Auster and Grossman. But writers talk less to each other about their craft than perhaps they should, so even in these cases what the interviews have to tell me is revealing. Auster talks about "reading with his fingers," the act of retyping the whole book once it's finished, and how valuable he finds it—"it's amazing." He marvels at "how many errors your fingers will find that your eyes never noticed." Then there's Grossman's paean to Hebrew, which I've already quoted.

Here too is John Ashbery being at once vague and sharp ("I have such an imprecise impression of what kind of a person I am," he mourns, but he also says, with some asperity, that he tries "to avoid the well-known cliché that you learn from your students"); and Philip

Roth being sufficient unto himself ("I don't ask writers about their work habits. I really don't care. Joyce Carol Oates says somewhere that when writers ask each other what time they start working and when they finish and how much time they take for lunch, they're actually trying to find out 'Is he as crazy as I am?' I don't need that question answered"); and Stephen Sondheim admitting that he uses the Clement Wood rhyming dictionary and *Roget's Thesaurus;* E. B. White on *Charlotte's Web* ("Anyone who writes *down* to children is simply wasting his time. You have to write up, not down"); Ezra Pound talking about Disney's "squirrel film" *Perri* and praising "the Confucian side of Disney," an "absolute genius"; Marilynne Robinson on how *Housekeeping* grew out of a "stack of metaphors"; Marianne Moore, interviewed on the day before the election of President Kennedy, but belonging to another age entirely; and Haruki Murakami, as contemporary a writer as it's possible to be, admitting his fear of Toni Morrison and Joyce Carol Oates.

If you aren't a writer, don't worry: This book won't teach you how to be one. If you are a writer, I suspect it will teach you a lot. Either way, it's a treasure chest, and a delight.

# AUTOBIOGRAPHY
# AND THE NOVEL

---

## (i)

Let's take a look at the title pages of three of the greatest novels of the eighteenth century—for many of us the golden age of the English novel.

Here it what it says on the title page of *Robinson Crusoe:* "The LIFE and STRANGE SURPRIZING ADVENTURES of *ROBINSON CRUSOE* of *YORK,* MARINER: Who lived Eight and Twenty Years, all alone in an un-inhabited Island on the Coast of AMERICA, near the Mouth of the Great River of OROONOQUE (Orinoco); Having been cast on Shore by Shipwreck, wherein all the Men perished but himself. WITH An Account how he was at last strangely deliver'd by PYRATES. *Written by Himself.* LONDON: Printed for W. Taylor at the Ship in *Pater-Noster-Row.* MDCCXIX (1719)."

And this is the complete text on the title page of *Gulliver's Travels:* "TRAVELS into several REMOTE NATIONS of the WORLD. In Four PARTS. By *LEMUEL GULLIVER,* First a SURGEON, and then a CAPTAIN of several SHIPS. Vol. I. *LONDON: Printed for* BENJ. MOTTE, *at the Middle* Temple-Gate *in* Fleet-street. MDCCXXVI (1726)."

And this, thirdly, is what it says on the title page of the first volume of *Tristram Shandy:* "The LIFE and OPINIONS of TRIS-

TRAM SHANDY, GENTLEMAN." Then there is a quotation from Epictetus, given in Greek. *"Tarassei tous Anthropous ou ta Pragmata, alla ta peri ton Pragmaton, Dogmata,"* which is to say, "What upsets people is not things themselves, but their theories about things." After that it says simply "VOL. I," gives the number of the edition, and the printing details, "LONDON: Printed for J. DODSLEY, in *Pall Mall,*" and the date (1759, for the first edition of the first two volumes).

What is striking about all three title pages is the absence of the true authors' names. *Robinson Crusoe* purports to have been written by Robinson Crusoe, *Gulliver* by Gulliver, and *Tristram Shandy* by poor Tristram himself, that hapless narrator who takes so long to tell us his story, who digresses so easily and so often, that the account of his life proceeds more slowly than the life itself, so that the more he writes, the more of his life lies ahead of him to write about. The names of Daniel Defoe, Jonathan Swift, and Laurence Sterne are absent from their books. Just two hundred and fifty years ago it was possible for books to become famous and celebrated, as all these books were in their day, and for the author to remain in the shadows. The personality and life story of the author was not deemed to be of any relevance to his work. *Robinson Crusoe* was not thought to have its origins in Defoe's childhood feelings of being marooned in a friendless world (except on Fridays). Nor was Dean Swift ever asked if he had had close encounters with very small people, very big people, or talking horses. And Laurence Sterne's parents were never doorstepped by journalists asking about their sexual habits and whether Mr. Sterne Senior had in fact forgotten to wind up that clock. Fiction was fiction; life was life; two hundred and fifty years ago, people knew that these were different things.

This is no longer the case. And if there is a writer we may blame for this, it is probably Charles Dickens. If Dickens did not wholly invent the cult of the writer as public personality, he certainly did a great deal to popularize it. On his first speaking tour of America in 1842—he liked speaking in America, because he was paid more—he used his fame to become a passionate and prominent antislavery advocate and also spoke vehemently in favor of the establishment of international copyright laws. Above all, however, he became a legendary performer of famous scenes from his own work, acting out all the parts, even the female ones; his enactment of the death of Little Nell from *The Old Curiosity Shop* was a particular success, and his portrayal of the expiring Nell was not, apparently, made any less convincing by his wispy beard. His skill as a performer greatly increased his celebrity, but it was probably also the cause of his sudden death, in 1870, after his return in poor health from his second American tour. (One moral of this story is, therefore, that while some writers are good at public speaking . . . it kills them.)

With the publication of *David Copperfield*, the eighth of his fifteen novels—or, to give it its full title, *The Personal History, Adventures, Experience, and Observation of David Copperfield the Younger of Blunderstone Rookery (Which He Never Meant to Be Published on Any Account)*—Dickens also explicitly used his own life, his own experiences as a child laborer, his first love, and his aborted legal career as the basis for his fiction. By this time, 1850, the author's name is prominently displayed on the title page. Dickens was uninterested in disguising his authorship; neither did he make any attempt to conceal the novel's autobiographical origins, and a year before he died he called it his "favorite child." Writers, after Dickens, may not have become more willing to fictionalize their own stories, but readers have certainly begun to believe that they do. Nowadays, there is a prevalent assumption that all novels are really autobiographies in disguise.

Every contemporary novelist will tell you that the question he or she is most frequently asked is the autobiography question. "How autobiographical is it?" The novel may be about a man lusting sexually after an underage girl, or it may be about a man who wakes up one day to find himself transformed into a giant dung beetle, or it may be about an American who has, in his own words, "gone spastic in time" and bounces uncontrollably between different ages, or it may be about a man trying to get out of the army by claiming to be insane, only to be told that there's a catch, namely that a man who wants to get out of the army cannot be insane; but the question is always the same, and so are the underlying assumptions. If Nabokov wrote *Lolita*, then he must have been, at the very least, exploring his own submerged pedophilic lusts. If Kafka wrote *The Metamorphosis*, then he must have seen himself as a disgusting, rejected insect. And Billy Pilgrim, the hero of *Slaughterhouse-Five*, must be Kurt Vonnegut in disguise, and *Catch-22*'s Yossarian must be Joseph Heller, and so on. The imagination, in our unimaginative times, is no more than a costume that the facts put on. If you write about a serial killer like Hannibal Lecter, then perhaps you, Mr. Harris, have secret murderous fantasies. If your hero is a dwarf, like Oskar Matzerath in *The Tin Drum*, then Günter Grass must think of himself as dwarfish. And if you often write about bears, as John Irving did earlier in his career, then there must—must there not?—have been a bear that was important in your life.

"How autobiographical is it?" As it happens, there is a right and a wrong answer to this question. The wrong answer first: "It's not really autobiographical. I suppose there are bits of me in there, bits of things that really happened, but they've all been changed around and jumbled up with other things that I just made up, and there are bits of people I know, but they are all mixed up with other bits I invented. You know, it's fiction?" This answer has the merit of usually being true, but it is still the wrong answer. The right answer is: "It's completely autobiographical. Yes! Everything in this novel happened either to me or to close friends or family members!" Only this answer will satisfy, and even impress, the person asking the question. Only this answer will allow you to move past the autobiography question to other, arguably more interesting questions about the work itself. This became clear to me when I published my novel *Fury*, whose central character was sexually abused as a child; who finds himself from time to time in the grip of inexplicable rages whose source he does not understand; who, in the grip of one such bout of fury in London, almost murders his sleeping wife and small child with a kitchen knife; and who, later, in New York City, experiences nocturnal memory blackouts that coincide oddly with the killings perpetrated by a serial murderer . . . and every journalist who interviewed me said, "So, this is, is it not, your most autobiographical novel?" For a long time I kept giving the wrong answer—"No, not really"—until I worked out that if I said, "Yes, of course," the journalist and I could both heave a sigh of relief and begin to have a proper conversation.

Nor is this autobiographical obsession limited to journalists. Readers have it too, and anyone who writes even a moderately successful novel will experience the phenomenon of people wanting to be characters in your books, people assuming they actually are characters in your books, even if you have never met them. After a lecture I gave in Bombay in the early 1980s, a woman, a rather grand, bejeweled woman, a woman carrying a fan, came up to me, closed her fan, and smacked me with it on my arm: *whack!* "Naughty boy," she said. "Never mind, I forgive you." I was thinking, Madam, who the hell are you? Then she identified herself as the "obvious" model for a particular character in my work. "Madam," I protested, "you have to accept that this is the first time we have ever met." She clucked her tongue impatiently. "I don't see why you're still going on about it," she said. "I have already forgiven you."

Not all readers are so forgiving. After the publication of *The Ground Beneath Her Feet*, a forgotten Indian starlet and jazz singer of long ago, one Asha Puthli, gave a series of newspaper interviews in which she accused me of actually stalking her in order to use her life as the basis for the character of Vina Apsara in my novel. The following is from *The Times of India* in July 2002: "There are fifty similarities between Vina Apsara and me," she says. "But he won't admit it. I could have sued him, but I didn't." (This was after I had explained to the papers that she had never crossed my mind when I was writing my book.) "You know, people say that only to avoid lawsuits," she fumes. At the same time, she affirms that if the book is ever turned into a film, she will have to put her foot down. "His style is magic realism and that's a distortion of facts. If I want something based on my life, I'd rather do it myself." So, anyone who wants to film my book had better watch out. Asha Puthli and her fifty similarities are on our trail.

The problem with this kind of foolishness is that it obscures the many ways in which a writer's life does inform his work. It is true that many fictional characters have real-life models. But if a real person—which includes the writer himself—is a writer's starting point and a fictional character is the result, the journey from one to the other, we may say, is the imaginative act. It is in that transformative journey that the art lies. This is most particularly true of those instances in which a writer chooses a "me character" to place at the heart of his work. It is plain that Stephen Dedalus is close to James Joyce and that Marcel in *À La Recherche du temps perdu* shares a good deal with his creator, Marcel Proust. And yet Stephen and Marcel are not flesh-and-blood creatures. They are made of words, and a life lived in language is quite other than a life spent breathing air. Stephen is not Joyce, though he went to the same school and shares his author's modest desire to "forge in the smithy of my soul the uncreated conscience of my race"; and Marcel is not Proust—for one thing, he's heterosexual, and for another, he seems a good deal less frightened of the world, and gets about a great deal more, than his author in his famous cork-lined room. Every literary version of the real—a real place, a real family, a real man or woman—is just that, a version, and it is dangerous to equate it with that slipperiest of ideas, "truth."

In James Atlas's recent biography of Saul Bellow, he tells us about the source material for *Herzog*. We discover that Bellow's own wife ran away with a friend of his, just as Madeleine Herzog does. Real life and fiction mirror each other to a remarkable degree. Here's a question, though: *So what?* To know things like this is undeniably interesting, it's a form of higher gossip, and gossip certainly has its place. But after you've been told that Madeleine Herzog is based on Sondra Bellow, and that her monopod lover, Valentine Gersbach, has his roots in Bellow's friend Jack Ludwig, and even after you've intuited that poor, crazed, letter-writing Herzog must be a figure of the author, what, in fact, have you learned? The answer is: nothing that enriches or enlightens your reading of the novel. Madeleine, Valentine, and Moses do not inhabit the same continuum as we do. They live in a world of words, and the critics who have seen in Gersbach an echo of the character of Dr. Tamkin in *Seize the Day* are wiser than the biographer who assumes that art emerges from life in some—what shall I say—literal, prosaic way. Bellow was fascinated by what he called "reality instructors," Deepak Chopra–like gurus, or what Alfred Kazin defined as "the very personification[s] of a kind of modern urban know-it-all, the quack analyst, the false guide to the many afflicted by their terrible uncertainty." Bellow's determination as an artist to portray and debunk such hollow men is the source of the power of his characterization of Valentine Gersbach. Merely being cuckolded is a far less potent fuel.

Yet the higher gossip is all around us. To understand *To Kill a Mockingbird*, we must first know that Harper Lee based her book on her observations of people she knew, including her own family, that Atticus Finch is a version of her own father, Amasa Coleman Lee, that the character of Dill is based on Truman Capote, and that the story of Boo Radley grew out of a house on the Lees' street that was always boarded up. To understand *The Sound and the Fury* we must be shown—as I was shown—the picket fence in Oxford, Mississippi, where the mentally troubled boy from whom Faulkner supposedly drew the character of Benjy used to stand. To appreciate fully Flannery O'Connor's terrifying story "Good Country People" we ought to see—and I was able to see it last year—the barn in Milledgeville that is an important setting for the tale. And so on. The life is the key to the work.

I repeat: I find this stuff interesting too. And I too think that, for example, Kurt Vonnegut's experience in Dresden profoundly affected his views on everything—on war, absurdity, irrationality, technology, death, and human nature. But many people experienced the firebombing of Dresden, just as many people lived in Oxford, Mississippi, along with Faulkner. Yet only Vonnegut wrote *Slaughterhouse-Five*, and only Faulkner was Faulkner. The question I ask myself is this: Why these men and not the men standing next to them? Why Flannery O'Connor or Harper Lee and not the women living next door, looking out on the same streets, seeing the same world go by? Why Roth and nobody else from Weequahic High, New Jersey? Why Joyce and none of the other boys who suffered through an education at the hands of the Jesuits of Clongowes Wood? A life may offer some of the raw material of a work. It does not offer the spark, the thing that makes the creative leap, the journey into the actual words.

Here's a taste of what I mean by the actual words. Let's talk about Joyce, let's talk, in particular, about "Stately, plump Buck Mulligan"—not only the first character to appear in *Ulysses* but also the first four words of the book. Joyce's biographer Richard Ellmann tells us that Buck Mulligan, Stephen's pal and the author of "The Ballad of Joking Jesus" and other such blasphemies, is based on Joyce's friend Oliver St. John Gogarty, a medical student, swimmer, poet, and wit, who lived with Joyce in the famous Martello Tower (which I also visited and, standing atop it, succumbed as we all do in these biographically obsessed days to the powerful sentimental lure of the higher gossip, the feeling of having walked into the pages of the great book). That's as may be. But my point is this. If he weren't "stately, plump Buck Mulligan," if he were, for example, "slow-moving, overweight Buck Mulligan," he would not exist as he does. The magic of the character lies not in its point of origin but in the precise language in which it is captured. "Mr. Leopold Bloom ate with relish the inner organs of beasts and fowls." This sentence is the open-sesame that brings Bloom to life in the pages of Joyce's verbal Dublin, his "new Bloomusalem." He could have been first described as an advertising salesman, or as a Jew, or as the husband of an unfaithful wife, and that would not have done the business. It is his eagerness to place himself outside those inner organs that creates him for us. Nothing in Joyce's biography prepares us for, or enriches our understanding of, these magic words.

There are good reasons why writers so often choose characters who are avatars, incarnations of themselves. It is helpful to be able to speak, think, and act through a shadow, an alternative "I," to go down a road not taken, to make a variation on the theme of yourself. I've done it twice. Saleem Sinai in *Midnight's Children* and Malik Solanka in *Fury* share a fair amount with their author. Saleem / Salman: not so far apart. In addition, Saleem lives in my house (although I renamed it), wanders through my neighborhood, goes to my school, and his boyhood friends are made up of bits of mine. (Another hazard of autobiography. In Bombay again, a man my age came up to me and said, "Hello, Salman, I'm Hairoil." In *Midnight's Children,* Saleem has a friend nicknamed Hairoil, a very clean and tidy boy with well-oiled and neatly parted hair. Now, as it happens I did borrow the hair from a boyhood friend, though the life of the fictional boy under the hair was quite unlike the real boy's. And here indeed, standing before me, was that old friend, very oddly identifying himself not by his real name, not even by a nickname we used to use, but by a nickname I made up for the book. How puzzling, I thought, that he found it easier to introduce himself as a fictional character rather than himself. And how sad, in addition, that he had lost all his hair.)

It's also true that Saleem's family has a similar structure to my maternal family. I too had a grandfather who was a doctor, an aunt who married a Pakistani general, an uncle involved in the Bombay movie industry, and a Goan ayah or nanny. I had thought that if I gave the novel a skeleton that I knew very well, it would be easier to control its immense length and scale. But during the writing of the novel I made an interesting discovery. When I tried simply to portray these people as they actually were—that is, when I allowed my autobiography too much power—they obstinately refused to come to life and remained inertly non-fictive. It was only when I pushed them away from their models—when Saleem's grandparents met through a hole in a perforated bedsheet (my grandparents did not meet in this way), when Saleem's uncle invented, to combat the censors, the innovative technique known as the Indirect Kiss (my uncle was not so inventive), when Saleem's uncle the general took part in a military coup (my own uncle might have wanted to, but probably did not), and, above all, when Saleem's Goan ayah Mary swapped two newborn babies in a nursing home as a political gesture (no, I was not swapped in my cradle at birth) and later rose to become an eminent pickle-factory boss—that I had a novel to write. It was the imaginative leap, and not the true-life source material, that mattered: to use the famous distinction of Lévi-Strauss, not the raw, but the cooked. And this, finally, is what I am defending: cookery. The joy of cooking.

Speaking of cookery, one more word about Saleem Sinai, who, like his old ayah Mary, ends up in a pickle factory. It's true that Saleem's early childhood echoed mine. However, as he gets older, our life stories diverge sharply and so do our personalities. Saleem gets more and more passive as he grows up, becoming, more and more, a person *to whom things are done* rather than a man who acts to take control of his own destiny. To be frank, there were times when this irritated me, and I tried more than once to write scenes in which he was less passive. These scenes were no good, and I learned another great lesson of fiction. The author can create character, but once the character has been created, the author is no longer free. He must operate within the limits of the human being he has invented. In short, I had to let Saleem be Saleem and stop trying to make him someone he wasn't—for example, me.

When *Fury* was published and people noticed that its central character was about my age and, like me, of Indian origin and, also like me, had recently moved to New York, the higher gossip drowned out everything else, and the assumption of autobiography became overwhelming. Not only was an entirely imaginary young Serbian woman assumed to be someone I was having an affair with—to which my reaction was, "If only!"—but, in addition, all Professor Solanka's views were thought to be mine. In fact, I had concentrated in Dr. Solanka's grumpy mind all the grouchy attitudes I could muster about life, America, and everything, and then attempted to surround him with a carnival of New York that would, I thought, balance, argue with, contextualize, his disenchanted internal monologue. I had forgotten the first rule about autobiography in fiction, the one that I have already taught you: "it's fiction," wrong; "it's completely autobiographical," right. The reception of *Fury* shocked me into realizing that I would have to avoid "me characters" in my books from now on. To put it bluntly, I have a particular problem in this regard. Too much of my life story has found its way into the public domain already; there has been, one could say, altogether too much of the "lower gossip," and for readers of a certain kind it is impossible not to try to "decode" my fiction in terms of what they know, or believe they know, about my own character and private life. This is, I have to say, a little horrifying, and I recoil from it. In the two novels that followed *Fury, Shalimar the Clown* and *The Enchantress of Florence*, there is no trace of an autobiographical character. These shadows are not mine. Nor will any image of the author be discernible in any future fiction I may succeed in writing. I have learned my lesson.

## (ii)

I want to talk a little bit about the ways in which an author's life *does* affect his work indirectly, by shaping his sensibility, by pointing him in one direction or another, and I guess I'll continue to focus on the author whose life I'm most closely acquainted with. I was born and raised in a big city and have spent most of my life in big cities and so it will come as no surprise that I see myself as essentially an urban writer. Also, to begin with, a postcolonial one. An empire does not end on the day the imperialists leave, and as I grew up there was still a strong after-influence of the British. In many ways—the law, the school curriculum, the railways, the civil service, the land reclamations—the British were still with us; on the other hand, we were raised to be proud of the new, independent India whose children we were. My parents used to joke that I was born and eight weeks later the British ran away—and really, how funny is that joke?—but I grew up in a city built by the British on Indian soil, itself a mixture of East and West, and that mingling forever shaped the way I saw the world.

I was also the product of a division, the Partition of the Indian subcontinent into the new states of India and Pakistan, and was raised in the aftermath of the massacres that followed, unable to forget the stories of the trains of slaughtered men, women, and children arriving in railway stations in Amritsar and Lahore. The Partition divided my family down the middle: Both my aunts were on the Pakistani side of the border, while we, more Indian than Muslim, preferred to stay on the Indian side. This gave me an accidental privilege as a writer: I could see the Partition, and the massacres, and the history of the subcontinent, from both sides. I took pride in the fact that Pakistani readers used *Midnight's Children* to "enter" India, and Indian readers used *Shame* to "enter" Pakistan, and I have always felt a close affinity for those writers, like the great Urdu short-story writer S. H. Manto, who had one foot in Karachi and the other in Bombay.

The first great writer I knew, who became for me a model of what a writer should be, was the Pakistani Urdu poet Faiz Ahmed Faiz. Faiz was a lifelong Communist, a winner of the Lenin Prize, and a heavy whiskey drinker, and in these things I did not follow him. But he was like an extra uncle to me, a close family friend, perhaps the best friend of my mother's older sister, and I was literally dandled on his knee. As I grew up I was struck by his determination to be, like Pablo Neruda, both private and public, the author of beautiful, somewhat jaundiced and disenchanted love poems in the form of the *ghazal*, many of which, set to music, brought him immense popularity, and also a body of public, political poetry, also jaundiced and disenchanted; and this double project, the public and the private, was one I assumed was quite simply what the job entailed. I believed then, and continued to believe, that this two-sided approach was what writing should be.

After the blood-drenched birth of Pakistan, Faiz wrote the famous poem "Subh-e-Azadi" ("Freedom's Morning"): "This trembling light, this night-bitten dawn, / This is not the dawn we were waiting for," a poem whose clear-eyed realism contrasts starkly with the much rosier vision of India's Nehru in his even more famous "freedom at midnight" speech. This clear-sightedness made him, inevitably, the target of the patriotically blind, and on one occasion, which may remind you of a scene in *Midnight's Children*, one of my aunts hid him in the cellar, rolled the living room rug over the trapdoor, placed a settee on top of the rug and her very ample self on top of the settee, and then faced down the mob that came looking for him and shooed them away.

Faiz was not a religious man, to put it mildly. Nor was my father. Nor am I. However, in India and Pakistan, just about everyone else is, and if you want to create that world credibly in your pages, you have to reckon with religion all the time, because your characters will be religious even if you aren't. And if you're writing about India, you have to reckon with an enormous number of gods. There have been attempts by Indian scholars to enumerate all the gods of India, not just the famous, superstar, above-the-title deities but all the little local gods of Indian households and neighborhoods, of woodland grove or mountain stream. These scholars have come up with the astonishing, magic-realist figure of three hundred million. Three hundred million gods. The population of the United States in supernatural form. The population of India is over 1.35 billion people, so that makes, very approximately, one god to four and a half human beings.

And it's even stranger than that, because while the divine population is presumably reasonably stable—one assumes divine birth control to be better than the human variety—the human population has been growing at high speed; in fact it has more than doubled since I was at school in Bombay in the 1950s. So if we project that population curve backward, we see that it was probably only sometime in the 1930s that the human population of India grew larger than the divine population for the first time. What does it do to a writer's sensibility and his artistic imagination to grow up in a world in which the supernatural and the quotidian rub up against each other in approximately equal numbers? What does it do to his understanding of the word "realism"? In my case, the answer is that it liberated me, showing me early on that kitchen-sink naturalism is only one way, and perhaps quite a limited way, of describing the world.

This realization was a part of what I call "the given." All writers start out with a "given," some little or large nugget of good or bad feeling, funny-ha-ha or funny-peculiar stories, some little moral or sexual twistedness, some unexpected angle on the language, some unscratched itch that makes them want to write in the first place. Some writers are able to mine that seam for a lifetime. Others—most of us, I believe—eventually feel that we have exhausted what we started out with and have to find a second act.

I have been unusually fortunate as a writer, in that my life has given me more than one such golden nugget. To begin with I had India, that inexhaustible horn of plenty, that endlessly nourishing well. After that I had migration, because the journey I made from East into West was made by millions of others. Migration is an old subject in America, but now it's the world's subject too. At the time of the India–Pakistan Partition, that was the greatest mass migration in human history, and since then there have been others to rival it. For good or ill this is the age of the migrant, the time in human history in which more people than ever before have ended up in places in which they did not begin, driven by economic necessity, political turmoil, or simply the lure of the big city's bright lights. This too became my subject, thanks to the accidents of my life. And then there is a third, the one that preoccupies me more and more—the desire to show how the world joins up, how *here* connects to *there*, how the little boxes we live in now open out into other little boxes, often very far away, and how, in order to explain our lives, we often need to understand things happening on the other side of the world. I once wrote that the British didn't fully understand their own history because so much of it happened overseas. This is true of us all now, and I find myself wanting more and more to reduce that incomprehension by finding the stories that connect the dots.

Here's one such story. In May 1662, the Infanta Catarina of Portugal, more familiar to history as Catherine of Braganza, married King Charles II of England, the extrovert Restoration monarch well known for his carousing, philandering ways. Sad to say, Catherine was not beautiful, so, in order to make her attractive to King Charles, a man partial to a pretty face, the dowry had to be pretty damn good, and the British managed to persuade Portugal to part with their early colonial possession, the islands and harbor of Bombay. This may well have been the underlying motive for the marriage all along. At any rate, the British immediately built a fort on Bombay island, set about the immense land-reclamation project that would join the Seven

Isles to one another and to the mainland as well, and a city grew that became the major port and economic powerhouse of British India. Meanwhile in America, two new boroughs were being marked out for development across the river from Manhattan Island. They were originally called the King's Borough, after Charles II, and the Queen's Borough, after Catherine of Braganza. Today they are called Brooklyn and Queens. You see how unexpectedly the world joins up? It turns out Bombay and New York, at or near their births, had the same queen.

The story has a sad postscript. In 1988, there were plans to erect a statue of Catherine of Braganza, a thirty-five-foot statue on a fifteen-foot base, at Hunters Point in Queens. She would have been the second-largest statue in New York, second only to Liberty herself. The sculptor Audrey Flack won a competition for the right to make the statue. She decided—perhaps after looking at portraits of Catherine—not to make a true likeness but rather a "multicultural image" with thick lips, a broad nose, and ringletted hair that could easily be taken for dreadlocks. Then things got even worse. Local historians objected. The Irish objected. Antislavery groups branded Catherine a slaver, though there's no evidence that she personally owned or traded in human beings, whereas several American presidents who did have slaves do have their statues. And in the end poor Catherine was denied the right to stand in glory gazing out across at Lady Liberty. Today she languishes in that limbo reserved for unwanted art and forgotten princesses. (Actually, she's in a foundry in Beacon, in upstate New York, where she has not yet been cast in bronze; and there she waits, and waits.)

## (iii)

All this talk of the journey beyond the source material, of inexplicable writerly idiosyncrasy that seems to come from nowhere, of the complex formation of artistic sensibility and the indirect influence on the creators of fiction of people, places, histories, and crowds, will not impress those who firmly believe novels to be thinly disguised autobiographies. And it's a small step from that belief to the conclusion that undisguised autobiographies are preferable anyway. Better, perhaps, to turn away from fiction to the apparently greater authenticity and authority of lives retold as facts. In these nonfictional times the proliferation of memoirs and autobiographies bears witness to people's growing suspicion that fiction is, well, *so not true,* and therefore somehow unworthy. And it is beginning to seem that the old adage about everyone having a book in them is going to come literally true, because these days, it's plain, anyone can have their name on a book, even if they haven't written it themselves, even if as seems likely in some cases they haven't even *read* it themselves. Look in the windows of the bookstores. There are tales of finding oneself through breast-reduction surgery or finding happiness through colossal weight loss; accounts of sporting triumph, triumph on television reality shows, and the overcoming of dreadful disadvantages through the beauty of the body, or of the soul, or the unadulterated purity of the memoirist's blind ambition. And there are the eternal tales of fall and redemption, of the self brought low through crime, drugs, and the intervention of evildoers and then raised back toward the light by good friends, family, Jesus, and detox clinics.

Self-regard has never been so well regarded. Self-exposure has never been so popular, and the more self that is exposed the better. Amid such promiscuity of revelation, how can art compete? How can truth fail to be stranger than fiction?

Nor is it by any means certain that what is on offer in these sad volumes is the truth, as the awful but also laughable case of Mr. James Frey reveals. You remember James Frey, the author of *A Million Little Pieces*—a prophetic title, revealing, as it does, the current condition of his reputation—James Frey, first Oprah's darling and then her whipping boy, two such arousing things to be. What you have, instead of truth, in these million little volumes, is what Stephen Colbert has unforgettably dubbed "truthiness." If real life isn't sexy enough, the answer—the very novelistic answer, it must be said—is, obviously, to sex it up. Or to put it another way, to lie.

I once knew a "truthy" writer, a consummate liar, a truly brilliant, even majestic liar, who, when faced with the obvious untruthfulness of her statements, responded with a straight face, "It was a metaphor of how unhappy I felt." Not to know the difference between a metaphor and a lie is one definition of insanity. It is also, perhaps, a necessary ignorance if one is to write "truthy" books rather than truthful ones.

If one were in a death-of-the-novel sort of mood, one might conclude that this time of confessional Knausgaardery, this flood of memoir-abilia, and the apparent readiness of readers to turn toward such books with pleasure is not merely a short-term fashion but might in fact soon supplant the subtleties of fiction altogether. What's a novelist to do? I suppose the options are (a) to carry on regardless; or (b) to hang oneself; or (c) to admit grudgingly that many of the new memoirs are superb—at least as good as, if not better than, most novels; or (d) to write a memoir. In the case of Elias Canetti, the 1981 Nobel laureate, we may have to admit that his three-volume autobiography, *The Tongue Set Free, The Torch in My Ear,* and *The Play of the Eyes,* is his masterpiece. And in America, African American writers are claiming the memoir form as their own. Margo Jefferson's *Negroland,* Sarah M. Broom's *The Yellow House,* Tracy K. Smith's *Ordinary Light,* Kiese Laymon's *Heavy,* and Roxane Gay's *Hunger* are just some examples of this new *richness.*

These memoirs, at the literary end of the spectrum, do what the New Journalism of George Plimpton and Tom Wolfe did in the sixties and seventies: They steal the techniques of novelists to create a new kind of nonfiction. This is not the "truthiness" of the self-glorifier but an effort, through craft, to convey more of the truth.

Full disclosure: I myself have joined the memoirists' number, but I continue to find it more satisfying to imagine what Plato disparagingly called "the thing that is not" than merely to recount the way I was. More and more I envy the freedom of those eighteenth-century masters to allow their books to be celebrated while they kept themselves to themselves. More and more I admire the strength of those authors who destroy their private papers—and I say *this* as an author who has just placed his manuscripts, journals, and idle doodlings in the hands of, and at the tender mercies of, the good people at MARBL, the Manuscripts and Rare Books Library at Emory University in Atlanta. I'm thinking of Philip Larkin, who instructed his lover Monica Jones to arrange for the destruction of more than thirty volumes of his private diaries. Oddly, she didn't do it herself but asked another of his lovers, his former secretary Betty Mackereth, to do the work of shredding the books page by page during the course of a long afternoon in December 1985.

Shakespeare's plays don't tell us much about his life. Was Anne Hathaway the model for Lady Macbeth or a Merry Wife of Windsor? We can't say. Shakespeare's only son, Hamnet, died, perhaps from the plague, in 1596, at the age of eleven. Did Shakespeare, in *Hamlet*, written three or four years later, transpose his grief and rage at the death of a child into a son's rage and grief at the death of a father? We don't know. We can extrapolate a few things about Shakespeare's character from such details of his life that survive. In an eccentric and no doubt suspect book called *How Shakespeare Spent the Day*, written in 1963, the British scholar Ivor Brown points out that even after he became the most successful and wealthiest playwright of the Elizabethan age, Shakespeare lived in or close to Southwark until the day of his retirement—raunchy Southwark with its whorehouses, gambling dens, bear pits, cockfights, alehouses, and theaters, thus revealing himself to be a downtown kind of guy, happiest when plunging into the roughneck wildness of life. The point about Shakespeare is that he can be endlessly speculated about in this way, but he can never be pinned down. And so the attention turns again, as it must and should, away from the life and back to the work.

But I am one of those who has failed to follow his glorious example, and Emory University's Manuscripts and Rare Books Library has all my papers. I've seen something of the diligence and care with which they have been cataloged, and I know they could not be in better, more responsible, more careful hands, and the day has now come when the papers are open to scholarly inquiry; and all I can say is, thank you to everyone at MARBL, thank you, Emory, and God help me.

# ADAPTATION

ADAPTATION, THE PROCESS BY WHICH ONE THING DEVEL-
ops into another thing, by which one shape or form changes into a
different form, is, of course, a commonplace artistic activity. Books
are turned into plays and films all the time; plays are turned into
movies and also sometimes into musicals; movies are turned into
Broadway shows and even, by the ugly method known as "noveliza-
tion," into books as well. We live in a world of such transformations
and metamorphoses. Good movies—*Lolita*, *The Pink Panther*—are
remade as bad movies; bad movies are remade as even worse movies—
Ang Lee's *Hulk* (2003) returns as *The Incredible Hulk* five years later;
British TV comedy series are turned into American TV comedy series, so that *The Office* becomes a different *The Office*, and Ricky Ger-
vais turns into Steve Carell, just as, long ago, the British working-class
racist Alf Garnett in *Till Death Us Do Part* turned into the American
blue-collar bigot Archie Bunker in *All in the Family*. British reality
programs are adapted to suit American audiences as well: *Pop Idol*
becomes *American Idol* when it crosses the Atlantic; *Strictly Come
Dancing* becomes *Dancing with the Stars*, a program that, it may interest you to know, once invited me to appear on it, an invitation I
declined, believing, rightly or wrongly, that appearing on the show
would be a career-ending move.

Songs by great artists are covered by lesser artists; on Obama's
Inauguration Day in January 2009, Beyoncé performed her version
of Etta James's classic "At Last" to the considerable irritation of Etta

James herself (but, then, Ms. James seemed even more irritated by the election of Barack Obama, so perhaps she was just in a bad mood). All of these are examples of the myriad variations of adaptation, an insatiable process that can sometimes seem voracious, as if we now live in a culture that endlessly cannibalizes itself, so that, in the end, it will have eaten itself up completely. Anyone can make a list of the many catastrophic adaptations they have seen, my personal favorites being David Lean's ridiculous film of *A Passage to India*, in which Alec Guinness in brownface as a Hindu wise man dangles his feet blasphemously in the waters of a sacred water tank; and the Merchant–Ivory emasculation of Kazuo Ishiguro's *The Remains of the Day*, in which Ishiguro's guilty-as-hell British Nazi aristocrat is portrayed as a lovable, misguided, deceived old bugger more deserving of our sympathy than our scorn.

But adaptation can be a creative as well as a destructive force. Rod Stewart singing "Downtown Train" is the equal of Tom Waits, and Joe Cocker singing "With a Little Help from My Friends" achieves the rare feat of singing a Beatles song better than the Beatles did, which becomes a less impressive achievement when you remember that the original singer was Ringo Starr. And after Aretha Franklin sang "Respect," it was her song, even if Otis Redding wrote and recorded it first. I've taught a course highlighting some of the instances in which fine books have been adapted into equally fine films. Edith Wharton's *The Age of Innocence* mutated successfully into Martin Scorsese's *The Age of Innocence;* Giuseppe di Lampedusa's portrait of Sicily in 1860, *The Leopard,* turned into Luchino Visconti's greatest film; Flannery O'Connor's *Wise Blood* was well filmed by John Huston; and, in his film of *Great Expectations,* David Lean produced a movie classic that can stand alongside the Dickens novel without any sense of inferiority, a film that allows this filmgoer, at least, to forgive him for the later blunder of *A Passage to India.*

There are many other examples of successful adaptation. Few English-language readers today will know Jan Potocki's nineteenth-century Franco-Polish masterpiece *The Manuscript Found in Saragossa,* but I urge you to discover it for its playfulness and bizarrerie, its surreal, supernatural, gothic, picaresque world of gypsies, thieves, hallucinations, inquisitions, and a pair of unbelievably beautiful sisters who are, unfortunately for the men they seduce, only ghosts. Its qualities are perfectly captured by the Polish film director Wojciech Has in his 1965 film *The Saragossa Manuscript*. Across the world in Bengal, India, Satyajit Ray's 1955 film *Pather Panchali*, "The Song of the Little Road," not only equaled but bettered the 1929 Bengali classic by Bibhutibhushan Bandopadhyay from which it was adapted. John Huston seems to have been a particularly gifted adapter of good literature, and his film of Joyce's "The Dead," perhaps the greatest short story in the English language, brings it vividly, passionately to life; although right at the end, when the camera moves out through a window to watch the falling snow, and Joyce's famous words take over from Huston's images, speaking of the snow that was "general all over Ireland," the snow that was "falling faintly through the universe and faintly falling, like the descent of their last end, upon all the living and the dead," we are reminded of the difference between excellence and genius. *The Dead* is an excellent film, but the last lines of Joyce's story surpass it effortlessly.

The film that explores the idea of adaptation most radically is probably Spike Jonze and Charlie Kaufman's 2002 *Adaptation*, a film that takes exceptional liberties with its source material, Susan Orlean's nonfiction book *The Orchid Thief*, which began as a text for *The New Yorker* magazine, telling the story of Orlean's investigation of the arrest of a man named John Laroche, who was caught poaching rare orchids in Florida, in the Fakahatchee Strand State Preserve. The film plays fast and loose with the truth, obliging the "Susan Orlean" character to have an affair with the "Laroche" character, both of them being presented as figments of the actual screenwriter's fictional alter ego, who is also named Charlie Kaufman and is blessed, or cursed, with an imaginary twin brother named Donald. The film is a maze of mirrors and pretenses and self-conscious metafictional devices and in the end moves into a crazy thriller world of drugs, sex, and gunplay; and this John Laroche, the movie's John Laroche, winds up being eaten alive by an alligator, like Captain Hook. I have to say that the person I admire most in all this is Susan Orlean, not the character portrayed by Meryl Streep but the actually existing Susan Orlean, who allowed her work and, even more courageously, her own character to be treated in this creatively savage, this almost appallingly cavalier fashion. She becomes, so to speak, the sibling of John Malkovich, who allowed himself to be so ruthlessly and comically Malkoviched in Jonze and Kaufman's earlier film, *Being John Malkovich*.

The question raised by the adaptive excesses of *Adaptation*, the movie, is the question at the heart of the entire subject of adaptation, the activity: that is to say, the question of essence. "Poetry is what gets lost in translation," said Robert Frost, but Joseph Brodsky retorted, "Poetry is what is gained in translation," and the battle lines could not be more clearly drawn than that. My own view has always been that whether we are talking about a poem moving across a language border to become another poem in another tongue, a book crossing the frontier between the world of print and celluloid, or human beings migrating from one world to another, both Frost and Brodsky are right. Something is always lost in translation; and yet something can perhaps also be gained. You will see that I am defining adaptation very broadly, to include translation, migration, and metamorphosis, all the means by which one thing becomes another. In my novel *Midnight's Children* the narrator, Saleem, discusses the making of pickles as this sort of adaptive process: "I reconcile myself," he says, "to the inevitable distortions of the pickling process. To pickle is to give immortality, after all: fish, vegetables, fruit hang embalmed in spice-and-vinegar; a certain alteration, a slight intensification of taste, is a small matter, surely? The art is to change the flavor in degree, but not in kind; and above all (in my thirty jars and a jar) to give it shape and form—that is to say, meaning."

The question of essences remains at the heart of the adaptive act; how to make a second version of a first thing, of a book or film or poem or vegetable, or of yourself, that is successfully its own new thing and yet carries with it the essence, the spirit, the soul of the first thing, the thing that you yourself, or your book or poem or film or your mango or lime, originally were.

Is it impossible? Is the intangible in our arts and our natures, the space between our words, the things seen in between the things shown, inevitably discarded in the remaking process, and if so can it be filled up with other spaces, other visions, that satisfy or even enrich us enough so that we do not mind the loss? To look at adaptation in this broad-spectrum way, to take it beyond the realm of art into the rest of life, is to see that all the meanings of the word deal with the question of what is essential, in a work adapted to another form, in an individual adapting to a new home, in a society adapting to a new age. What do you preserve? What do you jettison? What is changeable, and where must you draw the line? The questions are always the same, and the way we answer them determines the quality of the adaptation, of the book, the poem, or of our own lives.

I'M WRITING THIS ON Oscars night 2009, so let's take a look at a couple of recent highly praised adaptations of books into films, both up for multiple Academy Awards.

To begin with, there is the curious case of F. Scott Fitzgerald and Brad Pitt. In 1921, F. Scott Fitzgerald wrote an odd little story called "The Curious Case of Benjamin Button," about the birth, to "young Mr. and Mrs. Roger Button," of a male baby who is born as a seventy-year-old man and who then lives backward, getting younger all the time, until at the end of his life, baby-sized and shrinking slowly in his white crib, he is sucked away into nothingness. In 2008, this little squib of a tale was turned by Brad Pitt and the director David Fincher into a $200 million motion picture, which, as I write, is in contention for no fewer than thirteen Academy Awards. (A note from the future: It ended up winning just three, for Best Art Direction, Best Makeup, and Best Visual Effects.)

However, the difference between the story and the film is unusually great. In Fitzgerald's story, Benjamin is born as a full-sized septuagenarian male. It is never explained how Mrs. Button managed to give birth to such a large baby without being torn in half. Indeed, Mrs. Button never gets a look-in, and it is several pages before a casual reference to her shows that she somehow survived her magnificent parturition. The manner of her survival is not discussed. In the film, however, Benjamin is born old but baby-sized; he is a seventy-year-old robot baby that looks a little like Brad Pitt. And Mrs. Button, regrettably, does not survive, even though her baby has been so helpfully downsized. In the story, Mr. Button undertakes the work of raising and educating his child; in the film, Mr. Button, horrified by the swaddled little monster he has helped to bring into the world, abandons it on a doorstep to be raised by Taraji P. Henson. In the story, Benjamin's life is lived largely in the private sphere, apart from an excursion to fight in the Spanish–American War, while in the movie he becomes involved in so many of the public events of his time that the picture might almost have been called *Zelig in Reverse*, or perhaps *Forrest Gump Goes Backward*. (The screenwriter of *Forrest Gump*, Eric Roth, who adapted Winston Groom's novel, is also responsible for the screenplay of *Benjamin Button*.)

Perhaps the biggest difference between the two works is that, other than sharing the idea of a man who lives backward in time, their stories are entirely different; the film is not really an adaptation of the book but almost entirely Eric Roth's creation. And while Roth and Fincher's film is essentially a bravura special-effects display helped by two fine acting performances, by Pitt and Cate Blanchett, it doesn't finally have anything in particular to say, while Fitzgerald's story is at least a comedy of snobbery and embarrassment that, while maintaining a deliberately frothy and light tone, enjoyably satirizes the social attitudes of late-nineteenth- and early-twentieth-century Baltimore.

To call the movie *Button* an adaptation of the "Button" story is to strain to the limit the meaning of the word "adaptation," capacious as that meaning is. To *adapt* is, just to recapitulate the most common definition, to make something suitable for a new use or purpose by modifying it, as when, for example, an old hospital is adapted for modern medicine. More specifically for our present purposes, an adaptation "alters a text to make it suitable for filming, broadcasting, or the stage." Everyone accepts that stories and films are different things and that the source material must be modified, even radically modified, to be effective in the new medium. The only interesting questions are "how?" and "how much?" However, when the original is virtually discarded, it's difficult to know if the result can be called an adaptation at all.

There are, after all, other well-known stories of time reversal that precede the Fincher-Roth film. In Martin Amis's 1991 novel *Time's Arrow*, the story of the Holocaust is told in reverse, so that, in one extraordinary scene, kindly Nazi doctors in a concentration camp fetch gold from their private hoards and use it to put fillings into the teeth of Jewish dental patients. But in *Time's Arrow* everything, and not just one single life, goes backward. Perhaps the best-known example of another *Button*-style reversal is the character of the wizard Merlyn in T. H. White's 1938 classic *The Sword in the Stone*, itself the subject of a Disneyfied adaptation, over which it would be best to draw a veil. Merlyn, the teacher of the boy known as Wart, the future King Arthur, lives backward in time and thus has the great advantage of knowing the future while being confused about the past. Benjamin Button has no such luck. He's old and robotic but as ignorant as any newborn babe. On the other hand, he grows into Brad Pitt, so things are not all bad.

What can one say about Danny Boyle's *Slumdog Millionaire*, the film that won a lot of Oscars? Eight Oscars! To quote Wallace Shawn in *The Princess Bride:* "Inconceivable!" The film was adapted by Simon Beaufoy from the novel *Q&A* by the Indian diplomat Vikas Swarup and directed by Danny Boyle and Loveleen Tandan. Many of you will have seen it, and liked it, because a feel-good movie about the dreadful Bombay slums, an opulently photographed movie about extreme poverty, a romantic, Bollywoodized look at the harsh, unromantic underbelly of India—well, it feels good, right? And, just to clinch it, there's a nifty Bollywood dance sequence at the end. (Actually, it's a pretty second-rate dance sequence even by Bollywood's standards, but never mind.) It's difficult and probably pointless to go up against such a popular film, but let me try, anyway.

The problems begin with the work being adapted. Vikas Swarup's novel is a corny potboiler, with a plot that defies belief: A boy from the slums somehow (how?) manages to get onto *Kaun Banega Crorepati,* the hit Indian version of *Who Wants to Be a Millionaire,* and answers all the questions correctly because the random accidents of his life have, in a series of outrageous coincidences, given him the information he needs, and the questions are conveniently asked in the order that allows his flashbacks to occur in chronological sequence. This is a patently ridiculous conceit, the kind of fantasy writing that gives fantasy writing a bad name. This plot device is faithfully preserved by the filmmakers and lies at the heart of the weirdly renamed *Slumdog Millionaire.* As a result, the film too beggars belief.

The movie piles impossibility upon impossibility, exceeding even the crassness of the book. Two boys from the Bombay slums, who grow up speaking Hindi and Marathi, flee a fire and suddenly acquire perfect English, good enough to talk to (and hoodwink) Western tourists. Oh, and when they run away from the burning slum, they demonstrate extraordinary fitness, because the next thing you know they are at the Taj Mahal, which is in Agra, hundreds of miles away. A moment later they are back in Bombay and the older boy has miraculously acquired a gun, and bullets, and the skill and courage to use both. How did he get a gun? It is never explained. India is not the United States, and consequently it isn't easy for anyone there to acquire a weapon, unless they are already in one of the criminal mafias, and at this point in the story that is not the case. To watch your hometown's story being told in this comically absurd, tawdry fashion is, finally, to grow annoyed. The sentimentality of *Slumdog Millionaire,* were its setting somewhere more familiar to Western audiences, would be recognized as the banal fluff it is. Do we seriously believe that the moll of a Mafia godfather would be able to escape him and live happily ever after with her childhood sweetheart? Would Don Corleone put up with such a thing? No? Well, nor would the godfathers of D-Company or any of the other criminal gangs of Bombay.

And while I am well aware of the potential for brutality lurking in Indian police forces, the idea that a game-show contestant would be hung upside down and tortured because he was getting too many questions right . . . Let's just say, it strains credulity. The Indian police aren't interested enough in TV game shows to do that. They have many other people they prefer to torture.

It used to be the case that Western movies about India were about blond white women arriving there to find, almost at once, a maharajah to fall in love with, the supply of such maharajahs being apparently endless and specially provided for English or American blondes; or they were about European women accusing non-maharajah Indians of rape, perhaps because they were so indignant at being approached by a non-maharajah; or they were about dashing white men galloping about the colonies firing pistols and unsheathing sabers, to varying effect. Now that sort of exoticism has lost its appeal; people want, instead, enough grit and violence to convince themselves that what they are seeing is authentic; but it's still tourism. If the earlier films were Raj tourism, maharajah tourism, then today we have slum tourism instead. In an interview conducted at the 2008 Telluride Film Festival, Danny Boyle, when asked why he had chosen a project so different from his usual material, answered that he had never been to India and knew nothing about it, so he thought this project was a great opportunity. Listening to him, I imagined an Indian film director making a movie about New York lowlife and saying that he had done so because he knew nothing about New York and had indeed never been there. He would have been torn limb from limb by critical opinion. But for a First World director to say that about the Third World is considered praiseworthy, an indication of his artistic daring. The double standards of postcolonial attitudes have clearly not yet wholly faded away.

I WANT TO CONSIDER for a moment the case against film adaptations in general, because there is a widely held view among movie lovers that films made from original screenplays are and must be held to be superior to films made by adapting plays or books. Many successful books of recent times have undergone cinematic transmutation, including—to offer a very incomplete list—Günter Grass's *The Tin Drum;* Gabriel García Márquez's *Love in the Time of Cholera, Innocent Eréndira,* and *Chronicle of a Death Foretold;* Philip Roth's *The Human Stain; Short Cuts,* from the stories of Raymond Carver; Donna Tartt's *The Goldfinch; The Joy Luck Club,* by Amy Tan; and the *Harry Potter* series, by J. K. Rowling. (*Independence Day,* the movie, was not an adaptation of Richard Ford's award-winning novel, which unfortunately came out at much the same time as the film, so that, according to legend, when customers in bookstores requested the book, the booksellers were obliged to ask, "With or without aliens?")

Of this particular list, however, perhaps only Volker Schlöndorff's film of *The Tin Drum* is worth talking about as a film, and this imbalance between good and bad adaptations strengthens the argument of the anti-adaptation lobby. The *Harry Potter* films, determined to remain utterly faithful to the books, suffer cinematically from that loyalty, apart, perhaps, from Alfonso Cuarón's *Prisoner of Azkaban. Short Cuts* betrays the vision of Raymond Carver by moving most of his characters up the social scale, where their barely suppressed despair looks like self-indulgence. The *Goldfinch* movie was, to put it politely, a colossal flop. And down at the very bottom of the barrel is the film of *The Human Stain,* which casts, in the role of a light-skinned African American man who manages to pass for white for much of his life, the actor Anthony Hopkins, a light-skinned Welshman. I suppose, as a great actor, he was expected simply to act the black part. The anti-adaptation, pro-original-screenplay argument was once expounded to me with immense vehemence by a somewhat inebriated British film producer, who had probably seen too many adaptations of the *Human Stain* type. He said, in plain language and with a certain amount of fist-pounding on our hosts' dinner table, that "all movies made from books are shit." It is certainly possible to make a strong argument for the Shit Position. *The Human Stain* does not stand alone. The films of all the books I mentioned a few moments ago are limp failures, whereas the originals are gripping, energetic, and taut. The films of García Márquez's masterpieces, in particular, are travesties, replacing the writer's imaginative precision with a lazy exoticism that betrays the originals profoundly without even knowing it is doing so.

However, Schlöndorff's *Tin Drum* stands as an exception to the Excremental Principle, with, at its heart, the electric performance of David Bennent as Oskar Matzerath, the Peter Pan among the million lost boys and murderous pirates of Nazi Germany; little, stunted Oskar, the other boy in classic literature who never grew up. There are more films that disprove the British producer's dictum—for example, the Coen brothers' *No Country for Old Men,* a film that (by contrast with the Potter cycle) actually succeeds by keeping very close, scene by scene, line of dialogue by line of dialogue, to Cormac McCarthy's novel, and Paul Thomas Anderson's *There Will Be Blood,* which succeeds by the opposite method, making only a free, loose, and largely successful adaptation of Upton Sinclair's novel *Oil!* But the odor lingers on, because the failures are so much more frequent than the successes.

THE *AUTEUR* THEORY OF filmmaking was first expressed by François Truffaut in *Cahiers du Cinéma* in the late 1950s and amplified, first as film theory and then in the making of actual films, by a group of critics who would turn into some of the world's most important filmmakers: François Truffaut himself, Jean-Luc Godard, Claude Chabrol, Eric Rohmer, and Jacques Rivette. But even though the idea of the superiority of scripts written as original screenplays rather than adaptations lay at or near the heart of the French New Wave, many of the finest works of French and indeed World Cinema in the 1950s and 1960s were, in fact, successful adaptations. Godard, a devotee of the original screenplay, had his greatest commercial success with *Le Mépris,* "Contempt," which was based on a novel by Alberto Moravia. Chabrol made a terrific film from the British poet laureate (and father of Daniel) Cecil Day-Lewis's pseudonymously written thriller *The Beast Must Die,* or, in French, *Que La Bête meure;* Eric

Rohmer brilliantly filmed the classic novella by Heinrich von Kleist, *Die Marquise von O*; Truffaut himself mingled original screenplays, such as *Les Quatre Cents Coups* (given the erroneous, literally translated English-language title "The 400 Blows," whereas the idiomatic French would be better rendered as "The Wild Life") and *La Nuit Américaine* ("Day for Night"), with adaptations such as *Fahrenheit 451*, from Ray Bradbury's celebrated book, and *Jules et Jim*, from the novel by Henri-Pierre Roché, a novel that, incidentally, was probably itself inspired by the real-life love triangle between Roché, Marcel Duchamp, and the American artist and potter Beatrice Wood, known as "Mama of Dada" because of her place near the center of the Dadaist world.

The immensely rich World Cinema of the period likewise went some distance toward exploding or at least diluting the "All Adaptions Are Shit" Principle. Kurosawa's early samurai masterpieces *Yojimbo* and *Sanjuro* had literary originals, though *Seven Samurai* came from an original screenplay, and *Rashomon* was made by combining two short stories by Ryūnosuke Akutagawa. Satyajit Ray took much from classic Bengali literature, and some of his greatest films, such as *Charulata* and *The Home and the World*, are adapted more or less faithfully from originals by Rabindranath Tagore. Ingmar Bergman and Federico Fellini invariably filmed their own original screenplays, but Luis Buñuel was less dogmatic and made some of his most successful films by allying his own anarchic, surrealist tendencies to classic European literature, adapting *Belle de Jour* by Joseph Kessel; *Tristana* and *Nazarín*, both novels by Benito Pérez Galdós; and *The Diary of a Chambermaid* by Octave Mirbeau.

The case against film adaptations thus remains unproven, and, when we look below the level of great literature, a plausible argument can be made that many cinematic adaptations are better than their prose source materials. At the risk of offending the enormous army of Tolkien fans, I would suggest that Peter Jackson's films surpass Tolkien's originals, because, to be blunt, Jackson makes films better than Tolkien writes; Jackson's film language, sweeping, lyrical, by turns intimate and epic, is greatly preferable to Tolkien's prose, which veers alarmingly between windbaggery, archness, pomposity, and an unbearable thee- and thou-ing faux-classicism, achieving something like humanity and ordinary English only in the parts about hobbits, the little people who are our representatives in the saga to a far greater degree than its grandly heroic (or snivelingly crooked) men.

MY FIRST PERSONAL EXPERIENCE of adaptation was the stage version of *Midnight's Children*, directed by Tim Supple, which the Royal Shakespeare Company performed both in England and in America. Theater is a different beast from film—it's so *present;* the play's being right there in front of you makes it such an insistently declaratory form (except in the hands of a Beckett or Pinter, who turn its normal rules upside down); and what is true of the theater in general is doubly true of epic theater. As a result, the stage adaptation of *Midnight's Children* differed in two striking ways from the book: Firstly, it was much more noisily, obviously political, putting the public material front and center instead of using it more suggestively, in the background, as the novel often does; and, secondly, there was a lot more sex. I mean: a *lot* more. In the novel most of the fornication is kept decorously offstage, but in the theater, it sometimes seemed that the actors never stopped leaping on one another and going at it with a will.

Speaking as the co-author of the adaptation as well as the author of the novel, I liked the differences. I thought of the play as a sort of cousin of the book, or perhaps its illegitimate child; its relative, not its mirror image. I thought its brasher, more aggressively in-your-face style was effective and properly theatrical, while remaining true to the book's spirit. The response from audiences was interestingly divided. It soon became clear that the people who most enjoyed the show were those who had not read the novel. If people came to the theater simply as theatergoers, bringing no literary baggage along, so to speak, just coming as people interested in seeing a new play, they usually left satisfied, even excited. The book's fans had more-complicated reactions, almost all of them finding something to argue with, either stylistically or in terms of what had been left out of the adaptation. Some of them liked the show, others hated it, but few of them were satisfied.

THE ESSENCE OF A WORK to be adapted may lie anywhere: in the frame stories that tell us, for example, how Superman became super, why Batman became batty, or why the Joker jokes. It may lie in a story's unique atmospherics—the Depression-era bigotries of a small Alabama town as seen through a young girl's eyes—or it may lie in a character's interiority, the inner life of Holden Caulfield or of Proust's narrator Marcel. That these essences can be understood and captured on film is exemplified by, for example, Raúl Ruiz's great film of Proust's *Time Regained,* or Robert Mulligan's film of *To Kill a Mockingbird,* or Heath Ledger's extraordinary incarnation of the Joker in *The Dark Knight.*

Most difficult of all for the adapter are those texts whose essences reside in language, and this may explain why all those García Márquez movies were so bad, why there have never been good films made from the work of Italo Calvino or Evelyn Waugh (though there are many snobbery-choked versions of *Brideshead Revisited*), why movies of Hemingway so often misfire (I'm thinking of *The Old Man and the Sea,* with Spencer Tracy cast horribly adrift with a dead fish), and why even a really good try like Joseph Strick's 1967 attempt to film Joyce's *Ulysses* doesn't fully match up to the original, even though it is perfectly cast, with Milo O'Shea as an uncannily good incarnation of Leopold Bloom, and Maurice Roëves as a more than adequate Stephen Dedalus. In the final scene of Strick's *Ulysses,* it must be said, when Barbara Jefford as Molly Bloom lounges and rolls promiscuously upon her marital bed and delivers in voiceover the grandest soliloquy in any novel, and as yes she says yes she says yes, the world of Joyce's tongue comes fully alive at last.

What is essential? It's one of the great questions of life, and, as I've suggested, it's a question that crops up in other adaptations than artistic ones. Before I finish, I'd like to return to the subject of these other, real-life adaptations, in which the "work" to be adapted is us. The text is human society and the human self, in isolation or in groups, the essence to be preserved is a human essence, and the result is the pluralist, hybridized, mixed-up world in which we all now live. Adaptation as metaphor, as *carrying across,* which is the literal Greek-derived meaning of the word "metaphor," and of the related word "translation," another form of *carrying across,* this time derived from the Latin.

What is essential? In little ways, all of us answer this question every day. What are the things we think of as essential in our lives? The answers could be our children, a daily walk in the park, a good stiff drink, the reading of books, a job, a vacation, a baseball team, a cigarette, or love. And yet life has a way of making us rethink. Our children move away from home, we move away from our favorite park, the doctor forbids us to drink or smoke, we lose our eyesight, we get fired, there's no time or money to take a vacation, our baseball team sucks, our heart is broken. At such times our picture of the world hangs crookedly on the wall. Then, if we can manage it, we adapt, we begin to like the idea of not having to be hands-on parents every day, we get used to a different daily walk, we don't need to drink or smoke anymore, we learn Braille, we find new work, we decide we don't need a vacation, we learn how to do without love, and then, maybe, we find it possible to fall in love again. Our baseball team still sucks, but that's life, we adapt to it, we survive, and what this shows us is that essence is something deeper than any of that, it's the thing that gets us through. The twelve separate varieties of finches that Charles Darwin found on the Galápagos Islands had all made local adaptations, but when the ornithologist John Gould examined Darwin's specimens in 1837, he could see that these were not different birds but twelve different species of the same bird. In spite of random mutation and natural selection, their finch-ness, their essence, was intact.

As individuals, as communities, as nations, we are the constant adapters of ourselves and must constantly ask ourselves the question.

Wherein does our finch-ness lie, so to speak: Of what does our essence consist; what are the things we cannot ever give up unless we wish to cease to be ourselves? We move to a new city, a new country; we find ourselves among people we do not know, who do not know us. Perhaps we do not speak their language perfectly, nor they ours. Perhaps their customs, their belief systems, are different from ours. Our children will grow up in these new streets, among these new people, speaking this new tongue. Should we too adapt to the new ways, so that our children do not find us strange? Or should we hold fast to the old ways, so that we can pass them on down the generations? If we are religious among non-religionists, should we accommodate our thinking to theirs so that we can live easily among them, or harden our own, even if it means we are forever thought of as outsiders? If we are radicals among conservatives, should we tone down our ideas? You see that the question of adaptation is at bottom the oldest of questions: *Who are we, and how shall we live?* The matter of essences is also, in the end, an ethical question—it raises, inevitably, the ancient argument between right action and wrong.

We can learn this much from the poets who translate the poetry of others, from the screenwriters and filmmakers who turn words on the page into images on a screen, from all those who *carry across* one thing into another state: An adaptation works best when it is a genuine transaction between the old and the new, carried out by persons who understand and care for both, who can help the thing adapted to leap the gulf and shine again in a different light. In other words, the process of social, cultural, and individual adaptation, just like artistic adaptation, needs to be free, not rigid, if it is to succeed. Those who cling too fiercely to the old text, the thing to be adapted, the old ways, the past, are doomed to produce something that does not work, an unhappiness, an alienation, a quarrel, a failure, a loss.

But those who do not know who they are are doomed too: individuals who sacrifice themselves for the sake of pleasing others; comedians who stop telling jokes because they find themselves in a humorless world; serious people who start trying to tell jokes because they fear being thought humorless; people in a new situation, a new relationship, a new country, who act against their natures because they think that's the way to make things easy for themselves.

Whole societies can lose their way through a process of bad adaptation. Striving to save themselves, they can oppress others. Hoping to defend themselves, they can damage the very liberties they believed to be under attack. Claiming to defend freedom, they can make themselves and others less free. Or, seeking to calm the violent hotheads in their midst, societies can try to appease them and so give the violent hotheads the notion that their violence and hotheadedness is effective. Wishing to create better understanding between peoples, they can seek to prevent the expression of opinions unpalatable to some of their members and so immediately make others even angrier than they were before.

Societies in motion, at a time of rapid change such as the present day, succeed, as all good adaptations do, by knowing what is essential, what cannot be compromised, what all their citizens must accept as the price of membership. For many years now, I'm sorry to say, we have lived through an era of bad social adaptations, of appeasements and surrenders on the one hand, of arrogant excesses and coercions on the other. Consequently, in times of crises—political, ecological, or medical—we may find ourselves ill-equipped to deal with them.

To attempt a note of optimism: The human race has shown itself to be a species capable of rapid adaptation when it is seriously threatened. We need that human ingenuity more than ever, to fulfill our hope that better times—and better movies!—may lie ahead.

# NOTES ON SLOTH:
# FROM SALIGIA
# TO OBLOMOV

----

## Saligia

"SALIGIA" IS ALL SEVEN DEADLY SINS ROLLED INTO ONE. I picture her as a Fellini grotesque, ample and fleshy, wobbling as she laughs. The camera falls toward her and she proffers her immense chest. She has bad teeth and greasy black hair pulled back in a bun. If she were sculpted, the artist would have to be Fernando Botero, the Colombian sculptor of outsized people (and animals). She terrifies adolescent boys in, perhaps, Federico Fellini's hometown of Rimini, or a town like it, but the same adolescents are also inexorably drawn to her, to the perfume of her mighty breasts. She initiates them into the mysteries of the flesh, and her sisters are Cabiria and Volpina and the rest. She stretches out her arms toward us, and we are lost.

She was probably born in the thirteenth century. In 1271 she appears in print, in the *Summa hostiensis,* the work of a certain Henricius de Bartholomaeis—a man of the port town of Ostia, where, centuries later, the whore Cabiria would ply her trade by night in the Fellini movie. Bartholomaeis brought Saligia into being by revising the traditional order of the seven deadly sins, the order laid down in the sixth century A.D. in the *Magna Moralia* of Gregory the Great: *superbia, invidia, ira, avaritia, accidia, gula, luxuria.* Pride, envy, anger, greed, sloth, gluttony, and lust. These are her seven components, but in Gregory's arrangement *SIIAAGL* she cannot yet be discerned. It is

Bartholomaeis who gives her life by rearranging her DNA. He is her Crick and Watson, her Pygmalion. Pride, greed, lust, envy, gluttony, anger, and sloth: that, the man from Ostia perceives, is the sequence that cracks her genetic code. *Superbia, avaritia, luxuria, invidia, gula, ira, accidia:* The acronym brings Saligia to vivid, palpable life.

Of the seven sins, the greatest and worst, given the right to close the show, positioned in the final place, the place of maximal dishonor, is sloth. *Accidia,* a.k.a. *acedia* or *pigritia,* and its shadow selves, *tristitia,* sadness, and *anomie,* an erosion of the soul. Fellini is the supreme artist of enervated sloth. His protagonist is, almost always, some sort of a *vitellone,* a loafer, sometimes poor, sometimes affluent, always a wastrel, whose supreme incarnation is the Mastroianni of *La Dolce Vita* and *8½,* alienated, melancholy, drifting, passive, lost. There he goes, Marcello of the tired eyes, handsome and weak, a cigarette in his hand and a woman by his side, a woman he is in the process of losing. Down the Via Veneto he wanders, down along dirty side alleys and up again into the world of the sweet life, into the homes of the rich. He meanders through slow, decadent parties, seized by inaction, by an inability to make choices or to move his life forward, a paralysis of the spirit. An inebriated movie star, pneumatically desirable, cavorts beside him in the Fontana di Trevi, and he tries to rise from the depths of his apathy to seduce her, but he fails, and all he earns for his efforts is a punch in the face from her boyfriend, which he deserves. Around him, in salons and restaurants and in the nighttown of the predatory photographer paparazzo, wander the denizens of his affectless world, bored beauties with glazed expressions and perfect coiffure. These incarnations of sloth are not just damned. They are already in hell, dancing with Saligia in the flames.

## Is Sloth a Sin?

A boy is sent to boarding school, in a foreign land, far away from home. He lacks the robust, extroverted temperament that thrives in such cold places; he is shy, intelligent, small, unathletic, subtle, quiet. Within moments he understands that these, when added to foreignness, are the seven deadly sins of boarding school life, and, being guilty of all seven, he is cast into the outer darkness; which is to say, without saying a word or doing anything, he becomes unpopular.

After a few days he begins to feel unwell, unwell in an unfamiliar way. When he wakes up each morning in his boardinghouse dormitory, his arms and legs feel heavier than they ought to be. It is actually difficult for him to get out of bed and dress, but once he has struggled to his feet, the burdensome extra weight slowly leaves him and he can function normally. Each day, however, the morning heaviness is worse than it was the day before, and it is harder and harder for him to overcome it.

The day comes when he can't get out of bed. The other boys in the dormitory, including the older boy who acts as dorm prefect, can't understand what he means when he complains of the heaviness and so, being boys, they begin to jeer and taunt. *"O ze no ze blimey!"* they yell, in appalling parody of his foreign accent and his supposed unfamiliarity with local idiom. *"O, O! Ze heaviness of ze limbs!"*

As his housemates caper and prance and parody his slothfulness a new feeling takes hold of the boy, and to his surprise this feeling has a beneficial effect on the crushing weight that has pinned him to his bed. The new feeling gives him strength and he throws the heaviness and lethargy away from him, as a hero in an ancient tale might push away the boulder under which his foes had pinned him. He rises from his bed, a soul on fire.

The new feeling is anger. The other boys see the wrath blaze from his eyes, and the jeers die on their lips. They back away from him, warily. From that moment on he understands how to live in this new world. The anger fuels him, and he excels at school, in the classroom, at least; and it defends him too. He is still unpopular, but he is handled with care now, as if he were a bomb that might explode if dropped.

A Christian person might say that the unhappy boy has used one deadly sin to overcome another. So he is still in a sinful state. His sin deprives him of the capacity for charity and so it takes him far from God. Another kind of religious person (Buddhist or Jain) might counsel him to search for the enlightenment that brings the world into proper balance and so creates inner peace. Other religions would no doubt come up with other kinds of godly nostrums. However, to the secular mind, governed by reason, schooled by psychoanalysis, it feels wrong to describe as sinful what is plainly a psychological disorder. Sloth is not the devil's work. It's not a metaphor, it's an illness. *The devil makes work for idle hands?* Well, yes, but he makes work for busy hands too. Or he would if he existed. Which he doesn't.

## Tyrone Slothrop

The two great, opposing ideas in the work of the reclusive American novelist Thomas Pynchon are paranoia and entropy. His many paranoid characters, such as Herbert Stencil in *V.* and almost everyone in *The Crying of Lot 49,* are convinced that the true shape and meaning of the world is concealed from them and that immense forces—governments, corporations, aliens—are at work, both ruling the world and hiding their existence behind impenetrable screens. These characters exist in counterpoint with another group of types, such as the sailor Benny Profane and his friends in the "Whole Sick Crew" in *V.,* for whom life appears to be a sluggish, almost catatonic beer party that is eternally winding down without ever managing to end.

The second law of thermodynamics tells us that heat will always flow from the warmer object to the cooler, so that, gradually, the warmer object will become less warm and the cooler object warmer. When this principle is applied on a universal scale, it suggests that the heat energy of all hot objects—that is to say, stars—will slowly dissipate, spreading itself to less hot matter, until in the end all matter in the universe will be at the same temperature, and there will be no usable energy left. The whole cosmos will be the victim of a terminal enervation. This is what William Thomson, the First Baron Kelvin (a real person, not a Pynchonian invention) in 1851 described as "the heat death of the universe." The universal dissipation of energy would bring about a time in which all motion ceased. Benny Profane's endless beer party would finally end.

Paranoia, in Pynchon, is presented as a form of higher sanity: not delusion but perception. His paranoiacs are people who strive to see through what Hinduism calls *maya*, the veil of illusion that prevents human beings from perceiving reality as it truly is. Thus we see that paranoia in Pynchon represents a kind of bleakly optimistic view of the world, suggesting that human life does indeed have meaning; it's just that that meaning is concealed from us, so we don't know what it is.

The metaphor of entropy is paranoia's bleakly pessimistic flip side. The entropic themes in Pynchon propose to us that the world is meaningless, that all our actions decay, our energy leaches from us, and we are doomed to wind slowly down, toward the Ultimate Absurdity.

The character in whom both these themes are united is Tyrone Slothrop, the protagonist of Pynchon's most complex and ambitious novel, *Gravity's Rainbow*. Slothrop's story contains many paranoiac elements—for example, his mysterious conditioning "beyond the zero" by one Laszlo Jamf, when he is still an infant. Above all there is the strange matter of the Poisson distribution.

A Poisson distribution is a statistical measure that expresses the probability of a number of events occurring in a fixed period of time if these events occur with a known average rate and independently of the time since the last event. In *Gravity's Rainbow*, the Poisson distribution in question plots the locations of Tyrone Slothrop's encounters with women in various parts of London. For incalculably profound and therefore hidden reasons, this chart predicts the locations that will be hit by German V2 rockets a few days later.

Insofar as Tyrone Slothrop has a character, however, he is more like one of Pynchon's gallery of entropics than a paranoiac, though both strains are present. He is a decaying, sloth-ridden wanderer, more done-to than doing, and at length his mind disintegrates into at least four separate personas, and he is lost to the book. This is his own private heat death.

What does Slothrop look like? I imagine him as tall, skinny, wearing a red-and-white-check lumberjack shirt and drainpipe blue jeans, with an Einstein-like halo of hair and protruding, Bugs Bunny–ish front teeth.

I once met Thomas Pynchon, but according to the terms of that meeting I am unable to say whether the above description matches that of the author.

I can say that the author has not yet fallen into entropic torpor but continues to deliver immensely energetic works about the loss of energy. I can also say that the name "Tyrone Slothrop" is an anagram, whose letters rearrange to form the phrase "sloth or entropy."

## The Elsinore Vacillation

In each of Shakespeare's great tragedies the author asks us, very close to the beginning of the work, to answer a nearly unanswerable question. For example: Why does Othello believe Iago and turn against his beloved Desdemona? He isn't even shown the supposedly incriminating handkerchief but murders his wife just because Iago tells him that the evidence exists.

There are many different possible answers to these questions. Perhaps Othello's wrath (*ira*) is too easily triggered, or perhaps he doesn't truly love Desdemona but thinks of her as a trophy wife, an aspect of his honor (*superbia*, in the sense of *amour propre*, vainglory), and so, when her fidelity is impugned, it is he who is shamed and must avenge the dishonor of the accusation. Neither of these analyses is definitively right, nor absolutely wrong, but if an explanation is not settled upon, the play is impossible to produce.

Some years ago I introduced Christopher Hitchens to a silly literary game: the renaming of the plays of Shakespeare in the manner of the novels of Robert Ludlum (*The Rhinemann Exchange, The Bourne Identity, The Holcroft Covenant*, or, in general, *The Someone-or-Somewhere Something*). This gives us, for example, *The Rialto Sanction* (*The Merchant of Venice*), *The Kerchief Implication* (*Othello*), and *The Dunsinane Afforestation* (*Macbeth*). And *Hamlet* would become *The Elsinore Vacillation*.

In *Hamlet*, the question concerns the Prince of Denmark's interminable delays, which go on long enough to turn this into Shakespeare's longest play. Why, then, after the ghost of his father clearly tells his son how he died, does Hamlet delay his revenge so long? Why so many uncertainties and divagations? In this case the author himself provides the answer. Hamlet is a victim of sloth.

> I have of late—but wherefore I know not—lost all my mirth, forgone all custom of exercises; and indeed it goes so heavily with my disposition that this goodly frame, the earth, seems to me a sterile promontory, this most excellent canopy, the air, look you, this brave o'erhanging firmament, this majestical roof fretted with golden fire, why, it appears no other thing to me than a foul and pestilent congregation of vapors. What a piece of work is a man! How noble in reason! How infinite in faculty! In form and moving how express and admirable! In action how like an angel! In apprehension how like a god! The beauty of the world! The paragon of animals! And yet, to me, what is this quintessence of dust? Man delights not me: no, nor woman neither . . .

It is *accidia,* or *acedia,* that paralyzes Hamlet, the despairing lethargy, the clinical depression that annihilates the will and can be triggered by an existential shock. Such as discovering that your uncle killed your father and then your mother married him.

And if this were to be understood as a sin, then maybe it would follow that Hamlet, the sinner, deserved to die. But this is not what Shakespeare makes us feel. Never a very godly writer, he rejects religious condemnations of his characters and gives us a very worldly tragedy instead.

## For and Against Sloth

Literature has not, on the whole, dealt kindly with sloth.

In the *Divina Commedia,* Dante thinks that those who have accomplished nothing in life aren't even worthy of being admitted into hell.

———

THE ROMAN POET OF LOVE, Gaius Valerius Catullus, addresses himself thus:

> *Otium, Catulle, tibi molestum est:*
> *Otio exsultas nimiumque gestis.*
> *Otium et reges prius et beatas*
> *    Perdidit urbes.*

("You have nothing to do, Catullus, that's your problem. Through idleness you run around, too cheerfully. Idleness has destroyed kings in the past, and their rich cities too.")

MICHEL DE MONTAIGNE PRAISES the Emperor Vespasian for continuing to govern his empire even as he lay upon his deathbed. "An emperor, said he, must die standing. . . . No pilot performs his office by standing still."

IN CONRAD'S *THE NIGGER OF THE "NARCISSUS,"* the title character, James Wait, a black West Indian sailor who falls fatally ill with tuberculosis while his ship is on its way from Bombay to London, is asked why he embarked on such a journey, knowing, as he must have known, that he was ailing, and makes the famous reply, "I must live until I die, mustn't I?"

*I must live until I die. No pilot performs his office by standing still.* In Montaigne and Conrad, as in Dante and Catullus, slothfulness is invariably reprehensible. Action is a good, inaction an evil, and that is all.

I AM GRATEFUL TO the writer Nassim Nicholas Taleb for introducing me to a contrary view: "George Spencer Brown," he writes, "has famously said about Sir Isaac Newton that 'to arrive at the simplest truth, as Newton knew and practiced, requires years of contemplation. Not activity. Not reasoning. Not calculating. Not busy behavior of any kind. Not reading. Not talking. Not making an effort. Not thinking. Simply bearing in mind what it is that one needs to know.'" Taleb goes on to endorse the value of a mental activity that he names "to glander," or *glandouiller:* "to idle, but not to be in a state of idleness ... Glander is what children without soccer moms do when they are out of school." And he further claims: "I glander whenever I am bored and I come up with some awesome ideas! Some of them are even viable product ideas which could be used to make major money."

Take *that*, Montaigne.

(But let us note that Montaigne, the author of "Against Sloth," used to accuse himself of being slothful, saying that this was the reason why he only wrote little essays rather than full-length books.)


AND SO WE COME to De Quincey. Ah, the English Opium-Eater, utterly unashamed of his slothfulness, who describes his account of opium eating, and of the hallucinations it induces, as "useful and instructive." He modestly calls himself a "philosopher" and an "intellectual creature" and acknowledges no guilt. He gives us accounts of his opium dreams, and they are fine enough, with enough phantasmagoria therein to satisfy the most gothic palate. But then he says, of South Asia, my place of origin, that it is "cruel," that its cultures make him "shudder," that "man is a weed in those regions."

It is the man that speaks here, not the drug. "I am terrified by the modes of life, by the manners, and the barrier of utter abhorrence and want of sympathy placed between us by feelings deeper than I can analyze. I could sooner live with lunatics or brute animals," he tells us—he tells *me*. After that confession, the stuff about his hallucinations feels oddly uninteresting, despite all the monkeys, the parrots, the gods that appear in them, to say nothing of the famous leering crocodile that haunts him constantly, the symbol of everything Eastern that he found so repulsive.

The problem lies not in the opium but in the eater. As the old sailor Singleton says in *The Nigger of the "Narcissus,"* "Ships are all right. It is the men in them." There are worse sins than the deadly ones. Bigotry is high on that list.

## Oblomovshchina

The best, strongest, funniest, most profound case in favor of sloth, without which no examination of the subject would be complete, can be summed up in a single word: Oblomov.

Ilya Ilyich Oblomov, most slothful of all Russia's indolent nineteenth-century landed gentry, and the hero—yes, the hero!—of the novel by Ivan Aleksandrovich Goncharov that bears his name, is the exact opposite of Proust's insomniac Marcel. Marcel, we know, for a long time, used to go to bed early, and then took an unconscionable age, dozens and dozens of drowsy, long-sentenced pages, actually to fall asleep. Oblomov, by contrast, lies in bed all day, sometimes wide awake, sometimes somnolent; he takes one hundred and fifty pages not to fall asleep but rather to get up. When he finally does get out of bed, he is not wrapped in the soothing cadences of the Proustian sentence; he is not contemplative but angry, and the reason for his wrath is plain enough. His long-suffering manservant, Zakhar, is to blame, having finally lost his patience with his horizontal master, and Oblomov's rage at the fellow is expressed in brief, direct utterances:

> "Get up! Get up!" he [Zakhar] roared at the top of his voice, seizing Oblomov with both hands by the skirt of his dressing gown and by the sleeve.
>
> Oblomov suddenly jumped out of the bed and rushed at Zakhar.
>
> "You wait," he said. "I'll teach you how to disturb your master when he wants to sleep."

We can understand Oblomov's sloth, his *Oblomovshchina*, his Oblomovism or Oblomovitis, as the product of his spoiled, effete childhood, or as a metaphor for the decay and torpor of the class he represents, and that is true enough, but such narrow exegeses miss the point—which is that a little Oblomov lives within us all, longing to be allowed to languish for the rest of our lives, to be freed from responsibilities and care, to be—yes!—happy parasites. Oblomov knows that his distant estates are in trouble, that their finances need attending to, and that he ought, he really ought, to travel a thousand miles to deal with the problems. But no! Like Bartleby, his American descendant, he prefers not to. And again, even though he is in love, and the young lady, Olga, is delightful, and he really ought to get married, he puts the decision off until she makes it for him and breaks off their engagement. He is procrastinating Hamlet as well as Bartleby, and he is all of us. We look at the state of the world, and we wish we could hide beneath the covers. Oblomov hides for us. We look at the opposite sex, and it overwhelms us. Oblomov retreats from it on our behalf. We know our own problems, and we wish they were one thousand miles away. Oblomov sends them there and refuses to face them, as we cannot but as we wish we could. Oblomovism justifies and validates our sloth.

## Linda Evangelista

Linda is a supermodel. No, Linda is *the* supermodel. Here are the important facts about her.

She is known in the industry as the Chameleon but is not, in fact, a lizard.

She was once called the Founder of the Supermodels' Union, but, in fact, no such trade association exists.

She told a *Vogue* journalist, Jonathan Van Meter, in 1990 that "We [the supermodels] don't wake up for less than ten thousand dollars a day." This is often misquoted as "I don't get out of bed for less than ten thousand dollars a day."

In this sentence, in either version, three of the seven deadly sins, *superbia, avaritia,* and *accidia*—pride, greed, and sloth—are combined; while a normal reaction to the statement, and indeed to Miss

Evangelista herself, might combine elements of *luxuria, invidia,* and *ira,* which is to say lust, envy, and anger. Only *gula,* gluttony, is absent. Not bad!

## Ilya Ilyich Oblomov and Linda Evangelista

I picture them in separate, adjacent beds in a light-filled, flower-perfumed, rococo bedchamber. Oblomov is trying anxiously not to read the messages of financial urgency his manservant brings him. Linda, feigning sleep, is waiting for the telephone to ring with an offer of more than ten thousand dollars, so that she can get up.

The telephone rings. The offer is for Oblomov. He will receive ten thousand dollars if he agrees to get out of bed. The offer is large enough to pay off all his estate's debts and leave him happily recumbent, without a care in the world.

He declines the offer. "I prefer not to," he says.

They remain in bed. Oblomov is content, and drowsy. Linda is unhappy, tense, wide-eyed. But character is destiny, as Heraclitus said, and they are both in the grip of the terrible fate of having to be themselves. The day drifts on. "Here we lie," they say silently, almost echoing Martin Luther at the Diet of Worms. "We can do no other." They do not move.

The manservant Zakhar brings food on a dented silver tray. But they are both in the grip of *accidia,* the sin of sloth—Linda because she has not received a phone call, Oblomov in spite of the one he did receive—and they do not eat.

# HANS CHRISTIAN
# ANDERSEN

———

ACCORDING TO THE GREAT GERMAN CRITIC WALTER BENjamin, the story and the novel did not begin in the same place. The story, he proposes, is a collective act, a tale told by many mouths, written down by many hands, passed down, hand to hand, mouth to mouth, down the generations. In this definition of the story it is the nearest thing we have to that holy grail of literary criticism, the authorless text. Sometimes, as stories come to be collected and codified, as this or that version comes to be thought of as canonical, we give them authors. To the *Iliad* and the *Odyssey* we give the authorial name of Homer; to the *Mahabharata* and *Ramayana* we add the names of the bards Vyasa and Valmiki. But these writers may or may not have existed, and if they did, they were telling stories whose origins preceded their tellings. The story is a tale told by everyone, and nobody owns it.

By contrast, Walter Benjamin suggested, "What differentiates the novel from all other forms of prose literature—the fairy tale, the legend, even the novella—is that it neither comes from oral tradition nor goes into it. This distinguishes it from storytelling in particular. The storyteller takes what he tells from experience—his own or that reported by others.... The novelist has isolated himself. The birthplace of the novel is the solitary individual." To which it may also be added that the story grows out of a sense of community, of locality; the novel out of a sense of nationhood. German stories, such as those collected by the Grimm Brothers, come from the Black Forest; German literature comes from Germany.

In spite of these very different origins, a strong interest in storytelling was for a long time incorporated in the novel—at, or near, the center of most of the best fiction. It's impossible to read the work of Dickens, or Austen, or Thackeray, without understanding that for the novelists of the eighteenth and nineteenth centuries, the story was the engine of the novel. Many of these novels were extremely long and needed a powerful storyline to drive them. I myself learned from these writers never to forget what a good strong story brings to a book. If you're building a big car, I've always thought, put a big engine in it.

To make a broad generalization: In the twentieth century, somewhere around the period of High Modernism, the novel separated itself from the storytelling tradition. I yield to no one in my admiration for *Ulysses* and *À La Recherche du temps perdu*, but nobody could honestly say that either of them is plot-driven. Story takes second place, in Joyce and Proust, to form, character, language, psychology, and social portraiture.

The separation of what has come to be called literary fiction from the storytelling tradition has always seemed to be both unnecessary and harmful. Popular fiction, pulp fiction, never forgets to tell a story. These books depend crucially on page-turning narrative, full of hooks, mysteries, and drama. It has always seemed to me that there is no reason for serious literature to dispose of these things. And I have been interested to see, in the literature of the last half century or so, a renewed and growing interest in the ancient art, even in its oldest forms, of the myth, the legend, the fable, and the fairy tale.

For this kind of contemporary literature, Hans Christian Andersen's work stands as an important signpost. The folktale, fairy tale, or fable, in its original European incarnation, very often pointed toward a moral. "Don't be greedy" was the moral of the Grimm tale of the fisherman and his wife and the talking flounder. In India, interestingly, many ancient folktales are less concerned with moralizing. In the grand narratives of the *Ramayana* and *Mahabharata*, heroes are flawed, and their adversaries not necessarily villainous but possessed of heroic virtues as well. Homer knew this too. Hector, the Trojan who falls in single combat to the Greek Achilles, is the lesser warrior but in many ways the better man.

Modern writers who have drawn on the fable and folktale for inspiration have on the whole eschewed the simple morality of, for example, Aesop. Italo Calvino is a fabulist and a collector of folktales, but he is no moralist. Separate the fable from its moral and you get what has come to be known, a little irritatingly, as magic realism, a thing of which I have been guilty myself.

What interests me about Hans Christian Andersen's stories, about where they stand in this literary journey from the past to the present, is that they look in both directions, backward to the religious, strict, good-and-evil morality of the past—the collective wisdom of the tribe, if you like—and forward to the flawed ambiguities of the modern, individualist sensibility: what Benjamin called the sensibility of the novelist. Some stories are openly—we may say, conservatively—religious, contrasting godly virtue with devilry, as, for example, in "The Red Shoes." In "The Little Mermaid," the heroine's romantic love for the prince does not win the day. But her spirit of self-sacrifice, or caring more for others than for herself, attracts divine benediction and gives the mermaid a chance of immortality.

In other stories, however, Andersen's morality becomes stranger. The princess in "The Princess and the Pea," able to discern and be discomforted by the presence of a single pea under many, many mattresses, is praised for her "sensitivity," which proves her to be a true princess. Reading this story today, we may less charitably conclude that the princess is a spoiled brat and probably a pain in the neck.

In "The Emperor's New Clothes," the story is more interested in giving the emperor and his courtiers their comeuppance than in punishing the swindlers who "made" the nonexistent garment while making off with substantial quantities of money. If they are indeed punished for their crime, the story omits to mention it.

Even darker, and therefore more modern, is the moral universe of "The Tinder Box." Near the beginning of the story the protagonist kills the witch and thinks nothing of it; at the end of the story the princess marries the hero even though the great dogs unleashed by the tinder box have just killed her parents. This is decidedly odd and therefore of great interest to our contemporary, disenchanted sensibility. The story's amorality makes it more attractive to us than a clear moral message would.

Two of Andersen's greatest stories may serve to illustrate his contrasting modes. "The Snow Queen," a genuinely frightening story, allows the reader the release of a happy ending. Gerda's love thaws Kay's frozen heart and the icy shard lodged there, and the tears she releases in him wash the other shard out of his eye. For all the terror in the story, it remains essentially a part of the conventional tradition of the fairy tale.

However, in what I think of as Andersen's greatest story, "The Shadow," the ending is more Kafka than happy-ever-after. The shadow detached from its owner not only supplants the human being in the affections of the princess, but the princess and the shadow arrange to have the real man executed on their wedding day. No trace here of Walter Benjamin's idea of the traditional storyteller. This is the solitary, individual, dark vision of the modern writer.

Hans Christian Andersen stands in an imaginative, fabulist tradition that stretches from the most ancient stories all the way to Kafka. That is the best measure of his worth.

# KING OF THE WORLD
# BY DAVID REMNICK

———

I NEVER WENT TO ANY OF ALI'S FIGHTS, BUT I SAW HIM twice. The first time was in the year 2000, almost twenty years after he lost that last bout to Trevor Berbick (who?), ten sad rounds that should never have happened against an opponent he'd once have beaten, as the Cowardly Lion might say, with his eyes closed, with one hand tied behind his back. But those days of leonine majesty were long gone, and two decades after Berbick (who?) ended Ali's fighting days, I was visiting a friend in Los Angeles and we went into a dry cleaner's in West Hollywood to pick up some garments and Ali was there, with only a small entourage, waiting like anybody else for his suits to come round on the motorized rail.

He wasn't like anybody else, obviously, and everyone in the dry cleaner's was starry-eyed and tongue-tied, myself included, but my friend was bold enough to say hi, how are you doing, and he grinned a tentative smile and put out a big trembling hand to be shaken. Fine, just fine, he said, which quite obviously wasn't true. How could it be, I thought, as many of us have thought, that the best, the fastest, the prettiest there ever was could have been dumb enough to fight on too long, to keep going until the unfixable damage was done. But they all go on too long. Even the smartest. "Your hands can't touch / what your eyes can't see," he sang, back in the day, but even the floatingest butterfly, the stingingest bee, finally slows down and gets swatted, hard, and the unfixable damage gets done.

"What are you doing in L.A.?" I asked him, though I had guessed the answer. The film director Michael Mann was shooting the biopic *Ali* in the city that year, with Will Smith in the lead. That probably had something to do with it. Ali's grin grew mischievous. "I'm gonna teach Mr. Will Smith how to do the Ali Shuffle," he said. "I'm gonna teach that boy how to dance." Then he got his suits and walked out and the starlight in everyone's eyes dimmed and was gone and I never met him again.

I saw him, though. I was at Yankee Stadium, one afternoon a couple of years later, sitting maybe two dozen rows back from third base, waiting for the ball game to begin, when a low roar started up on the far side of the ground and there he was, sitting in a golf buggy, being driven around the perimeter of the stadium, waving and nodding, and there was his name on the loudspeakers.

## MOOOOHAMMAD ALIIIIIIIII!!!!!!!!!

"Make some NOISE!" the jumbotron instructed us, and we did, but mixed in with the applause and cheers and chants of "ALI! ALI!" there were really quite a lot of boos. Not as many boos as cheers, but plenty. Enough to be shocking. After all this time, after the hero's return from exile to regain his crown, the Rumble in the Jungle and the Thrilla in Manila, "Ali Bomaye" and "This'll shock and amazeya / I'm gonna defeat Joe Frazeya," even after the long weakened years of Parkinson's disease, there were still people for whom the refusal to fight in Vietnam ("I ain't got no quarrel with them Vietcong"), the connection to Elijah Muhammad and Malcolm X, and the whole grand defiance that Ali had made of his life—these things, which made him a hero to many Americans and many more people beyond America, were still, in the minds of those booing spectators, unforgivable.

Until Ali came along, I had never been interested in boxing. I was familiar with a few names—Louis, Dempsey, Floyd Patterson, Ingemar Johansson—but I didn't really care about the fight game. In Bombay we preferred to watch wrestling, and the great wrestler Dara Singh had been my kind of hero. Just once, at school in Bombay, I had been forced into a boxing ring, terrified. I whispered to my opponent, "If you go easy on me I won't try to hit you," and he nodded okay. Then by pure accident in the first minute of the fight I bopped him on the nose and he came after me with murderous intent. I never made the mistake of climbing into any ring again.

However, for young fellows of my time this good-looking young boxer with the big loud mouth—the Louisville Lip, Cass the Gas—was a joy and an enchantment. I was sixteen at the time of the JFK assassination, still sixteen when, three months later, twenty-two-year-old Cassius Clay improbably defeated Sonny Liston to win the world heavyweight title, not only defeated him but humiliated him. And when he took his stand on the draft, refusing to go to 'Nam, sacrificing his title, risking jail, putting it all on the line for a principle, he became, well, awesome. In those days the word still meant what it was supposed to mean, "inspiring great admiration/awe," and Ali did that. "One, two, three, what are we fightin' for," we sang with Country Joe and the Fish, and Ali the fighter achieved, by refusing to fight, a heroism he could never have attained in the ring, even if he was, as he said he was, the Greatest.

"The sixties" were full of foolishness. The drugs were stupid and the Hare Krishna wisdom-of-the-East nonsense was stupid and the Vietnam War was the most stupid thing of all. But in among all the stupidity was courage that changed the world, feminist courage, the courage of the civil rights movement, and the courage of Muhammad Ali, and so the lesson we learned from "the sixties," if we weren't too stoned to learn it, was that it was possible, by one's own personal, direct actions, to bend the universe to your will and remake society, improve it, give it better music, higher ideals, and freedom. And Ali was a big part of all that.

As David Remnick tells us in *King of the World*, Ali was the first heavyweight champ to avoid the clutches of the mob, which made it possible for others to follow where he led, so that boxing was pried loose from gangsters' clutches. That revolution was largely invisible to the general public at the time, but his brashness, his refusal to be a good black man (a.k.a. Floyd Patterson, in Ali's opinion anyhow), the screaming half-crazy mouth on him, we heard that all right, and it was backed up by the power of his fists. And the Vietnam refusal, the fight he took all the way to the Supreme Court and won, persuading the Supremes to vote in his favor in spite of considerable pressure from the White House to do otherwise: that made him a part of the counterculture, even though he would probably not have approved of most of the things the counterculture got up to in its spare time. (Remnick is good at showing us Ali's puritanical streak.)

I remember reading Ali's autobiography, *The Greatest: My Own Story,* when it came out. It's not a good book, poorly ghostwritten, and *King of the World,* among its many virtues, performs the service of telling Ali's story better and more truthfully than he did.

In *The Greatest,* Ali tells how he was supposedly refused service in a Louisville restaurant when he came home from the Olympics with his gold medal around his neck and how he was so alienated by that act of local racism that he threw his medal into the river. Self-mythologizing was a part of Ali's stock-in-trade, and Remnick makes it clear that the story isn't true and that its presence in the book, in spite of the editorial presence at Random House of Toni Morrison, had a lot to do with the desires of Elijah Muhammad and the Nation of Islam that Ali portray himself in that way: as a black refusenik of the white man's culture. One of the great strengths of *King of the World* is its portrayal of Ali's relationship with the Nation of Islam, the half-cockeyed-comic, half-sinister, proto-Scientological, Islam-with-added-spaceships cooked up by Elijah Muhammad that se-duced Ali by its segregationist clarity (white man bad, black man good), as a result of which Ali kept his distance from the civil rights movement and its leaders, seeing them as people who were playing the white man's game. He also preached a sexual separatism that, perhaps inevitably, he did not practice. Remnick is excellent on the engulfing, smothering quality of the Nation people and Ali's depen-dence on them. His break with Malcolm X when Malcolm and Eli-jah fell out is a key moment in this story. Remnick is clear too that Ali's brand of "Islam" led him to treat the women in his life pretty restrictively, even unkindly. This is emphatically not a hagiography and we are left in no doubt of Ali's blemishes, but they humanize him, just as Sonny Liston is humanized by his many, and greater, flaws.

In these pages Liston comes to life as a rounded character more fully than in anything I've read. We remember Liston as the terrifying hulk, the killer, the wordless monster of whom the young Clay should have been terrified and mysteriously was not. We remember the sportswriters of the time unanimously worrying that Clay might actually be grievously, perhaps even mortally, harmed in the fight. But Liston the human being has been a great dark absence, until now. In Remnick's pages we see the damaged, inarticulate, ill-educated figure of the man, locked into his brutishness, managed by gangsters, his only language the language of his fists. It is a part of this book's very considerable achievement that Liston becomes almost as sympathetic a figure as Clay: his tragic silence set against Ali's heroic volubility, his doom and descent toward penury the counterbalance to Clay/Ali's date with destiny.

In the Cassius Clay we first got to know, there seemed to be an edge of madness, something genuinely unbalanced behind all that openmouthed shrieking, but again David Remnick takes us behind the façade and shows us how Ali used the ranting to psych himself up, to banish fear and the thought of defeat until victory was the only possibility, and also how calculated it was. He knew he was box office and his mouth brought in the dollars. But away from the cameras he was all professionalism. He worked and worked and worked. This too is an Ali we haven't seen so clearly before, the nonstop training, the commitment, the hard graft: the man who reached the top because he knew what it took and put in the hours that were needed to turn talent into glory.

It has been an age of great sportswriters and Remnick mentions several, but with this book he places himself alongside them— Plimpton, Talese, Mailer, and the rest. He takes pleasure in writing about the writing, showing the writers' part in the creation of the myths of boxing, the heroes and villains, the rises and falls. And in his account of the two Ali–Liston fights, his own prose becomes supreme. He takes us into the meat of the contests as if he were right there in the ring, hearing the blows land, being drenched in sweat and blood, bringing it to us from the inside. It's some of the best writing about combat I've ever read, and it makes you feel Ali's arrival at the pinnacle, moment by moment—the dancing, Liston's wild lunges swooshing through empty air, Ali's blows thudding home, the shock of Liston refusing to rise from his stool (first fight) or from the canvas (second fight), the truth about the illegal stuff on Liston's gloves that got into Ali's eyes and half-blinded him (first fight) and about the "phantom punch" that ended it once and for all (second fight). And the young champion screaming at the great sportswriters who had written him off. "Eat your words! Eat your words!" In short: It's a knockout.

# VERY WELL THEN
# I CONTRADICT MYSELF

---

I**N TOM STOPPARD'S PLAY** *JUMPERS,* **THE LEADING CHARACTER,** George Moore, a philosopher, says this: "Meeting a friend in a corridor, Wittgenstein said: 'Tell me, why do people always say it was *natural* for men to assume that the sun went round the earth rather than that the earth was rotating?' His friend said, 'Well, obviously, because it just *looks* as if the sun is going round the earth.' To which the philosopher replied, 'Well, what would it have looked like if it had looked as if the earth was rotating?'" It's a beautiful slow burn of a joke, the laughter building as the audience realizes that it would look exactly the same, because that, after all, is what is actually happening. This is the laughter of paradox, and without it literature, and life, would be grievously diminished; indeed, some critics have said that the connection between paradox and poetry is so intimate that they are the same thing.

Paradox begins in the Bible, where the idea of the Virgin Birth embodies the paradoxical nature of faith, and continues to the present day, where the most cursory search of the literature of pop culture reveals analyses of the "Paradox of the Beatles" (which is that they were young rebels who quickly became establishment figures with MBEs), the "Paradox of Oprah Winfrey" (which is that while she intimately advises us on our lives, as if she were a close family member, she remains aloof, mysterious, and unknown), and the "Paradox of Eminem" (which is that he both is and is not the real Slim Shady).

Don Quixote is a paradox on a broken-down horse, the knight errant whose wanderings undo the very idea of the knight errant, the chivalrous fool whose folly reveals the greater folly of the chivalric ideal. Borges's detective Erik Lönnrot in his story "Death and the Compass" solves the riddle of a mysterious series of murders and works out the time and location of the next murder, only to discover, too late to save himself, that he is the intended victim and that the other crimes have been committed to bring him to the killing place. Oscar Wilde, who said he could resist anything except temptation, incarnates the paradoxes of hedonism. And in Joseph Heller's novel *Good as Gold,* the character of the presidential aide Ralph Newsome, the embodiment of the dishonesties of politics, speaks entirely in oxymoronic sentences whose ends contradict their beginnings: "This President will back you all the way until he has to. We want to move ahead with this as speedily as possible, although we'll have to go slowly. This President doesn't want yes-men. What we want are independent men of integrity who will agree with all our decisions after we make them."

To my mind the most beautiful of paradoxes is the famous formulation found near the end of Whitman's "Song of Myself":

> Do I contradict myself?
> Very well then I contradict myself.
> (I am large, I contain multitudes.)

Human nature is contradictory, and the human self is a capacious and multiform thing. We can be, we are, many selves at once: We can be gentle with our children but harsh with our employees; we can love God but dislike human beings; we can fear for the environment and yet leave electric lights on when we leave the house; we can be peaceful souls who are driven, by our passion for a football team, to aggressive, sometimes even hooligan extremes. And no matter how strongly we may wish to defend the sovereignty of the individual self—an idea born in the Florentine Renaissance that may be Italy's greatest gift to world civilization—that self is, in reality, *simultaneously sovereign and invaded by other selves.* It is at once autonomous and not autonomous. None of us comes into the world empty-handed. We carry with us the baggage of our inheritance, both biological and cultural, and that inheritance both limits and enables us, both cripples and liberates. We may think of ourselves as free to choose and morally responsible for our choices, and it is right that we should so understand ourselves, but the way in which we frame those choices, and indeed the particular choices we feel we have to make, are not only ours to determine.

So we are paradoxical beings, both individual and social, both of our time and part of history's flow. We are mortal but have, like Shakespeare's Cleopatra, immortal longings in us; and contradiction is our lifeblood. There are great social benefits in such broad definitions of the self, for the more selves we find within ourselves, the easier it is to find common ground with other multiple, multitude-containing selves. We may have different religious beliefs but support the same team. Yet we live in an age in which we are urged to define ourselves more and more narrowly, to crush our own multidimensionality into the straitjacket of a one-dimensional national, ethnic, tribal, or religious identity. This, I have come to think, may be the evil from which flow all the other evils of our time. For when we succumb to this narrowing, when we allow ourselves to be simplified and become merely Serbs, Croats, Muslims, Hindus, then it becomes easy for us to see each other as adversaries, as one another's Others, and the very points of the compass begin to quarrel, East and West collide, and North and South as well.

Literature has never lost sight of what our quarrelsome world is trying to force us to forget. Literature rejoices in contradiction, and in our novels and poems we sing our human complexity, our ability to be, simultaneously, both *yes* and *no*, both *this* and *that*, without feeling the slightest discomfort. The Arabic equivalent of the formula "once upon a time" is *kan ma kan*, which translates "It was so, it was not so." This great paradox lies at the heart of all fiction. Fiction is precisely that place where things are both so and not so, where worlds exist in which we can profoundly believe while also knowing that they do not, have not, and will never exist. And in our age of oversimplification, this beautiful complication has never been more important.

# PART THREE

# TRUTH

---

"**W**HAT, ART THOU MAD? ART THOU MAD?" FALSTAFF DEMANDS of Prince Hal in Shakespeare's *Henry IV, Part I*. "Is not the truth the truth?" The joke is that he has been lying his head off, and the prince is in the process of exposing him as a liar.

In a time like the present, when reality itself seems everywhere under attack, Falstaff's duplicitous notion of the truth seems to be shared by many powerful leaders. In the three countries I've spent my life caring about—India, the UK, and the United States—self-serving falsehoods are regularly presented as facts, while more-reliable information is denigrated as "fake news." However, the defenders of the real, attempting to dam the torrent of disinformation flooding over us all, often make the mistake of yearning for a golden age when truth was uncontested and universally accepted and of arguing that what we need is to return to that blissful consensus.

The truth is that truth has always been a contested idea. As a student of history at Cambridge, I learned at an early age that some things were "basic facts," that is, unarguable events—the Battle of Hastings took place in 1066, and the American Declaration of Independence was made on July 4, 1776—but the creation of a historical fact was the result of a particular meaning being ascribed to an event. Julius Caesar's crossing of the Rubicon is a historical fact. But many other people have crossed that river, and their actions are not of interest to history. Those crossings are not, in this sense, facts. Also: The passage of time often changes the meaning of a fact. During the

British Empire, the military revolt of 1857 was known as the "Indian Mutiny," and as a mutiny is a rebellion against the authorities, that name, and therefore the meaning of that fact, placed the "mutinying" Indians in the wrong. Indian historians today refer to this event as the "Indian Uprising," which makes it an entirely different sort of fact, which means a different thing.

History is not written in stone. The past is constantly revised according to the attitudes of the present.

There is, however, some truth in the idea that in the West in the nineteenth century there was a fairly widespread consensus about the nature of reality. The great novelists of that time—Flaubert, George Eliot, and so on—could assume that they and their readers, broadly speaking, agreed on the nature of the real, and the grand age of the realist novel was built on that foundation. But that consensus was built on a number of exclusions. It was almost wholly middle class and almost entirely white. The points of view of, for example, colonized peoples, or racial minorities—points of view from which the world looked very different than the bourgeois reality portrayed in, say, *The Age of Innocence*, or *Middlemarch*, or *Madame Bovary*—were largely erased from the narrative. The importance of great public matters was also often marginalized. In the entire oeuvre of Jane Austen, the Napoleonic Wars are barely mentioned; in the immense oeuvre of Charles Dickens, the existence of the British Empire is only glancingly recognized.

In the twentieth century, under the pressure of enormous social changes, the nineteenth-century consensus was revealed as fragile; its view of reality began to look, one might say, fake. Some of the greatest literary artists sought to chronicle the changing reality by using the methods of the realist novel, as Thomas Mann did in *Buddenbrooks* or Junichiro Tanizaki in *The Makioka Sisters;* but gradually the realist novel seemed more and more problematic and writers from Franz Kafka to Ralph Ellison and Gabriel García Márquez, from Octavia Butler's science fiction to Margaret Atwood's nightmare dystopias, created stranger, more surreal texts, telling the truth by means of obvious untruth, creating a new kind of reality, as if by magic.

I have argued for much of my life as a writer that the breakdown in the old agreements about reality is now the most significant reality and that the world can perhaps best be explained in terms of conflicting and often incompatible narratives. In Kashmir and in the Middle East, and in the battle between progressive America and Trumpistan, we see examples of such incompatibilities. I have also argued that the consequences of this new, argumentative, even polemical attitude to the real has such profound implications for literature that we can't, or ought not to, pretend it isn't there. I believe that the influence on public discourse of more, and more varied, voices has been a good thing, enriching our literatures and making more complex our understanding of the world.

American literature, for example, now contains voices from everywhere—Junot Díaz, Yiyun Li, Nam Le, Jhumpa Lahiri, Edwidge Danticat, to name but a few. And a rising generation of African American writers in all forms—Tracy K. Smith, Ta-Nehisi Coates, Jesmyn Ward—offers its own multitudinous reality and makes it immensely influential.

And yet I now face, as we all do, a genuine conundrum. How can we argue, on the one hand, that modern reality has become necessarily multidimensional, fractured and fragmented, and, on the other hand, that it is a very particular thing, an unarguable series of things that are so, which need to be defended against the attacks of, to be frank, the things that are not so, promulgated by, let's say, the Modi administration in India, the Brexit crew in the UK, and the 45th president of the United States? How to combat the worst aspects of the Internet, that parallel universe in which important information and total garbage coexist, side by side, with, apparently, the same levels of authority, making it harder than ever for people to tell them apart? How to resist the erosion in public acceptance of even "basic facts," scientific facts, evidence-supported facts, about the coronavirus, or climate change, or inoculations for children? How to combat the political demagoguery that seeks to do what authoritarians have always wanted—to undermine the public's belief in evidence and to say to their electorates, in effect, "Believe nothing except me, for I am the truth"? What do we do about that? And what, specifically, might be the role of art, and the role of writers and the literary arts in particular?

I don't pretend to have a full answer. I do think that we need to recognize that any society's idea of truth is always the product of an argument, and we need to get better at winning that argument. Democracy is not polite. It's often a shouting match in a public square. We need to be involved in the argument if we are to have any chance of winning it (I can't forget that just under half of all registered voters in the United States failed to show up at the polls in November 2016, including many of the young people who afterward marched passionately to protest the result). And as far as writers are concerned, we need to rebuild our readers' belief in the argument from evidence and to do what fiction has always been good at doing: to construct, between the writer and the reader, an understanding about what is real. I don't mean to reconstruct the narrow, exclusive consensus of the nineteenth century. I like the broader, more disputatious view of society to be found in modern literature. But when we read a book we like, or even love, we find ourselves in agreement with its portrait of human life. Yes, we say, this is how we are, this is what we do to one another, this is true. That, perhaps, is where literature can help most. We can make people agree, in this time of radical disagreement, on the truths of the great constant, which is human nature. Let's start from there.

In Germany after World War II, the authors of what was called *Trümmerliteratur*, "rubble literature," felt the need to rebuild their language, poisoned by Nazism, as well as their country, which lay in ruins. They understood that reality, truth, needed to be reconstructed from the ground up, with new language, just as the bombed cities needed to be rebuilt. I think we can learn from their example. We stand once again, though for different reasons, in the midst of the rubble of the truth. And it is for us, writers, thinkers, journalists, philosophers, to undertake the task of rebuilding our readers' belief in reality, their faith in the truth. And to do it with new language, from the ground up.

# COURAGE

―――

WE FIND IT EASIER, IN THESE CONFUSED TIMES, TO ADMIRE physical bravery than moral courage, the courage of the life of the mind, or of public figures. A firefighter runs toward a burning building while others flee it: We readily salute his bravery, as we do that of servicemen returning from the battlefront, or men and women struggling to overcome debilitating illnesses or injuries.

It's harder for us to see politicians, with the exception of Nelson Mandela, as courageous these days. Perhaps we have seen too much, grown too cynical about the inevitable compromises of power. There are no Gandhis, no Lincolns anymore. One man's hero (Hugo Chávez, Fidel Castro) is another's villain. We can no longer easily agree on what it means to be good, or principled, or brave. When political leaders do take courageous steps—as France's then-president Nicolas Sarkozy did in Libya by intervening militarily to support the anti-Gadhafi uprising—there are as many who doubt as approve. Political courage, nowadays, is almost always ambiguous.

Even more strangely, we have become suspicious of those who take a stand against the abuses of power or dogma.

It was not always so. The writers and intellectuals who opposed Communism—Aleksandr Solzhenitsyn, Andrei Sakharov, Anna Akhmatova, Nadezhda Mandelstam, and the rest—were widely esteemed for their stand. *Samizdat* literature, disseminated by shaky underground networks, was honored as speaking the truth and showing up the official lies of the Soviet state. (True, Solzhenitsyn in

American exile turned out to be a cranky fellow, but that did not diminish our admiration for *The Gulag Archipelago*.) The poet Osip Mandelstam was much admired for his "Stalin Epigram" of 1933, in which he described the fearsome leader in fearless terms, turning his mustache into "the huge laughing cockroaches on his top lip," and adding, "He rolls the executions on his tongue like berries." It was a brave poem, which led to Mandelstam's arrest and eventual death in a Soviet labor camp.

As recently as 1989, the image of a man carrying two shopping bags and defying the tanks of Tiananmen Square became, almost at once, a global symbol of courage.

Then, it seems, things changed. The "Tank Man" has been largely forgotten in China, while the pro-democracy protesters, including those who died in the June 4 massacre, have been successfully redescribed by the Chinese authorities as counterrevolutionaries. The power of such redescription can obscure the heroism even of people like the Tiananmen martyrs; and the battle of descriptions continues, obscuring or at least confusing our understanding of how "courageous" people should be judged. This is how the Chinese authorities are treating their best-known critics, people such as Ai Weiwei and Liu Xiaobo.

The use of "subversion" charges against Liu Xiaobo and of alleged tax crimes against Ai Weiwei are deliberate attempts to blind people to their courage and to paint them, instead, as criminals.

The problem is by no means exclusively Chinese. Such is the influence of the Russian Orthodox Church that the jailed members of the Pussy Riot collective are widely perceived, inside Russia, as immoral troublemakers because they staged their famous protest on Church property. The point they were trying to make—that the leadership of the Orthodox Church is too close to Putin for comfort—has been lost on their many detractors, and their act is not seen as brave but improper.

In 2006 the Italian writer Roberto Saviano published *Gomorrah*, a detailed exposé of the workings of the Camorra, the "Mafia" of Naples. Since then he has lived under threat of death but has continued his work in spite of the appalling privations and risks of his day-to-day circumstances. He has been widely praised for this, but, as he himself points out, there is a continuing effort by some parts of the Italian power structure to discredit him. Silvio Berlusconi, when he was still prime minister, denounced him, and many other ministers and commentators have accused him of being unpatriotic. Not even Saviano is immune from the new anti-heroism. A right-wing politician, former interior minister Matteo Salvini, has attacked him repeatedly.

In 2011 in Pakistan, the former governor of Punjab, Salman Taseer, who had defended a Christian woman, Asia Bibi, wrongly sentenced to death under the country's draconian blasphemy law, was murdered by one of his own security guards, who shot him twenty-seven times. After the murder, the guard, Mumtaz Qadri, was widely praised and showered with rose petals when he appeared in court. The dead Taseer was equally widely criticized, and public opinion turned against him. His courage was obliterated by religious passions. The horrific blasphemy law proved more important to many Pakistanis than a principled stand for justice. It was the murderer who was called a hero.

In February 2012, a Saudi poet and journalist, Hamza Kashgari, published three tweets about the Prophet Muhammad:

"On your birthday, I will say that I have loved the rebel in you, that you've always been a source of inspiration to me, and that I do not like the halos of divinity around you. I shall not pray for you."

"On your birthday, I find you wherever I turn. I will say that I have loved aspects of you, hated others, and could not understand many more."

"On your birthday, I shall not bow to you. I shall not kiss your hand. Rather, I shall shake it as equals do, and smile at you as you smile at me. I shall speak to you as a friend, no more."

He claimed afterward that he was "demanding his right" to freedom of expression and thought. (He also criticized the condition of women in Saudi Arabia and supported the Arab Spring.) He found little public support and was condemned as an apostate, and there were many calls for his execution. He was finally released from jail on October 29, 2013.

The writers and intellectuals of the French Enlightenment also challenged the religious orthodoxy of their time and so created the modern concept of free thought. We think of Voltaire, Diderot, Rousseau, and the rest as intellectual heroes. Sadly, very few people in the Muslim world would say the same of Hamza Kashgari.

This new idea—that writers, scholars, and artists who stand against orthodoxy or bigotry are to blame for upsetting people—is spreading fast, even to countries like India that once prided themselves on their freedoms. In recent years, the grand old man of Indian painting, M. F. Husain, was hounded into exile, where he died, because he painted the Hindu goddess Sarasvati in the nude (even though the most cursory examination of ancient Hindu sculptures of Sarasvati shows that while Sarasvati is often adorned with jewels and ornaments, she is equally often undressed). Rohinton Mistry's celebrated novel *Such a Long Journey* was pulled off the syllabus of Bombay University because local extremists objected to its content. At the Jaipur Literary Festival, the scholar Ashis Nandy was attacked for expressing unorthodox views on lower-caste corruption. Kamal Haasan's film *Vishwaroopam* was censored because of Muslim objections. And in all these cases the official view—with which many commentators and a substantial slice of public opinion agreed—was, essentially, that the artists and scholars had brought the trouble on themselves.

America isn't immune from this trend. The young activists of the Occupy movement have been much maligned (though, after their highly effective relief work in the wake of Hurricane Sandy, those criticisms have become a little muted). Out-of-step intellectuals like Noam Chomsky and the late Edward Said have often been dismissed as crazy extremists, "anti-American," and in Said's case even, absurdly, as apologists for Palestinian "terrorism." (One may disagree with Chomsky's critiques of America, but it ought still to be possible to recognize the courage it takes to stand up and bellow them into the face of American power. One may not be pro-Palestinian, but one should be able to see that Said stood up against Arafat as eloquently as he criticized the United States.)

It's a beleaguered time for those of us who believe in the right of artists, intellectuals, and ordinary, affronted citizens to push boundaries and take risks and so, at times, to change the way we see the world. There's nothing to be done but to go on restating the importance of this kind of courage and to try to make sure that these oppressed individuals—Ai Weiwei, Pussy Riot, Roberto Saviano, Hamza Kashgari, and many more—are seen for what they are: men and women standing on the front line of liberty. How to do this? Sign the petitions against their treatment; join the protests. Speak up. Every little bit counts. In the words of the ancient Chinese philosopher Lao Tzu, "A journey of a thousand miles begins with a single step."

POSTSCRIPT. SINCE THIS ESSAY WAS WRITTEN, Liu Xiaobo has died of liver cancer. He was released from jail on medical parole in 2017, just seventeen days before his death.

# TEXTS FOR PEN

### 1. The Pen and the Sword: The International PEN Congress of 1986

IN JANUARY 1986 I CAME TO NEW YORK FOR A GATHERING OF writers that has become a literary legend. The 48th Congress of International PEN, the global writers' organization dedicated to spreading the word and defending its servants, was quite a show. Norman Mailer was president of PEN America back then and used all his powers of persuasion and charm to raise the funds that brought more than fifty of the world's leading writers to Manhattan to debate, with almost one hundred of America's finest, the exalted theme of "The Writer's Imagination and the Imagination of the State" and to be wined and dined at Gracie Mansion and the Metropolitan Museum's Temple of Dendur.

As one of the younger participants I was more than a little awestruck. Brodsky, Grass, Oz, Soyinka, Vargas Llosa, Bellow, Carver, Doctorow, Morrison, Said, Ozick, Paley, Styron, Updike, Vonnegut, and Mailer himself were some of the big names reading their work and arguing away at the Essex House and St. Moritz hotels on Central Park South. One afternoon I was asked by the photographer Tom Victor to sit in one of the park's horse-drawn carriages for a picture, and when I climbed in, there were Susan Sontag and Czesław Miłosz to keep me company. I am not usually tongue-tied, but I don't recall saying much during our ride.

The atmosphere was electric from the start. Much to the chagrin of many PEN members, Mailer had invited Secretary of State George Shultz to speak at the opening ceremony, at the New York Public Library. This prompted howls of protest by the South African writers Nadine Gordimer, J. M. Coetzee, and Sipho Sepamla, who accused Shultz of supporting apartheid. Other writers, including E. L. Doctorow, Grace Paley, Elizabeth Hardwick, John Irving, and many more, also disapproved of Shultz's presence, protesting that writers were being set up "as a forum for the Reagan administration," as Doctorow put it.

In the days that followed, there were more disputes. Cynthia Ozick circulated a petition attacking Bruno Kreisky, the Jewish ex-chancellor of Austria and a congress participant, because he had met with Arafat and Gadhafi. Kreisky's defenders pointed out that during his chancellorship, Austria had taken in more refugee Russian Jews than any other country. However, during a panel discussion, Ozick rose from the floor to denounce Kreisky, who handled the situation with such grace that the trouble passed.

Many women at the congress demanded, with much justification, to know why there were so few women on the panels. Sontag and Gordimer, both panelists, did not join the revolt. It was Susan who came up with the argument that "literature is not an equal-opportunity employer." This remark did not improve the protesters' mood. Nor, I suspect, did my own intervention. I pointed out that while there were, after all, several women on the various panels, I was the sole representative of the Indian subcontinent, which was to say, of one-fifth of the human race. (In 1986 the population of the world was approximately five billion people, and India alone accounted for eight hundred million. Add Pakistan and Bangladesh, and you had one billion people represented by this lone writer.)

Speak, memory: I remember Updike delivering, to a considerably bewildered audience of world writers, his paean to the little blue mailboxes of America, those everyday symbols of the free exchange of ideas. I remember meeting Donald Barthelme, whose work I loved, but who was so drunk that I had the feeling of not really having met him. (When I mentioned this to an American writer friend, he told me, "No, you met him. That's how he was.") I remember Rosario Murillo, the poet and *compañera* of the Sandinista president of Nicaragua, Daniel Ortega, standing next to the Temple of Dendur, surrounded by a phalanx of astonishingly beautiful, dangerous-looking Sandinista men. She invited me to come and see the Contra War for myself, an invitation I accepted later that year, making the journey that afterward turned into my book *The Jaguar Smile*. I didn't know, until I got to Managua, that Rosario Murillo—then as now—was probably the most hated woman in Nicaragua.

And I remember being dragged into a heavyweight prizefight between Saul Bellow and Günter Grass. After Bellow made a speech containing a familiar Bellovian riff about how the success of American materialism had damaged the spiritual life of Americans, Grass rose to point out that many people routinely fell through the holes in the American dream and offered to show Bellow some real American poverty in, for example, the South Bronx. Bellow, irritated to be told about American poverty by a German writer, spoke sharply in return, and when Grass returned to his seat, next to me, as it happens, he was trembling with anger.

"Say something," he ordered.

"Who, me?" I said.

"Yes. Say something."

So I got up and went to the microphone and asked Bellow why he thought it was that so many American writers had avoided—I think I actually said, more provocatively, "abdicated"—the task of taking on the subject of America's immense power in the world. Bellow bridled.

"We don't have tasks," he said majestically. "We have inspirations."

Enjoyable as such recollections are, the real significance of the congress lay deeper. In those last years of the Cold War, it was important for us all to hear Eastern European writers like Danilo Kiš and Czesław Miłosz, György Konrád and Ryszard Kapuściński, setting their visions against the visionless Soviet regime. Omar Cabezas, Nicaragua's deputy interior minister at the time, who had just published a memoir of his life as a Sandinista guerrilla, and Mahmoud Darwish, the Palestinian poet, were there to articulate views not often heard on American platforms; and American writers such as Robert Stone and Kurt Vonnegut did indeed offer their own critiques of American power, while the Bellows and Updikes looked inward at the American soul. Nadine Gordimer said: "The state sees imagination as something that can be put to service." And Toni Morrison spoke about alienation and the state: "Had I lived the life that the state had planned for me from the beginning ... I would have lived and died in someone else's kitchen on somebody else's land and never written a word. That is what the state planned for me as a black person and as a female person." So in the end it is the gravity of the event, not the levity, that insists on pride of place in the memory.

In 1986 it still felt natural for writers to claim to be, as Shelley said, "the unacknowledged legislators of the world," to believe in the literary art as the proper counterweight to power, and to see literature as a lofty, transnational, transcultural force. In our dumbed-down, homogenized, frightened present-day culture, under the thumbs of leaders who seem to think of themselves as God's anointed and of power as their divine right, it is harder to make such exalted claims for mere wordsmiths. Harder, but no less necessary.

In many parts of the world—in, for example, China, Iran, and much of Africa—the free imagination is still considered dangerous. At the heart of PEN's work is our effort to defend writers under attack by powerful interests who fear and threaten them. Those voices, Arab or Afghan or Latin American or Russian, need to be magnified, so that they can be heard loud and clear, just as the Soviet dissidents once were. Yet, in America, unlike in Europe, a lamentably small percentage of all the fiction and poetry published each year is translated from other languages. It has perhaps never been more important for the world's voices to be heard in America, never more important for the world's ideas and dreams to be known and thought about and discussed, never more important for a global dialogue to be fostered. Yet one has the sense of things shutting down, of barriers being erected, of that dialogue being stifled precisely when we should be doing our best to amplify it. The Cold War is over, but a stranger war has begun. Alienation has perhaps never been so widespread; all the more reason for getting together and seeing what bridges can be built.

Welcoming the 1986 delegates to New York, Norman Mailer wrote: "If it is one of the great cities of our civilization, it is, like that civilization, in peril from above, from below and on the flank." It's a greeting that could have been written yesterday. Against peril, writers offer no stale defenses, but we can, perhaps, offer this bruised and shaken city new thoughts, new angles of vision, moments of better understanding. New York, greatest of world cities, deserves no less.

## 2. The Birth of PEN World Voices

PEN America gave me invaluable support when I needed it most, after the attacks on *The Satanic Verses*, its author, publishers, translators, and booksellers. In the last two decades, ever since I came to live in New York, I've been deeply involved with PEN and have tried to do my best to pay back that support, by working in defense of free expression and of other writers, as I was defended over thirty years ago. And when I became president of PEN America in 2004, my memory of the Mailer conference in 1986 was one of the inspirations that led us to create the PEN World Voices Festival of International Literature.

In the aftermath of the 9/11 attacks and during what felt like the joint presidency of George W. Bush and Dick Cheney, a rift had appeared between America and the rest of the world, even between America and her natural allies in the West. It seemed sometimes as if the world had stopped being able to hear America singing, and America too had become deaf to what the rest of the world said and thought. We believed, at PEN, that that was probably bad for America, and bad for the rest of the world too, and we resolved to do what we could, at least at the level of literary and intellectual discourse, to restart that interrupted conversation.

The result was the PEN World Voices Festival, whose purpose was simply to allow the finest voices in world literature to spend a few days each year in New York City, in dialogue and debate with one another, and with the finest American voices too.

Mike Roberts, who was then the CEO of PEN America, and I went around New York, more or less cap in hand, raising money, because we agreed from the start that the festival should be something PEN did in addition to its normal work—that it should not make us cut back on any of that work—and that meant additional funds had to be raised. Mike and I turned out to be a good double act. I did the big-picture arm-waving song-and-dance performance, and Mike did the nuts and bolts. It seemed to work pretty well. And many other people helped get the festival off the ground. I remember in particular that Diane von Fürstenberg was a great ally, making introductions to people who gave donations and hosting a grand event to set us on our way. The PEN staff gave generously of their free time. And gradually the pipe dream became a reality.

We made one big change from the Mailer event. This time, all the events of our festival would be open to the public, not limited, as the Mailer conference had been, to the membership of PEN. We would open the doors and invite everyone in.

I always thought we were doing something Kevin Costner–esque by creating World Voices. It was PEN's own *Field of Dreams,* and our motto too was "If you build it, they will come." In fact, we weren't by any means certain that anyone would come. New York City's cultural calendar was crowded, and it wasn't easy to make room for yet another event. Nevertheless, we did build it, and they did come, and they have gone on coming, and we must thank them, our audiences, for that support, without which our work would have no meaning.

We should feel proud, all of us who are and have been a part of PEN America, to have created a stage on which the core values and the vital work of PEN have been able to reach and inspire a new generation of New Yorkers.

Think of this as a newish New Yorker's gift to his new hometown.

New York City too is a field of dreams, and within it, long may the dreams of literature thrive and the vital conversation between America and the world go on.

### 3. The Arthur Miller Lecture, PEN World Voices Festival 2012

I'm here, I guess, to talk about censorship, but no writer ever really wants to talk about censorship. Writers want to talk about creation, and censorship is anti-creation, negative energy, un-creation, the bringing into being of non-being, or, to use Tom Stoppard's description of death, "the absence of presence." Censorship is the thing that stops you doing what you want to do, and what writers want to talk about is what they do, not what stops them doing it. Writers want to talk about how much they get paid and to gossip about other writers and how much *they* get paid, and they want to complain about critics and publishers and gripe about politicians, and they want to talk about what they love, the writers they love, the stories and even sentences that have meant something to them, and, finally, they want to talk about their own ideas and their own stories. Their things. The British humorist Paul Jennings, in his brilliant essay on "Resistentialism," a spoof of Existentialism, proposed that the world was divided into two categories, "Thing" and "No-Thing," and suggested that between these two is waged a never-ending war. If writing is Thing, then censorship is No-Thing, and, as King Lear told Cordelia, "Nothing will come of nothing," or, as Mr. Jennings would have revised Shakespeare, "No-Thing will come of No-Thing. Think again."

Consider, if you will, the air. Here it is, all around us, plentiful, freely available, and broadly breathable. And yes, I know, it's not perfectly clean or perfectly pure but here it nevertheless is, plenty of it, enough for all of us and lots to spare. When breathable air is available so freely and in such quantity, it's redundant to demand that breathable air be freely provided to all, in sufficient quantity for the needs of all. What you have, you can easily take for granted, and ignore. There's just no need to make a fuss about it. You breathe the freely available, broadly breathable air, and you get on with your day. The air is not a subject. It is not something to be discussed.

Imagine, now, that somewhere up there you might find a giant set of faucets and that the air we breathe flows from those faucets, hot air and cold air, and tepid air from some celestial mixer unit. And imagine that an entity up there, not known to us, or perhaps even known to us, begins on a certain day to turn off the faucets one by one, so that slowly we begin to notice that the available air, still breathable, still free, is thinning. The time comes when we find that we are breathing more heavily, perhaps we are even gasping for air. By this time many of us would have begun to protest, to condemn the reduction in the air supply, and to argue loudly for the right to freely available, broadly breathable air. Scarcity creates demand.

Liberty is the air we breathe, and we live in a part of the world where, imperfect as the supply is, it is nevertheless freely available, at least to those of us who aren't black youngsters wearing hoodies in Miami, and broadly breathable, unless, of course, we're women in red states trying to make free choices about our own bodies. Imperfectly free, imperfectly breathable, but when it is breathable and free we don't need to make a song and dance about it. We take it for granted and get on with our day. And at night, as we fall asleep, we assume we will be free tomorrow, because we were free today.

The creative act requires not only freedom but also this assumption of freedom. If creative artists worry if they will still be free tomorrow, then they will not be free today. If they are afraid of the consequences of their choice of subjects or of their treatments of those subjects, then their choices will not be determined by talent but by fear. If we are not confident of our freedom, then we are not free. The air supply is turned off, and we cannot breathe.

And, even worse than that, when censorship intrudes on art, then it becomes the subject; the art becomes "censored art," and that is how the world sees and understands it. The censor labels the work immoral, or blasphemous, or pornographic, or controversial, and those words are forever hung like albatrosses around the necks of those cursed mariners, the censored works. The attack on the work does more than define the work; in a sense, for the general public, it becomes the work. For every reader of *Lady Chatterley's Lover* or *Tropic of Capricorn,* every viewer of *Last Tango in Paris* or *A Clockwork Orange,* there will be ten, a hundred, a thousand people who "know" those works as excessively filthy, or excessively violent, or both.

The assumption of guilt replaces the assumption of innocence. Why did that Indian Muslim artist have to paint that Hindu goddess in the nude? Couldn't he have respected her modesty? Why did that Russian writer have his hero fall in love with a nymphet? Couldn't he have chosen a legally acceptable age? Why did that British playwright depict a sexual assault in a Sikh temple, a *gurdwara*? Couldn't the same assault have been removed from holy ground? Why are artists so troublesome? Can't they just offer us beauty, morality, and a damn good story? Why do artists think, if they behave in this way, that we should be on their side?

> "And the people all said sit down,
> sit down you're rocking the boat."

At its most effective, the censor's lie actually succeeds in replacing the artist's truth. That which is censored is thought to have deserved censorship. Boat-rocking is widely deplored. This is the final victory of the censor: when people cease to be able to imagine a noncensorious society.

Great banned works sometimes defy the censor's description and impose themselves on the world. *Ulysses, Lolita, The Arabian Nights.* Sometimes great and brave artists defy the censors to create marvelous literature underground, as in the case of the *samizdat* literature of the Soviet Union, or to make subtle films that dodge the edge of the censor's knife, as in the case of much contemporary Iranian and some Chinese cinema. You will even find people who will give you the argument that censorship is good for artists because it challenges their imagination. This is like arguing that if you cut a man's arms off you can praise him for learning to write with a pen held between his teeth. Censorship is not good for art, and it is even worse for artists themselves. The poet Ovid was banished to the Black Sea by a displeased Augustus Caesar and spent the rest of his life in a little hellhole called Tomis, but the poetry of Ovid has outlived the Roman Empire. The poet Mandelstam died in one of Stalin's labor camps, but the poetry of Mandelstam has outlived the Soviet Union. The poet Lorca was murdered in Spain by Generalissimo Franco's goons, but the poetry of Lorca has outlived the fascistic Falange. So perhaps we can argue that art is stronger than the censor, and perhaps it often is.

Artists, however, are vulnerable.

Here at PEN, our task is to defend and try to protect the artist as well as the art, the writer in prison as well as his imprisoned or forbidden words. There are many countries in the world in which a gathering such as World Voices, where a hundred writers talk about all manner of things in all manner of different ways, simply couldn't happen. The air is unclean here, but it is breathable.

That is not a reason for complacency. In England recently, English PEN protested that the London Book Fair had invited only a bunch of "official," state-approved Chinese writers, while the voices of at least thirty-five writers jailed by the regime, including Nobel laureate Liu Xiaobo and the PEN member Zhu Yufu, remained silent and ignored. In the United States, every year, religious zealots try to ban writers as disparate as Kurt Vonnegut and J. K. Rowling—an obvious advocate of sorcery and the black arts—to say nothing of poor, God-bothered Charles Darwin, against whom the advocates of intelligent design continue to march. I once wrote, and it still feels true, that the attacks on the theory of evolution in parts of the United States go some way to disproving Darwin's theory, demonstrating that natural selection doesn't always work, or at least not in the Kansas area, and that human beings are capable of evolving backward too, toward the missing link.

Even more serious is the growing acceptance of the don't-rock-the-boat response to those artists who do rock it, the growing agreement that censorship can be justified when certain interest groups, or genders, or faiths declare themselves affronted by a piece of work. But great art—or let's just say, more modestly, original art—is never created in the safe middle ground but always at the edge. Originality is dangerous. It challenges, questions, overturns assumptions, unsettles moral codes, disrespects sacred cows or other such entities. It can be shocking, or ugly, or, to use the catchall term so beloved of the tabloid press, controversial. And if we believe in liberty, if we want the air we breathe to remain plentiful and breathable, this is the art whose right to exist we must not only defend but celebrate. Art is not entertainment. At its very best, it's a revolution.

## 4.  PEN World Voices Festival Opening Night 2014

There's a general election under way in India right now. Because of the immense size of the country it takes six weeks for everyone to vote. The election is largely fair, largely free, voting is peaceful, incidents are few, and the result will be a trustworthy reflection of the gigantic electorate's will. On this electoral process rests India's claim to be the world's largest democracy, a proud claim, for it is harder for a poor country to be a free country, and the long civil uncertainties and frequent unfreedoms of the citizens of all India's neighbors to the north, east, west, and south make the Indian boast all the prouder. This, we can all agree, is good.

But a democratic society is not simply one in which such a ballot takes place every four or five years. Democracy is more than mere majoritarianism. Democracy is freedom. In a truly free society, all citizens must *feel* free, all the time, whether they end up on the winning or losing side in an election: free to express themselves as they choose, free to worship or not worship as they please, free from danger and fear. If freedom of expression is under attack, if religious freedom is threatened, and if substantial parts of society live in physical fear for their safety, then such a society cannot be said to be a true democracy. In contemporary India, all these problems exist, and are getting worse.

The attack on literary, scholarly, and artistic freedoms has been gathering force. A. K. Ramanujan's classic essay "Three Hundred Ramayanas," for decades the foundational text of Ramayana studies in Delhi University, was attacked by Hindu extremists, and the authorities cravenly succumbed and removed it from the syllabus. Not only was James Laine's study of the Maratha warrior king Shivaji, an icon of the Shiv Sena party, attacked and banned, but the great library of ancient texts in Pune, where Laine had done some research, was attacked and many ancient manuscripts destroyed. And most recently the same fanatical Hindu who attacked Ramanujan's essay brought an action against Wendy Doniger's important scholarly work, *The Hindus,* accusing her, ludicrously and ungrammatically, of being "a woman hungry of sex," and instead of being laughed out of court he succeeded in scaring the mighty Penguin Books into withdrawing the work. And a gay artist, Balbir Krishan, was first threatened and then physically attacked in India's capital New Delhi, accused of "spreading homosexuality."

Episodes of this sort are multiplying, by the month, by the week, by the day, and the authorities are failing lamentably in their duty to protect free-speech rights. In fact, politicians and police officials alike have repeatedly blamed the victims for being the troublemakers. The climate of fear that has consequently been created is such that, as some of the examples I have given show, the hooligans' and censors' work is now often done for them by the collapse of those who ought to be free speech's defenders. Penguin Books, whose merger with Random House has created the world's largest and most powerful publisher, and who were prepared to defend my work back in 1988, this time gave in to Doniger's critics without so much as a fight.

This already lamentable state of affairs looks likely to become much worse if, as seems probable, the election results bring to power the Hindu nationalist BJP, so that the highly divisive figure of Narendra Modi, accused* of being responsible for an anti-Muslim pogrom

* He was later cleared of those charges by a Special Investigation Team appointed by India's Supreme Court.

in 2002 in the state of Gujarat, whose chief minister he is, a hard-liner's hardliner, becomes India's next prime minister. (Films dealing with the attacks have been banned in Gujarat ever since 2002.) Already the threats to free expression have begun to spread beyond the borders of Gujarat. Siddharth Varadarajan, the editor of the distinguished English-language daily *The Hindu,* was forced to resign because the paper's owners felt he wasn't pro-Modi enough. Soon afterward, the caretaker of his apartment was beaten up in a Delhi street, by thugs who told him, "Tell your boss to watch what he says on television." Sagarika Ghose, a leading anchor of CNN's Indian affiliate, IBN, was ordered by her bosses to stop posting tweets critical of Mr. Modi. In response, she tweeted what many journalists are thinking: "There is an evil out there, an evil which is stamping out all free speech and silencing independent journalists: journalists unite!"

Nor are the threats limited to free expression. Modi's campaign manager, Amit Shah, delivered a speech in early April in the northern town of Muzaffarnagar, the site of sectarian strife last year. He described the elections as an opportunity to seek "revenge" against the Muslim minorities. Giriraj Singh, a senior leader of the BJP, one of the most senior of Modi's Toadies, said in an election rally in the northern state of Bihar that those opposing Modi would have no place in India. "They will only find a place in Pakistan," he shouted. Another Hindu extremist figure, Praveen Togadia, told his supporters to prevent Muslims from buying property in Hindu-majority neighborhoods in Gujarat. The writing is on the wall.

A couple of weeks ago the sculptor Anish Kapoor and I, along with several other Indian artists, academics, and intellectuals, signed an open letter worrying about Mr. Modi's rise to power. Since then the attack on us in Indian social media has been relentless and paradoxically has validated our fears. We worried about the arrival of a bullying, intolerant new regime, and here are its early outriders: menacing, nasty, bile-spewing, vengeful, substituting *ad hominem* attacks for any real debate. There will not be less of this after a Modi victory.

Mr. Modi's supporters point back to the ballot box. He will win, they say, because he is popular, and they are right. A disturbingly high percentage of the Indian electorate wants a strongman leader, is willing to turn a blind eye to his past misdeeds even if those include genocide, believes that dissenting intellectuals should be put in their place, critical journalists should be muzzled, and artists should behave themselves. This willingness to bet the farm on Mr. Modi's alleged economic genius, about which many commentators have doubts, and to risk everything that is beautiful about a free society, may indeed provide the wave that sweeps Mr. Modi to victory.

It would be easy to say, then India will get the government it deserves. But all those who value what is being lost, all those who want a country free of fear, an open society, not a stifled one, all those Indians will get an India they don't deserve. Those who value the India for which Rabindranath Tagore yearned in his great poem "Let My Country Awake" will get an India that would have horrified the poet.

Tagore wrote:

> Where the mind is without fear and the head is held
>   high;
> Where knowledge is free;
> Where the mind is led forward by thee into ever
>   widening thought and action
> Into that heaven of freedom, my Father, let my country
>   awake.

India is in danger of betraying the legacy of its founding fathers and greatest artists, like Rabindranath Tagore.

A POSTSCRIPT. A LOT has happened in India since this piece was written, including another general election and another resounding victory for Prime Minister Narendra Modi and his BJP. As Aatish Taseer wrote in *The Atlantic* in April 2020, "India is no longer India." The old secular ideals are being demolished day by day. Mr. Modi and his crony Amit Shah, buoyed by electoral success, have been pushing through legislation—notably the CAA, or Citizenship Amendment

Act—that serves their agenda of increasing discrimination against non-Hindus. And the state of Kashmir, its Internet services cut off, its citizenry at the mercy of often brutal security forces, is suffering from an authoritarian rule that surely has no place in any democracy.

I used to argue that the BJP had invented a "Hinduism" that isn't Hindu at all. "Hinduism" is an amalgam of belief systems. It has no single holy book, no single god, and no requirement for collective acts of worship. In its place the new ideology declares the *Ramayana* to be the book of books (why? The *Vedas* are older and have at least an equal claim), Ram to be the most important god, and the return of "Ram Rajya," the rule of Ram, to be the most desirable happening (this, even though there are many parts of India where Ram, an incarnation of Vishnu, has no such history of preeminence); and mass acts of worship, resembling nothing so much as Nuremberg rallies, have become regular events. This argument has the merit of being true, but Mr. Modi and his people have created a movement out of this new Hinduism that makes the old truths irrelevant. The new Hinduism is Hinduism now, and its intolerance has become India's intolerance.

If there is hope, it lies with the uprising against the excesses of the government, in particular against the CAA—an uprising led by women and university students which has defied threats and actual violence. What is most heartening is to see and hear the protesters returning to the language of the independence struggle, the language and ethos of Nehru and Gandhi and of Indian secularism, and to set that language against the coarser tongue of those presently in power. There is a battle under way for the soul of India. I have no idea who will prevail, but I know whose side I'm on.

## 5. PEN World Voices Festival Opening Night 2017

PEN World Voices was born in 2005, in part because we believed it was absurd that New York City, which has international festivals of everything, didn't have an international literary festival. That first year the writers at World Voices included Chimamanda Ngozi Adichie from Nigeria, Paul Auster from Brooklyn, Breyten Breytenbach from South Africa, Nuruddin Farah from Somalia, Ryszard Kapuściński from Poland, Elif Shafak from Turkey, Hanan al-Shaykh from Lebanon, Wole Soyinka from Nigeria, Ngugi wa Thiong'o from Kenya, and Chico Buarque from Brazil. From the very beginning, however, this has been a little more than just a literary festival. It was and is also a place where the PEN mission is advanced and where abuses of power abroad or in America are challenged and opposed.

At the beginning of the thirteenth iteration of World Voices, we face a new challenge at least as great, if not greater, than the George W. Bush–era challenges of 2005. From the highest and most powerful places in America we face an attack on the arts, and beyond the arts on journalism, and beyond journalism on the idea of truth itself: truth as objective, beyond personal opinion or prejudice, truth meaning the primacy of facts—facts backed up by evidence. We face a moment in which untruth pollutes our lives on a daily basis and in which bigots—bigoted against the media, yes, but also against immigrants, Mexicans, minorities, the LGBTQ community, women, and so-called elites—seem to have been set free by the result of the presidential election, and consequently our public discourse has already been greatly disfigured.

May I parenthetically object to the distortion in the meaning of the word "elites"? How is it allowed to happen that a government of billionaires and bankers, in which is accumulated more wealth than in any previous government in American history, is able to dismiss its adversaries as elites while claiming to speak for the masses? Very few novelists or journalists own private planes or clubs in Florida or New Jersey. Very few of these supposed out-of-touch elites live lives so utterly sequestered from ordinary people as this cabinet of billionaires. And yet *we* are the elites? Let's start by reclaiming this single word. Let's call things by their proper names. We are facing the most shamelessly elitist administration in the history of the United States. Anyone who doesn't see that, to paraphrase something Stephen King said the other day, isn't paying attention.

I worry for the future of this festival if the administration succeeds in making entry into America a much more difficult and unpleasant experience. Will the world's writers want to brave U.S. immigration? Already there is much anecdotal evidence of bullying at the points of entry, of people at the border being asked by immigration officers what they think of the president, as if that were a criterion by which their right to enter America was to be determined. Already we hear of a probable drop in visitors to America, this year by 20 percent or more. That rift between this country and the world, which led us to launch World Voices in 2005, is reopening. I hope writers will not be deterred from joining us here, so that we can go on doing what we can to speak across that gulf.

I believe that in this time, when the idea of a better America, diverse, open, tolerant, and civilized, is everywhere under assault, it falls to us, to all of us, writers, publishers, booksellers, readers, citizens, to be the guardians of the culture. To be, in what we say and how we act, embodiments and protectors of that better America. Because America is better than Trumpistan. America is better than these people for whom the Second Amendment is sacrosanct but the First Amendment, not so much. America is better than bullying and bigotry and hatred. If one good thing has come out of this dark moment, it is that so many Americans are politically galvanized, perhaps as never before. So perhaps there is an army of the good, an army of peace and justice, united against hate, that will stand in the way of the forces unleashed against us. I believe there is, and, to use an old form of words, we shall not be moved.

# CHRISTOPHER HITCHENS
## (1949–2011)

———

Written on December 15, 2011,
the day Christopher died

O N JUNE 8, 2010, I WAS "IN CONVERSATION" WITH CHRISTOPHER Hitchens at the 92nd Street Y in New York in front of his customary sellout audience, to launch his memoir, *Hitch-22*. Christopher turned in a bravura performance that night, never sharper, never funnier, and afterward at a small, celebratory dinner the brilliance continued. A few days later he told me that it was on the morning of the Y event that he had been given the news about his cancer. It was hard to believe that he had been so publicly magnificent on such a privately dreadful day. He had shown more than stoicism. He had flung laughter and intelligence into the face of death.

*Hitch-22* was a title born of the silly word games we played, one of which was "Titles that don't quite make it," among which were *A Farewell to Weapons, For Whom the Bell Rings, To Kill a Hummingbird, The Catcher in the Wheat, Mr. Zhivago,* and *Moby-Prick.* And, as the not-quite version of Joseph Heller's comic masterpiece, *Snag-* or *Hitch-22*. Christopher rescued this last title from the slush pile of our catechism of failures and redeemed it by giving it to the text that now stands as his best memorial.

Laughter and Hitchens were inseparable companions, and comedy was one of the most powerful weapons in his arsenal. When we were both on *Real Time with Bill Maher* along with Mos Def, and the rapper began to offer up a series of cockeyed animadversions about Osama bin Laden and Al Qaeda, Christopher became almost ferally polite, addressing Mos, as he tore into his ideas, by the faux-respectful moniker "Mr. Definitely," a name so belittlingly funny that it rendered even more risible the risible notions that Mr. Def was trying to advance.

Behind the laughter was what his friend Ian McEwan called "his Rolls-Royce mind," that organ of improbable erudition and frequently brilliant, though occasionally flawed, perception. The Hitch mind was indeed a sleek and purring machine trimmed with elegant fittings, but his was not a rarefied sensibility. He was an intellectual with the instincts of a street brawler, never happier than when engaged in moral or political fisticuffs. When I became involved in a public disagreement with John le Carré, Hitchens leapt unbidden into the fray and ratcheted the insult level up many notches, comparing the great man's conduct to "that of a man who, having relieved himself in his own hat, makes haste to clamp the brimming chapeau on his head." The argument, I'm sorry to report, grew uglier after the Hitch's intervention.

The le Carré dispute took place during the long years of argument and danger that followed the publication of my novel *The Satanic Verses* and the attack upon its author, publishers, translators, and booksellers by the minions and successors of the theocratic tyrant of Iran, Ruhollah Khomeini. It was during these years that Christopher, a good but not intimate friend since the mid-1980s, drew closer to me, becoming the most indefatigable of allies and the most eloquent of defenders.

I have often been asked if Christopher defended me because he was my close friend. The truth is that he became my close friend because he wanted to defend me.

The spectacle of a despotic cleric with antiquated ideas issuing a death warrant for a writer living in another country, and then sending death squads to carry out the edict, changed something in Christopher. It made him understand that a new danger had been unleashed upon the earth, that a new totalizing ideology had stepped into the down-at-heel shoes of Soviet Communism. And when the brute hostility of British and American conservatives (John Podhoretz and Charles Krauthammer, Hugh Trevor-Roper and Paul Johnson) joined forces with the appeasement politics of sections of the Western left, and both sides began to offer sympathetic analyses of the assault, his outrage grew. In the eyes of the right, I was a cultural "traitor" and, in Christopher's words, an "uppity wog," and in the opinion of the left, the People could never be wrong, and the cause of the Oppressed People, a category into which the Islamist opponents of my novel (and of the "hegemonic power of the United States") fell, was doubly justified. Voices as diverse as the pope, the cardinal of New York, the British chief rabbi, and John Berger and Germaine Greer "understood the insult" and failed to be outraged; and Christopher went to war.

He and I found ourselves describing our ideas, without conferring, in almost identical terms. I began to understand that while I had not chosen the battle, it was at least the right battle, because in it everything that I loved and valued (literature, freedom, irreverence, freedom, irreligion, freedom) was ranged against everything I detested (fanaticism, violence, bigotry, humorlessness, philistinism, and the new offense-culture of the age). Then I read Christopher using exactly the same everything-he-loved-versus-everything-he-hated trope, and I felt . . . *understood.*

He too saw that the attack on *The Satanic Verses* was not an isolated occurrence, that across the Muslim world, writers and journalists and artists were being accused of the same crimes: blasphemy, heresy, apostasy, and their modern-day associates, "insult" and "offense." And he intuited that beyond this intellectual assault lay the possibility of an attack on a broader front. He quoted Heine to me: "Where they burn books, they will afterward burn people." (And reminded me, with his profound sense of irony, that Heine's famous line, taken from his play *Almansor,* had referred to the burning of the Qur'an.) And on September 11, 2001, he, and all of us, understood that what began with a book-burning in Bradford, Yorkshire, had now burst upon the whole world's consciousness in the form of those tragically burning buildings.

During the campaign against the *fatwa,* the British government and various human-rights groups pressed the case for a visit by me to the Clinton White House, to demonstrate the strength of the new administration's support for the cause. A visit was offered, then delayed, then offered again. It was unclear until the last minute if President Clinton himself would meet me or if the encounter would be left to the national security adviser, Anthony Lake, and perhaps Warren Christopher, the secretary of state. Hitch worked tirelessly to impress on Clinton's people the importance of POTUS greeting me in person. His friendship with George Stephanopoulos was perhaps the critical factor. Stephanopoulos's arguments prevailed and I was led into the presidential presence. Stephanopoulos called Christopher at once, telling him triumphantly: "The Eagle has landed."

(On that visit to D.C. I stayed in the Hitchens apartment, and he was afterward warned by a State Department spook that my having been his houseguest might have drawn the danger toward him; maybe it would be a good idea if he moved house? He remained contemptuously unmoved.)

Christopher came to believe that the people who understood the dangers posed by radical Islam were on the right, that his erstwhile comrades on the left were arranging with one another to miss what seemed to him like a pretty obvious point; and so, never one to do things by halves, he made what looked to many people like a U-turn across the political highway to join forces with the war-makers of George W. Bush's administration. He became oddly enamored of Paul Wolfowitz. One night I happened to be at his apartment in D.C. when Wolfowitz, who had just left the administration, stopped by for a late-night drink and proceeded to deliver a critique of the Iraq War (all Rumsfeld's fault, apparently) that left me, at least, speechless. The Wolfowitz doctrine, Wolfowitz was saying, had not been Wolfowitz's idea. Indeed, Wolfowitz had been anti–Wolfowitz doctrine from the beginning. This was an argument worthy of a character from *Catch-22*. I wondered how long Christopher would be able to tolerate such bedfellows.

Paradoxically, it was God who saved Christopher Hitchens from the American right. Nobody who detested God as viscerally, intelligently, originally, and comically as Hitchens could stay in the pocket of God-fearing American conservatism for long. When he bared his fangs and went for God's jugular, just as he had previously fanged Henry Kissinger, Mother Teresa, and Bill Clinton, the resulting book, *God Is Not Great*, carried Hitch back toward his natural, liberal, ungodly constituency. He became an extraordinarily beloved figure in his last years, and it was his magnificent war upon God, and then his equally magnificent argument with his last enemy, Death, that brought him "home" at last from the misconceived war in Iraq.

LAST THINGS.

When I completed a draft of my memoir, *Joseph Anton*, I sent a copy to Christopher, who was by this time very unwell. I didn't expect him to do more than glance at it. Instead, I received a longish email containing a full critique of the text, pointing out errors of fact and misquotes of Rupert Brooke and P. G. Wodehouse.

There was a last dinner in New York, at which the poet James Fenton and I, by previous agreement, set out to make him laugh as much as possible. Distressingly, this unleashed, at least once, a terrifying coughing fit. But he enjoyed himself that evening. It was the only gift his friends could give him near the end: an hour or two of being himself as he had always wished to be, the Hitch mighty and ample among the ones he loved, and not the diminishing Hitch having the life slowly squeezed out of him by the Destroyer of Days.

Richard Dawkins wrote to Christopher ten days before he died, telling him that an asteroid had been named after him. Christopher was greatly delighted and told all his friends about the Asteroid Hitchens. "Finally!" he emailed us. "Twinkle, twinkle, little bat!" I replied, paraphrasing the last line of Lewis Carroll's verse, "Bravo! You're a teatray in the sky!" It was our last exchange.

On his sixty-second birthday—his last birthday, a painful phrase to write—I had been with him and Carol and other comrades at the Houston home of his friend Michael Zilkha, and we were photographed standing on either side of a bust of Voltaire. That photograph is now one of my most treasured possessions; me and the two Voltaires, one of stone and one still very much alive. Now they are both gone, and one can only try to believe, as the philosopher Pangloss insisted to Candide in the elder Voltaire's masterpiece, that "everything is for the best in this best of all possible worlds."

It doesn't feel like that today.

# THE
# LIBERTY INSTINCT

————

WHEN CHRISTOPHER HITCHENS FINISHED HIS BOOK *God Is Not Great,* he sent it to me to read, and I told him, only half joking, that the title was one word too long; he could usefully delete the "great." He ignored my advice.

Godlessness is unusual in America. In England and Europe it's so commonplace that to announce that one doesn't believe in God is to make people scratch their heads and wonder why you're being so banal. To express one's atheism feels like stating the obvious. To express religious belief is what seems weird. (Unless you're Muslim. Muslims have difficulties with atheism.) In England, when Tony Blair was prime minister, his spin doctors went to great lengths to conceal the fact that he was deeply religious, because if that were generally known, it would be electorally disadvantageous. Public godliness, profound religious faith, was a recipe for political defeat.

Last year I was invited to a "global atheist" conference in Australia, with many well-known headline speakers billed to appear: Richard Dawkins, Daniel Dennett, etc. Then later I heard that they had to cancel the conference because they had failed to sell any tickets. Impressively, they had sold *almost no tickets at all.* It seems that the Aussies didn't want to pay to hear a bunch of us lecturing them about what they took for granted. They preferred to go to the beach and, like Judge Brett Kavanaugh, drink a few beers and not be responsible for what happened after that. In America, sadly, we are not yet as advanced as Australians, except in the beer-and-afterward department.

In America, if you dismiss religion from a lecture podium, you often hear noises of shock: gasps, sharp intakes of breath. In America, you can't get elected dogcatcher if you can't prove that you go to church every Sunday and have a close relationship with the priest there. (Just to be clear, not that close. He probably prefers younger people anyway.)

Even Donald Trump has had to pretend to be religious, which has not been easy for him, because, as video footage from the National Cathedral has demonstrated, he appears not to know the words to the Lord's Prayer. (Parenthetically: Knowing things is not, on the whole, Trump's strong point. As a conservative commentator pointed out, it's not just that Trump doesn't know things, it's that he doesn't know what "knowing things" is.)

Some years ago, before the last Iraq War, I found myself in D.C. addressing groups of Democratic and Republican senators. One of the striking differences between the two groups was that the Democrats spoke in the secular language of politics, whereas the Republicans were full of references to prayer meetings and faith. During the Republican meeting, one GOP senator announced, with great indignation, that he had seen Osama bin Laden quoted as saying that America was a godless nation. "How can he say that?" the senator asked me, genuinely affronted. "We are incredibly godly!" I was struck by his vehemence. He felt that something essential about his identity was under attack. I thought that Osama bin Laden probably had larger targets in mind than the senator's self-image, but I kept that thought to myself.

I did, however, come away wondering why, in the Land of the Free, people were everywhere imprisoned by the antique ideology called God. Here is the explanation, the two-dollar theory I came up with. It has a lot to do with the way people think about freedom. In Europe, the battle for freedom of thought and expression was fought against the Church more than the state. The Church, with its apparatus of oppression—excommunication, anathema, the *Index Expurgatorius*, torture, the drowning of witches, the dismemberment or burning of dissidents—was in the business of placing limiting points upon what could be thought and said, and if you crossed those frontiers you might, like Giordano Bruno, like Savonarola, find yourself being burned at the stake or, at the very least, being forced, like Galileo, to recant what you knew to be true. So in European thought, "freedom" came to be understood as "freedom from religion." The writers and philosophers of the French Enlightenment understood this very well, made it their business to erode the power of the Church to silence expression, using blasphemy as one of their weapons, and it's their work that ended up being the cornerstone of our modern ideas about liberty.

However, the early settlers who came to America from Europe were in many cases escaping from religious persecution, and America, their newfound land, was to them the place where they would be free to practice their faith as they chose, without fear. Thus "freedom" in America was from the earliest times thought of not as freedom from religion but as freedom *for* religion. Religion and freedom were not on opposite sides but on the same side. And when the First Amendment was framed, those two things were yoked together forever. "Congress shall make no law respecting an establishment of religion, or prohibiting the free exercise thereof; or abridging the freedom of speech, or of the press; or the right of the people peaceably to assemble, and to petition the Government for a redress of grievances." You see that freedom of religion precedes freedom of speech. It is of the first importance, and free expression is of the second importance. This has something to do with why atheism has such shallow roots in America. Religion and freedom got married on the northern American continent, the First Amendment was the marriage certificate, and the United States was the result.

The American example, in which the desire for religious liberty was extended to include the freedom of all thought and expression, is, I believe, an exception to the rule. More commonly, religion and liberty have been at odds. And even in today's America, the fault lines between liberty and religion are not hard to see. On the one hand, the First Amendment fails to protect the religious freedoms of Pittsburgh Jews from the gun insanity of America sanctified by present-day interpretations of the Second Amendment. On the other hand, some religious folks can perpetrate attacks on other folks' freedoms by redefining the word "liberty" to mean something like "divinely authorized bigotry." Refusing to serve gay people in stores, or to certify their weddings, is an example of this kind of Bible Belt "liberty." We live in a violent age in which the meanings of words are everywhere being dishonestly distorted, in which those distorted meanings can lead to violence, and of no words is that more true than of "freedom" and "liberty." I'll circle back to this in a little while. But first I want to go back to the origins both of religion and of the idea of individual liberty.

The gods were born because human beings did not understand the world. What was the sun and how did it rise in the sky? What were the moon and the stars? Did we live beneath a great dome with holes in it that let in mysterious light? Who made it rain, and why did we live and die? How did we get here, and how did *here* get here before we did? From the earliest times, we suffered from the anthropomorphic fallacy—the belief that nonhuman things like plants and oceans had human characteristics, such as emotions, that the sky could be angry and the breeze could be kind—and, also from the earliest times, we were narrative animals. We told ourselves stories to try to explain everything we did not understand. We invented larger, more powerful versions of ourselves, hidden in the sky, hurling thunderbolts at us from mountaintops, churning the sea's surface from a throne in the water's depths. And we made the gods the centers of discussions about love and fear. Sometimes the gods loved us, they had favorite people and favorite cities, but when their favoritisms clashed, when one god liked the Greeks and another preferred the Trojans, look out. Sometimes the love of a god, when a human woman was involved, looked very like sexual assault. And very often the gods were just frightening and vengeful, especially toward those daring humans who dreamed of being their equals, as Arachne did, considering her weaving to be the equal of Athena's. She was turned into a spider as a result. The gods never liked it when humans rivaled their powers or when anyone tried to steal their magic. The punishment of the Titan Prometheus for stealing fire was intended to be an example to us all. "Know your place" was the message of the gods from the earliest times. But liberty is precisely the idea that one need not know one's place but rather construct for oneself a place that feels right.

Fear, on the whole, trumped love in the early polytheisms. True, these included gods of love, gods whose job it was to oversee the lives of lovers and to be adored in return; but on the whole our ancestors saw divinity as the embodiment of power. It was the answer to the great unanswerable question: Who made everything, including us? And there was no nonsense about human liberty. We were the gods' creatures, required to worship them and abase ourselves, or else. It's true that many of the stories our ancestors invented are very beautiful and strange: the god Indra churning the primal milk of the universe and creating the galaxies from it; the giant turtle holding up the world (but what held up the giant turtle?); the elephant-headed Ganesh sitting at the feet of India's Homer, the sage Vyasa, and writing down the *Mahabharata* as the poet recited it; the Twilight of the Gods. But the dead religions whose stories we now find so beautiful were once living religions, with all the apparatuses of repression that living religions possess, and you blasphemed at your peril. These religions only became "beautiful stories" when people no longer believed in them as being literally true. The idea of the literal truth of this or that holy text remains one of the most dangerous of notions.

Let's be clear. The gods did not create us in their image. We created them in ours. And if the first reason for this act of creation was our desire to provide explanations for the larger creation we did not understand, our desire, in the absence of science, to answer the first great question, the question of origins—then the second reason was to provide an ethical framework for our lives, to answer the second great question, the question of ethics: Now that we are here, how shall we live? What is right action and what is wrong action? What is evil and what is good? Interestingly, the polytheistic religions, the Egyptian, Norse, Greek, Roman, Hindu pantheons, weren't very concerned about the second question. Their gods were not moral exemplars and offered no theories of morality. These gods were like us, only enlarged. They did not behave well. They were greedy, sexually predatory, vain, petty, vengeful, treacherous, and lewd. (Come to think of it, human beings, even back in the mists of time, were probably a better bunch than their deities.) The point is that these gods did not say to their devotees, do as we do. They did not say, we are showing you the way to behave. They simply said, we are the gods, we can do whatever we like, and your job is to adore us, or else.

Fascism was born on Mount Asgard. And Mount Kailash. And Mount Olympus.

It was the great monotheisms that took on the subject of ethics. Now what came down from the mount was not a thunderbolt but a sermon. Now began the business of the carrot and the stick, what one might call the Santa Claus approach to ethics. Keep off the naughty list and there will be presents under the tree. But if you're not on the nice list, Judgment Day will be, let's say, disappointing. Be good, and Eden awaits. Here's a picture of that: clouds, nightgowns, wings, harp music, bliss. Be bad, and here's a picture of the inferno for you to look at. And, by the way, here are a bunch of earthly punishments for you to endure while you're taking a look. These pictures of hell and earthly punishments, which all the monotheisms love, are what we might today call trailers. And the question they ask is, now that you've seen the trailers of heaven and hell, which movie would you like to see? Here's a carrot. Here's a stick. You choose.

This sounds like old-fashioned parenting. When we are born, we understand very little, and we need a great deal. Before we have language, we need protection and care. As we grow up, we turn toward our protectors, if we are lucky enough to have protectors, and we look to them for the laws by which we must live. All children push against parental boundaries, but all children need to know where the boundaries are. We bask in the approval of our parents and we fear their disapproval. They are like gods to us. Until they're not.

Growing up is our first experience of the phenomenon of liberty, for which another term might be "thinking for oneself." At a certain point we all begin to formulate our own picture of the world, and if it is at odds with the picture our parents made for us, then very often we discard the old picture in favor of the new one, and if this causes problems between ourselves and our parents, then we have to face those problems. (Or run away from them.) The gods cease to be gods, and we begin to be autonomous beings.

Several of the old religious stories actually tell us that the time will come when human beings will have to do without their gods. "The Twilight of the Gods" is a phrase derived from what is almost certainly a typographical error. In the "Völuspá," the poem in the so-called *Poetic Edda* that describes these events, the word used to name them is, throughout, spelled *Ragnaråk*, and this means the fall or destruction of the gods. Only once is the word spelled *Ragnarøk*, which changes the meaning to "twilight." But the gods are not waiting for us in some beautiful twilight. Odin slays, and is slain by, the Fenriswolf; Thor kills the World Serpent that rises from the Sundering Seas but is also killed by the serpent's poisonous bite; Freyr faces Surtr and falls beneath the giant's flaming sword. At the end, the ogres are dead, but so are the gods. This is no twilight. This is a fall. After it, we're on our own.

In Buddhism there are no gods to begin with. So we can cut right to the chase.

I confess that I find this aspect of the old faiths attractive: the idea that in the end religion contains its own built-in destructibility, like an old washing machine. That the time comes when we have to throw it away.

This seems infinitely preferable to me to the "eternity" beloved of monotheisms, the eternity of God, and the eternity of the reward-and-punishment systems he puts in place for us.

Outgrowing the gods is the birth of individual and social liberty.

So what do we do about the two great questions after that? Well, as regards the first question, the question of origins, the one thing we can say with a high degree of certainty is that the answers given by every one of the world's great religions and all of the smaller, cockeyed ones too are 100 percent wrong. No, the world was not created in six days by an entity who rested on the seventh. No, there was nobody called Xenu, the tyrant ruler of the "Galactic Confederacy," who brought billions of people to earth 75 million years ago in space-craft resembling Douglas DC-8 airliners, stacked them around volcanoes, and detonated hydrogen bombs in the volcanoes, thus creating "thetans" who stuck to the bodies of the living. No, there were no gigantic Australian "ancestors" or *Wandjina* walking the surface of the earth, creating the landscape as they went. These stories may be attractive stories—well, except for the Scientology nonsense—but they are not true.

We are no longer ignorant. We don't need these stories. Science has better stories and many of them are verifiable. The ones that aren't are recognized as working hypotheses. How much better it is to adhere to a system of knowledge that concedes its limitations! We don't know everything about everything. But to admit that is not to say that we know nothing about anything. In the matter of the origins of the universe, we already know a great deal. I'll take the Big Bang over the World Turtle, any day of the week.

As for the second question, the question of ethics, I decided long ago that I didn't need the advice of Catholic priests or Wahhabi mullahs on that subject. The child-abuse scandals in the Catholic Church, and the authoritarian and even murderous crimes carried out by Wahhabi Islam's most powerful patrons, the Saudi ruling family, would convince me that the ideologies to which they adhere are not the best resources from which to develop an ethical worldview. Even peace-loving Buddhism, the faith without a God, has revealed, in the attacks by Buddhist monks on the Rohingya population of Burma/Myanmar, that it's capable of the worst as well. But my basic reason for rejecting the ethical guidance of religion has to do with the question of liberty.

Ethics change as societies change, and one definition of a free society is that in such a society, morality advances through discussion, argument, and the examination of new ideas. A society can accept slavery at one moment and reject it at another. It can deny women the right to vote at one moment and accept the error of that position at another time. It can discriminate against LGBTQ people in one period and begin to roll back those discriminations at another time. For all the faults of this system, which one might call "democracy"—and the biggest fault, as we are witnessing today, is that the argument can lead to movements in retrograde directions, not only in progressive ones—I still find it the best available method by which an ethical society can be created. As Winston Churchill said, democracy is the worst form of government, except for all the others.

Liberty relies on the constant interrogation of any ethical system's first principles. When one is not allowed to question the first principles of the dominant system of thought, and when the penalties for doing so are dire, one finds oneself trapped in a tyranny. This problem is not unique to religions. The penalties for questioning Stalinism then and the Chinese regime now were and are brutal and severe. But religion adds a twist to the tale by claiming unarguable authority from this or that divine source and arguing, further, that without such a supreme arbiter to establish right and wrong, it is impossible to lead an ethical life. Thus atheists are by definition amoral. This point of view is widespread in the Islamic world today, and by no means only among fanatics.

(Parenthesis. In 2006, during the administration of Tony Blair in the UK, he tried to introduce a law that would have made it illegal to criticize religion. I was one of the people leading the protest against that bill, which eventually failed in the House of Commons by a single vote. Another of the protesters was the comedian Rowan Atkinson. I went with him to meet with government ministers and civil servants, and at one point Rowan said, in his quiet, dignified voice, that he had recently had a sketch on this TV comedy show in which he had used stock footage of Friday prayers in Tehran. "And over this footage, I had this voiceover, you see," he said, "which went, 'And the search goes on for the ayatollah's contact lens.'" Would that be permissible under the proposed new law, he mildly asked, or would it be banned? The ministers and servants hastened to assure Mr. Bean that they loved comedy and it would be fine. "But how would I know that?" he asked. They had no good answer for him.)

I was raised in Bombay in the 1950s: a nonreligious place and time. My parents moved from Delhi to Bombay before independence, not long before I was born, because they feared that there would be religious conflict in Delhi; and there was. Bombay had the reputation of being different; and it was. There was very little Hindu–Muslim trouble there that year, while hundreds of thousands were dying elsewhere on the subcontinent. Bombay people were proud of that, proud that ours was a city where people lived side by side in harmony, observing each other's religious festivals, the many becoming one, and, somehow, canceling each other out, so that the city was strongly secular in spirit. That this is no longer the case, that the rise of Hindu nationalism has led to a sharp increase in sectarianism in what is now Mumbai, is a source of sadness for people of my generation.

So: I grew up in a family, place, and time in which we assumed we had the liberty to argue about everything, to question everything, even the first principles of religion. Nobody would be "offended." Certainly nobody would think about banning such speech. Most certainly nobody would think of launching reprisals against free thought. This was the makeup of the young man who began, in the mid-1980s, to write his fourth novel, *The Satanic Verses*.

It wasn't really even about religion. It was about migration, which to me is the great subject of our time, and a central subject for my own work. Migration from South Asia to Britain, and the condition of migrants in London, in the period we now know as High Thatcherism. Migration, I told myself, unleashes a radical questioning of the self, and so the novel itself must embody that act of questioning. And one of the things it must challenge is religion, the assumption of the rightness of one's faith.

This is where we come to the interrogation of first principles. I asked myself: If I had been standing on the mountain next to the Prophet when he saw the Angel Gabriel bringing the revelation, would I have seen the angel too? Gabriel is described as being very large indeed. He "stands on the horizon and fills the sky." Big angel. And yet I was pretty sure that I wouldn't have seen him. Maybe a religious person would say, that is because your faith was weak. I would say, it's because revelation is an internal event, not an external one. And once one has said that to oneself, one can tell the story of the Prophet and his prophecy as the story of a human being, a *character*, shaping his revelation out of his own experiences, in response to the circumstances of his particular place and time. A person and an idea within history, not outside it. Which brings one up against the first principle. If the revelation is the uncredited word of God, it can't also be a product of the Prophet's character and circumstances, and to say so is to blaspheme. One can protest and say, but the currently canonic version of the Qur'an wasn't established for quite a while. The Qur'anic verses on the Dome of the Rock in Jerusalem differ in certain respects from this canonical text. Nobody will listen. In the end, the novelist says, I must do it this way because that's who I am.

My questioning of the origin story caused problems. But it is an essential aspect of the secular humanist worldview that no set of ideas be ring-fenced and placed beyond question. My assumption was that that included the ideas of Islam. That remains my assumption.

RELIGIOUS DOCTRINE SAYS: SUBMIT. Accept what the great books say. They have all the answers already, with the authority of God behind them. Your faith in those answers will set you free. Without it, you are not free. You are lost.

The nonreligious thinker says: I do not submit. I do not accept. The question must be asked. Questioning is itself the answer. The ability to have the argument is liberty. To give up that liberty is to put oneself in chains.

In both cases, an idea of freedom is the goal.

But, as I said near the beginning, what a treacherous word it is, "freedom," and what strange things it can be made to mean. To call French fries "freedom fries" is not to say that they contain freedom. It is a way of saying, we do not like the French right now. To call the new One World Trade Center building the "Freedom Tower" is not so much a philosophical statement as a kind of patriotic slogan-making. The "Land of the Free" itself contains many groups for whom "freedom" is both a thing hard won—from slavery, from poverty—and a thing constantly in doubt, as the daily problems encountered by African Americans, and the bitter history of Native Americans, whose ancient freedoms were so thoroughly violated, can amply attest.

And yet the word is powerful. Is there, then, such a thing as a requirement for freedom in our makeup, a need to be unshackled from restrictions and limitations? Are we hardwired to seek it? Steven Pinker says we possess a language instinct that allows us to make sense of the sounds we hear when we come into the world, to decode and master language without the help of a Rosetta stone. Can we say that we possess a similar instinct for liberty and that our natural inclination tends toward it and chooses it?

There is powerful anecdotal evidence to support the idea.

Wherever liberty has been suppressed, people want it back. In the Taliban's Afghanistan, in both the shah's and the ayatollahs' Iran, in the Egypt of the Arab Spring, in the Soviet Union where the desire for freedom brought walls crashing down, people, young and old, have wanted the same things, the freedom to speak their minds, to hold hands with the people they love, to dress as they choose, and to make a better, less restricted life for themselves and their families. Their demands for freedom do not always succeed. The failures of the Arab Spring and of the Green Revolution in Iran, the return to authoritarianism in Russia and much of the former Soviet Union, are evidence of that. But we see, everywhere, a will to liberty. That man standing with his shopping bags in front of the Chinese tanks.

However, it's also true that we, all of us, have a second desire, which sometimes contradicts the first. This is the desire for community, for togetherness, our sense of ourselves as parts of something larger than ourselves, which can be race, nation, and, yes, religion. This is the eternal struggle within us: between the social and the individual, between the autonomous self perceived by the humanist philosophers of the Italian Renaissance and the self as part of, and finally lesser than, some kind of group: the battle, one might say, between the singular and the plural. Revolutionary ideologies have often suggested that the revolution can lead to the emancipation of an entire nation, or at least an entire class. I was born eight weeks before the Indian independence movement succeeded in expelling the British Empire, so I understand that there can be some truth to such assertions. But that was also, as I mentioned, the time of the Partition massacres, so I also know that for many people the promises of revolutions can be false.

Both John F. Kennedy and Nelson Mandela told us that freedom is indivisible. "When one man is enslaved, all are not free," President Kennedy said, and Mandela echoed him: "The chains on any one of my people were the chains on all of them; the chains on all of my people were the chains on me."

This is my own view and also the view enshrined in the First Amendment. But we live in a censorious age, in which many people, especially young people, have come to feel that limitations need to be placed on freedom of expression. The idea that hurting people's feelings, offending people's sensibilities, is going too far now has wide credence, and when I hear good people saying such things, I feel that the religious worldview is being reborn in the secular world—that the old religious apparatus of blasphemy, Inquisition, anathematization, all of that, may be on the way back.

I can and do argue that an open society must permit the expression of opinions that some members of that society may find unpleasant; otherwise, if we agree to censor unpleasant sentiments, we get into the problem of who should be given the power of censorship. *Quis custodiet ipsos custodies,* as the Latin has it. "Who will guard us from the guardians?"

WE LIVE IN THE AGE of an unprecedented attack on truth itself, in which deliberate lies are masked by the accusation that those who would unmask them are the liars. We live in the age of the world turned upside down. The lunatics are running the asylum. This is a time that poses a great test of the notions of free expression for which I've been arguing. But in the end I'll hold to my position. I have nothing but admiration for the diligence with which the news media, under ferocious attack, have held to a vital idea—that the truth is the truth and lies are lies—and have continued to do their work. If these are the enemies of the people, then I am happy to be named among them, for the truth is that the truth, and its tellers, are the people's greatest friends.

If I had stood before you a decade ago, I might have argued here that religious extremism was the greatest threat to liberty we faced. I did not foresee what seems to me to be a secularization of that fanaticism. The Trump phenomenon has all the qualities of a religious cult, in which truth becomes what the leader says it is, and only what he says it is, and in which evil becomes everything that is outside the cult. The cult has its servants, on Fox and on Gab, on Breitbart and in Gingrichland, and they are powerful servants indeed. The cult makes threats, and the threats have consequences, as we are beginning, in this time of horrors, to understand. This is the religion that we must now confront, the delusion we must undo, the prophet we must now debunk. Like the little child at the end of Hans Christian Andersen's story "The Emperor's New Clothes," we too must find a way to say, "But he hasn't got anything on!" Those words broke the spell, you recall, and then the whole town cried out, "But he hasn't got anything on!"

This is the magic that needs to be worked. The magic of the languages of truth is the only magic in which I believe. And I have to believe, we must all believe, that in the end the truth will set us free.

# OSAMA BIN LADEN

O SAMA BIN LADEN DIED IN 2011 JUST AFTER *WALPURGISNACHT*, the night of black Sabbaths and bonfires. A good time for the Chief Witch to fall off his broomstick and perish in a fierce firefight. One of the most common status updates on Facebook after the news broke was "Ding, dong, the witch is dead," and that spirit of Munchkin celebration was apparent in the faces of the crowds chanting "U.S.A.!" outside the White House and at Ground Zero and elsewhere. Almost a decade after the horror of 9/11, the long manhunt had found its quarry, and Americans felt less helpless when they heard the news, and pleased at the message that his death sent: "Attack us and we will hunt you down, and you will not escape." True closure, however, may require more than the killing of one man.

Many of us didn't believe in the image of bin Laden as a wandering Old Man of the Mountains, living on plants and insects in an inhospitable cave somewhere on the porous Pakistan–Afghan border. An extremely big man, six feet four inches tall in a country where the average male height is around five foot eight, wandering around unnoticed for ten years while half the satellites above the earth were looking for him? It didn't make sense. Bin Laden was born filthy rich and died in a rich man's house, which he had painstakingly built to the highest specifications. The U.S. administration confesses it was "shocked" by the elaborate nature of the compound.

We had heard—I certainly had, from more than one Pakistani

journalist—that Mullah Omar was being protected in a safe house run by the powerful and feared Pakistani Inter-Services Intelligence agency, or ISI. (Omar's death was finally announced in 2015, though he may have died as much as two years earlier.) It seemed likely that bin Laden too would have acquired a home of his own, and so he had.

In the aftermath of the raid on Abbottabad, all the big questions need to be answered by Pakistan. The old flimflam ("Who, us? We knew nothing!") isn't going to wash, must not be allowed to wash by countries such as the United States that have persisted in treating Pakistan as an ally even though they have long known about the Pakistani double game—its support, for example, for the Haqqani network that has killed hundreds of Americans in Afghanistan.

This time the facts speak too loudly to be hushed up. Osama bin Laden, the world's most wanted man, was found living at the end of a dirt road eight hundred yards from the Abbottabad military academy, Pakistan's equivalent of West Point or Sandhurst, in a military cantonment where soldiers are on every street corner, just sixty miles from the Pakistani capital, Islamabad. This extremely large house very suspiciously lacked a telephone and an Internet connection. And in spite of this we are supposed to believe that Pakistan didn't know he was there and that the Pakistani intelligence, and/or military, and/or civilian authorities did nothing to facilitate his presence in Abbottabad, while he ran Al Qaeda from his luxury pad, with couriers coming and going, for five years?

Pakistan's neighbor India, badly wounded by the 26/11 terrorist attacks launched from Pakistan against Mumbai, is already demanding answers. As far as the anti-Indian jihadist groups are concerned—Lashkar-e-Toiba, Jaish-e-Muhammad—Pakistan's support for such groups, its willingness to provide them with safe havens, its encouragement of such groups as a means of waging a proxy war in Kashmir and in Mumbai, is established beyond all argument. In recent years these groups have been reaching out to the so-called Pakistani Taliban to form new networks of violence, and it is worth noting that the first threats of retaliation for bin Laden's death have been made by the Pakistani Taliban, not by any Al Qaeda spokesman.

India, as always Pakistan's unhealthy obsession, is the reason for the double game. Pakistan is alarmed by the rising Indian influence in Afghanistan and fears that an Afghanistan cleansed of the Taliban would be an Indian client state, thus sandwiching Pakistan between two hostile countries. The paranoia of Pakistan about India's supposed dark machinations should never be underestimated.

For a long time now, America has been tolerating the Pakistani double game in the knowledge that it needs Pakistani support in its Afghan enterprise and in the hope that Pakistan's leaders will understand that they are miscalculating badly. Pakistan, with its nuclear weapons, is a far greater prize than poor Afghanistan, and the Pakistani generals and spymasters who are playing Al Qaeda's game today may, if the worst were to happen, become the extremists' victims tomorrow.

There is not very much evidence that the Pakistani power elite is likely to come to its senses anytime soon. Osama bin Laden's compound provides further proof of Pakistan's dangerous folly. As the world braces for the terrorists' response to the death of their leader, it should also demand that Pakistan give satisfactory answers to the very tough questions it must now be asked. If it does not provide those answers, perhaps the time has come to declare it a terrorist state and expel it from the comity of nations.

POSTSCRIPT. SINCE HE BECAME PRESIDENT, Donald Trump has talked tough about Pakistan. In August 2017 he declaimed, "We have been paying Pakistan billions and billions of dollars at the same time they are housing the very terrorists that we are fighting. But that will have to change, and that will change immediately. No partnership can survive a country's harboring of militants and terrorists who target U.S. service members and officials." And in January 2018 he tweeted, "They have given us nothing but lies & deceit, thinking of our leaders as fools.... No more!" In practice, however, American policy toward Pakistan hasn't changed, and for the same reason as the one given above: Afghanistan. Washington thinks of Islamabad as a crucial partner in any Afghan peace and reconciliation process, because of the influence Pakistan has over the Taliban—after all, it provided them with safe havens during the war. *Plus ça change.*

# AI WEIWEI AND OTHERS:
## THE 2011 CRACKDOWN
## IN CHINA

———

THE GREAT TURBINE HALL AT LONDON'S TATE MODERN GALLERY, a former power station, is a notoriously difficult space for an artist to fill with authority. Its immensity can dwarf the imaginations of all but a select tribe of modern artists who understand the mysteries of scale, of how to say something interesting when you also have to say something really big. Louise Bourgeois's giant spider *Maman* dominated the hall when it first opened in 2000; Anish Kapoor's *Marsyas*, a huge, hollow trumpet-like shape made of a stretched substance that hinted at flayed skin, triumphed over it majestically in 2002, as, in 2019, did Kara Walker with her giant fountain, the *Fons Americanus*.

In 2010 the leading Chinese artist Ai Weiwei covered the floor with his *Sunflower Seeds* installation: over one hundred million tiny porcelain objects, each handmade by a master craftsman, no two identical. *Sunflower Seeds* is a carpet of life, multitudinous, inexplicable, and in the best surrealist sense, *strange*. The seeds were intended to be walked on, but further strangeness followed. It was discovered that when trampled they gave off a fine dust that could damage the lungs. These symbolic representations of life could, it appeared, be dangerous to the living. The exhibit was cordoned off and visitors had to walk carefully around the perimeter.

Art can be dangerous. Very often artistic fame has proved dangerous to artists themselves. Ai Weiwei's work is not polemical—like *Sunflower Seeds* it tends toward the mysterious—but his immense public prominence as an artist (he was a co-designer of the Bird's Nest Stadium for the Beijing Olympics and was recently ranked at number 13 in *ArtReview* magazine's list of the 100 most powerful figures in art) has allowed him to take up human-rights cases and to draw attention to China's often inadequate responses to disasters (the plight of the child victims of the Sichuan earthquake or those afflicted by the huge fire at Jiaozhou Road, Shanghai). He has embarrassed the authorities and been harassed by them before, but now they have gone on the offensive against him.

On April 4, 2011, Ai Weiwei was arrested by the Chinese authorities as he tried to board a plane to Hong Kong. He disappeared from view. His studio was raided, and computers and other items were removed. The regime allowed hints of his "crimes" to be published—tax evasion, pornography. These accusations are not credible to those who know him. The Chinese regime, irritated by the outspokenness of its most celebrated art export, whose renown had protected him for a long time, had decided to silence him in the most brutal fashion.

On the same day, Wen Tao, a freelance journalist and one of Ai's partners, was kidnapped by several unidentified persons on a street in Beijing, but the police refused to say who was responsible for his disappearance.

The disappearance of Ai Weiwei was made worse by reports that he had started to "confess." His release became a matter of extreme urgency. Nor was Weiwei the only Chinese artist in dire straits that year. The writer Liao Yiwu was denied permission to travel to the United States to attend the PEN World Voices Festival in New York, and we feared that he could be the regime's next target. He was asked to sign a document pledging not to publish any more of his "illegal" works outside China (all of his works, including the great book we know as *The Corpse Walker*, have been banned inside China for years). Publication of a new collection, *God Is Red*, was then imminent in the States and Europe, and there were real worries that he might soon disappear as well. However, he succeeded in leaving China overland, by crossing the border with Vietnam, in 2011, and is now living in Germany.

The writer Ye Du was picked up in February 2011 and, like Weiwei, disappeared. No charges were laid against him. He was not allowed to contact his family or lawyers.

Teng Biao, a writer and human-rights lawyer, was one of several prominent human-rights lawyers who disappeared since February.

Liu Xianbin, a writer, was sentenced to a ten-year prison term for incitement to subversion, the same charge that was laid against the Nobel Peace Prize laureate Liu Xiaobo, who remained in jail until just before his death. Other writers, artists, and activists who were arrested or disappeared in the draconian crackdown include Zhu Yufu, detained since March 5 and formally arrested on April 10; Liu Zhengqing, illegally held incommunicado at an unknown location since March 25 (his wife was also impossible to contact); and Yang Tongyan (sentenced to twelve years) and Shi Tao (ten years).

Not all writers or artists seek or ably perform a public role, and those who do—Harold Pinter, Susan Sontag, Günter Grass, Graham Greene, Gabriel García Márquez, Amos Oz—risk obloquy and derision, even in free societies. Sontag, an outspoken commentator on the Bosnian conflict, was giggled at because she sometimes sounded as if she "owned" the subject of Sarajevo. Pinter's "champagne socialism" was much derided. Grass's high visibility as a public intellectual and scourge of Germany's rulers led to a degree of *schadenfreude* when it came to light that he had concealed his brief service in the Waffen SS as a conscript at the tail end of World War II. García Márquez's friendship with Fidel Castro, and Greene's earlier chumminess with Panama's strongman ruler Omar Torrijos, made them political targets. Amos Oz's determined fight for a two-state solution to the Israeli–Palestinian conflict made him a hate figure for Israeli right-wingers.

When artists venture into politics, the risks to reputation and integrity are ever present. But outside the free world, criticism of power is at best difficult and at worst all but impossible—there are no Chinese Friedmans, Dowds, or Krauthammers. Such creative figures as Ai Weiwei and his colleagues are often the only ones with the courage to speak the truth against the lies of tyrants. We needed the *samizdat* truth-tellers to reveal the ugliness of the Soviet Union. Today the government of China ranks high among the world's biggest threats to freedom of speech, and so we need Ai Weiwei, Liao Yiwu, and Liu Xiaobo.

# THE
# HALF-WOMAN GOD

———

ACCORDING TO GREEK MYTHOLOGY, HERMAPHRODITUS, THE
child of Hermes and Aphrodite, fell so passionately in love with a
nymph named Salmacis that they beseeched Zeus to unite them for
all time and were joined in a single body in which both sexes remained manifest. The Hindu tradition contains, if anything, a more
powerful version of this story, elevated to the very summit of the
Hindu pantheon and glorifying not merely the beauty of the physical
union of the sexes but the union of the male and female principles in
the universe, a metaphor reaching far beyond biology. In a cave on
Elephanta Island in Bombay Harbor is a sculpture of the deity named
Ardhanari, or Ardhanarishvara, a name composed of three elements—
*ardha*, half, *nari*, woman, *ishvara*, god; thus Ardhanarishvara, the
half-woman god. One side of the Elephanta carving is male, the
other female, and it represents the coming together of Shiva and
Shakti, the being and doing forces, the fire and the heat, in the body
of a third, double-gendered deity. A cultural history so rich in the
mighty possibilities of sexual admixture ought by rights to find it
easy to understand and accept not only biological hermaphrodites
but also such contemporary gender-blenders as the hijra community.
Yet hijras have always been, and still are, treated with a mixture of
fascination, revulsion, and fear.

I remember feeling both fascination and fear when, as a young
boy in Bombay long ago, I watched the tall, garish figure of a hijra
mendicant, dressed like a queen of the sea and carrying a long silver

trident, striding proudly through the traffic on Marine Drive. And like everyone else, I saw hijras performing their celebratory blessings at weddings, only half-tolerated by the hosts and guests. They seemed then like visitors from a louder, harsher, brighter, more dangerous world. They seemed . . . alien.

A part of the problem is, of course, the Operation, the reality of which, with its curved knife and long, painful aftermath, is hard to stomach. In John Irving's 1994 novel *A Son of the Circus,* there is a graphic description of what happens. "A hijra's 'operation'—they use the English word—is performed by other hijras. The patient stares at a portrait of the Mother Goddess Bahuchara Mata; he is advised to bite his own hair, for there's no anesthetic, although the patient is sedated with alcohol or opium. The surgeon (who is not a surgeon) ties a string around the penis and the testicles in order to get a clean cut—for it is with one cut that both the testicles and the penis are removed. The patient is allowed to bleed freely; it's believed that maleness is a kind of poison, purged by bleeding. No stitches are made; the large, raw area is cauterized with hot oil. As the wound begins to heal, the urethra is kept open by repeated probing. The resultant puckered scar resembles a vagina." *Ouch.*

Irving also says, "Whatever one thought or said about hijras, they *were* a third gender—they were simply (or not so simply) another sex. What was also true was that, in Bombay, fewer and fewer hijras were able to support themselves by conferring blessings or by begging; more and more of them were becoming prostitutes." These words are still accurate today. And consequently the world of the hijras, already beset by the larger world's distrust, dislike, and distaste, is now also threatened by the increasing danger of HIV infection, and so of AIDS.

THESE ARE THE THREE traditional forms of hijra work: *manti* (or *basti*), that is to say, begging; *badai,* the marriage celebration; and *pun,* the selling of sex. In today's Bombay, with its high-rises, its guards at the gates, its loss of interest in hijra *badai,* its police force that is prepared to arrest beggars and implement the laws against *manti,* which impose a Rs. 1,200 ($15) fine for the offense, only *pun* now offers the chance of earning enough to survive. There is a law against begging, but there are looser laws against sex work. But there are other, greater risks, the risks of infection and death.

The hijra world is remarkably structured and hierarchical. There are seven hijra gharanas (literally "households") in India, like the "families" we know of from Mafia movies, though far less powerful, far less ruthless, far more vulnerable. At the head of each gharana is a naik, or head guru, and these are scattered across India; only one of the naiks lives in Bombay. In each gharana, there descends from the head guru a pyramid of lesser gurus and chelas (disciples), locked together in relationships of protection and exploitation. If a disciple is arrested, the guru will provide bail; if there are quarrels between hijras, and there are often quarrels, the guru will adjudicate and re-solve them. It is not easy to change gurus. It is not easy to alter the hierarchy in any way. To enter the hijra community you need to be introduced by other hijras and given the blessings of naiks and lesser gurus. Once you are in, there is really no way out. The hijra gharana is like a family; and you can't resign from your family.

This family structure is what gives a hijra's life meaning and con-stitutes its greatest appeal. This, they say, more than the transgender-ing, is what draws them in. Only about 60 percent of Bombay hijras actually have the Operation, although, they say, "in Gujarat it is in-sisted upon." (And, by the way, *pace* John Irving, it is not always called "the Operation" in English. The most common word for it is "Nir-vana.") Even more surprising, there are female hijras, women who were born women, who are drawn into the gharanas by the attraction and apparent safety of the hierarchies' substitute for family life. This, they told me over and over again, is what it means to be a hijra: to be a part of your gharana and to serve your guru. The gender thing is secondary. The family rules.

And sometimes the family can be a part of the problem. At the bot-tom of the gharana pyramid, a small guru will give disciples the task of bringing back a certain amount of money every day, and that guru has to pay her guru, and so on up the pyramid. The pressure to earn the daily requirement forces hijras into agreeing to five or six sex acts daily, often hurried and careless. If the client doesn't want to use a condom, sometimes there is no time to argue. And so their vulnerability increases. Those who are there to protect them are in part responsible for their exposure to deadly infection. Such is hijra family life.

Hijras exaggerate their numbers, claiming that there are one hundred thousand of them in Bombay alone. The real figure is probably nearer five thousand for Bombay, with one hundred thousand being closer to the total figure for hijras in the whole of India. They travel a great deal, moving from event to event around the country—one hijra told me she had been in Ghaziabad, Haryana, Nepal, Ajmer, and Gujarat in the previous two months—and, it seems, few hijras settle in their places of origin. Only one of the hijras I met in Bombay was from Bombay, and this is not atypical. Family rejection and disapproval probably accounts for the uprooting. Having re-created themselves as beings whom their original families often reject, hijras will usually take those new identities to new places, where new families form around them and take them in.

MALWANI IN MALAD IS a rough part of town, a dumping ground for convicts half a century ago, a slum zone in which many Bombay hijras now live. Proper housing is a problem. "In Andhra, the chief minister gave housing to hijras, but not here," I was told by the hijras I met. Ration cards are a problem, and, if you can get hold of one, it's a treasure. Without a ration card, or an income-tax card, or a voter-identity card, or a bank account, you don't exist, and the state can ignore you. Not surprising, then, that hijras feel vulnerable, that they fear not only policemen but hospitals too. Doctors are often rude and unhelpful, although, I was told, there are signs of improvement, even among policemen. "Now they call us Madam and don't only give us *galis* (insults)."

A *gut* is a self-help group set up to combat the various risks to hijras, health risks above all. The Aastha *gut* in Malwani is one such group. "It has been very successful. When fifteen people go to the police station because one person has been arrested, then the police behave better." With the help of a *gut*, a group of hijras can become "peer educators" and spread the word through the community. Today there are perhaps seven thousand such peer educators in India, each of whom "tracks" fifty community members, and as a result more and more hijras are being made aware of, and persuaded to visit regularly, health clinics, to be blood-tested.

But much work remains to be done. Condom use by hijras' clients is still low, perhaps only at 50 percent, and even though the fall in gonorrhea and chlamydia infections to below 5 percent shows that the use of condoms is improving matters, the risks remain. The Aastha *gut* makes and disseminates *paan* (betel nut) flavored condoms, and hijras are trained (with the help of attractive wooden penises) to hold the popularly flavored condoms in their mouths and then apply them quickly to the client's member. (I was given a couple of impressively swift and skillful demonstrations of the technique, on, I hasten to add, the wooden members only.)

THE HIJRAS OF MALWANI are worried about their image. "The police have misapprehensions about us."

They are concerned especially about "those people who wear male dress at night but in the daytime, dressed as women, they rob and steal, and so hijras get a bad name." This animosity toward the fake, or *naqli*, hijras was widespread.

"Of course we can all tell the *naqlis*. They run when they see us."

"They smoke beedis and drink alcohol on the street."

"When we ask them who is their guru, they cannot reply."

"They walk like men."

"They do not know the special language." (Hijras have a coded communication made up of words and signals that they can use, for example, to warn of danger.)

"We are not bad," they say. They concede that they are not perfect either. "Even if a few hijras do wrong, do not judge us all by them."

"Nobody goes to steal children from villages [to turn them into hijras]. They say it, but it doesn't happen."

THE HIJRAS I MET mostly "became aware" around puberty; some discovered their nature a couple of years later. Rejection and fear often followed.

"As a child I followed girlish ways and was laughed at and scolded for my girlishness."

"I often thought I should live like a boy, and I tried hard, but I couldn't do it."

"It's in the genes."

"My family always knew but are still in denial."

"Because of family *izzat* (honor), they cast me out."

"My father beat me when I was at college. I said, hit me, what can you do."

"I wouldn't have stayed alive if not for the community. At home I was shouted at, sworn at, everything."

But there are rare exceptions. "I only go at night to visit my family, but I do go."

And there is the beginning of political consciousness. "Women's rights have advocates, but we have no advocates, not even as 'second-grade women.'"

"We also are part of creation."

THANE, THE CITY OF the Lakes, is an altogether more attractive setting than the slums of Malwani, or the red-light district of Kamathipura, where there is a special hijra alley. (It is said that the hijras once owned the whole of the red-light district but had to sell it off, alley by alley, as the gharanas grew poorer.) I went to Thane to meet an exceptional hijra named Laxmi, a hijra of extreme articulacy and force of character. By the Talao Pali Lake in Thane, Laxmi, a local star of sorts, did her "ramp walk" every evening in the old days when she started out. Laxmi is a rarity among hijras; she lives at home and, to avoid upsetting her parents, dresses as a man when she is with them. They call her by her male name, Laxmikant, or by her family nickname, "Raju," and, as a man, she works at home as a *bharat-natyam* teacher. But when she leaves home she is Laxmi, and everyone in Thane knows her.

She is a voluptuous person with purple-black lips; hard to miss. Her beginnings are not unusual. "At nine to ten I told people I'm gay. I was called names. 'Gur.' *Sugar.* 'Meetha.' *Sweetie.* One day in the Maheshwari Gardens I met Ashok. 'Something is wrong with me, what should I do,' I said. 'The world is abnormal,' he told me. '*You* are normal.'"

While she was still at school she went to gay pubs and started to dance for money. "Then fifteen years ago I became First Drag Queen of Bombay." Soon after that she met the woman, Gloria, who opened the door into the hijra world. "My brother is like you," Gloria said. Laxmi met Gloria's brother, the hijra Shabina, at a phone booth in Victoria Terminus in Bombay (now renamed Chhatrapati Shivaji Terminus, or CST, though the old "VT" is still used). "Normally she wore saris, but that day in VT she was wearing jeans." Laxmi took Shabina to the Café Montecarlo. Shabina didn't want to go in. "I took her by the hand. 'You are yourself and should enjoy yourself,' I said. But in the café I told Shabina I used to hate hijras. 'Why do you clap and beg?' I asked her. 'You should do proper work.' Then Shabina explained about the structure, the gharanas. This was attractive to me. This was more than just sex talk."

Shabina took her to meet other hijras, notably Manjula Amma, a.k.a. Fat Manjula, of the Lashkar gharana, of which Lata Naik was the head. Laxmi joined the family. "In Byculla I entered the hijra world. Lata Naik was also there. I was sweating. An old man told me where to go. I saw Lata Naik. She was fifty-five but looked forty-five. There were six frightening hijras around her. They reminded me of Ravana." Ravana is the demon king of the *Ramayana*, who abducted Ram's wife, Sita, to his kingdom, Lanka. "I said, 'I want admission. How much fees? Donations?' Lata Naik laughed. She accepted me, for no money, orally. At that time nothing was written. Lata Naik was the one who later began the process of keeping records. She had beautiful writing; I have seen it in the hijrotic books, which she now maintains."

Before Lata Naik there was Chand Naik. Another naik wanted to be Chand's chela but was abusive to her, and Chand refused her. So there was a split between their two gharanas, which lasted several years, but afterward the two houses were reunited. "When there are such disputes, the Lashkars are always the mediators." Then, thirteen years ago, the splits began again. "When I became a chela, it was the very day before we split. Three of the gharanas on one side, four on the other. The split lasted until just recently. So now people are very excited. There is a big change in mood. The war is over. There is no competitiveness anymore."

LAXMI'S FATHER IS A "U.P. Brahmin military type." He found her transformation very hard to accept, especially as Laxmi was from the beginning a very forward sort of hijra, giving interviews to Zee News and so on. After the Zee TV interview, her father wanted to marry her off. She fought against the marriage and in the end her father wept and gave in. "My father, the pillar of my house. He wept." Her mother's love was never in doubt. "For me, my world is my mother."

Now her parents have accepted her, even to the point of being curious about her breast implants. Once at home she sat bare-chested, having forgotten to put on a T-shirt. Her father scolded her. "If you have made it," he said, "then learn to respect it." "Now," Laxmi says, "my father is my best friend."

LAXMI IS VOCAL, CONFIDENT, self-assured. She wants to be a voice in the HIV/AIDS campaign and to help save what she too calls "the third gender of India." "Hijras have become more vocal," she says, "but the problem is that activists are trying to put us inside the MSM culture." (MSMs are Men who have Sex with Men, and they are of three kinds: *Kothis,* who go on top, *Panthis,* who go on the bottom, and Double Deckers, who need no explanation.) "The MSM sector is getting so strong," Laxmi says. "But we are not simply MSMs. We are not even simply TGs." (Transgendered persons.) "We are . . . hijras. I am carrying a whole culture with me. It's that collective aspect, the hijra culture, that is important. We cannot sacrifice it. We are different."

THE HIJRAS OF BOMBAY and the rest of India are held to be the community most at risk of HIV infection. There have been improvements in organization, outreach, education, and self-help, but for many hijras their lives continue to be characterized by mockery, humiliation, stigmatization, fear, and danger. Laxmi of Thane and the "peer educators" of Malwani may be success stories, hijras who have taken charge of their destinies and are trying to help their fellows, but many hijras are mired in poverty and sickness.

According to the poet–saints of Shaivism, Shiva is *Ammai Appar*, Mother and Father combined. It is said of Brahma that he created humankind by converting himself into two persons: the first male, Manu Svayambhuva, and the first female, Satarupa. India has always understood androgyny, the man in the woman's body, the woman in the man's. Yet the walking Ardhanaris among us, the third gender of India, still need our understanding, and our help.

# NOVA SOUTHEASTERN UNIVERSITY COMMENCEMENT ADDRESS, 2006

THE GREAT FRENCH NOVELIST GUSTAVE FLAUBERT, IN HIS last novel, *Bouvard and Pécuchet*, published in 1881, tells us of the dangers of too much book-learning. The heroes, a pair of foolish, retired clerks, try to run their lives by information gleaned from how-to books, with comic and catastrophic consequences. As you have all spent several years learning things from books, it may strike you as inappropriate that I should commend to you this seditious foreign text containing so radical a denunciation of such studies. Nevertheless, I do commend it to you, if only because of the appendix that Flaubert attached to the main body of the story, the justly celebrated "Dictionary of Received Ideas." Flaubert was fascinated by the general stupidity of most human beings, by their ability to absorb and parrot clichés and other nuggets of fool's gold as if they were the wisdom of the gods. In this dictionary he offers us some fine instances of what Wyndham Lewis named the Moronic Inferno. Here are a few excerpts:

> AMERICA: Fine example of injustice. Columbus discovered it and it is named after Amerigo Vespucci. If it weren't for the discovery of America, we shouldn't have syphilis. . . . Praise it all the same, especially if you've never been there.

ARTISTS: All charlatans ... What artists do can't be called work.

AUTHORS: One should "know a few authors." No need to know their names.

BASES (OF SOCIETY): i.e., property, the family, religion, respect for authority. Show anger if these are attacked.

BEETHOVEN: Don't pronounce Beatoven.

BRUNETTES: Hotter than blondes.

CELEBRITIES: Find out the smallest details of their private lives, so that you can run them down.

CENSORSHIP: A good thing, whatever people say.

DEVOTION: Complain how little other people show.

DOCTRINAIRES: Despise them. Why? Nobody can say.

ENGLISHWOMEN: Express surprise that they can have pretty children.

FRENCH: The greatest people in the world.

GLOBE: Genteel way of referring to a woman's breast.

HOMER: Never existed.

IDIOTS: Those who think differently from you.

IMAGINATION: Be on your guard against it.

INNOVATION: Always dangerous.

ITALY: Is very disappointing.

JUSTICE: Never worry about it.

KORAN: Book by Mohammed, which is all about women.

LIBERTY: "Liberty, what crimes are committed in thy name!" We have all the liberty we need. "Liberty is not license." (Conservative saying.)

STUDENTS: ... never study.

YOUTH: What a wonderful thing it is!

Enough. Life was very different in 1881. Or perhaps not so very different at all.

The real world, to which you are about to return after these years in Florida, is full of wonders and brilliance, I am happy to report, but you will also find yourself beset from every quarter by dreariness and folly.

You may come across genuinely original minds, like the Indian Nobel laureate Professor Amartya Sen, who argues that when we define our identities too narrowly in terms of race, or religion, or class, or nation, or tribe, we "miniaturize" ourselves and make conflict and violence more likely. On the other hand, you may encounter a rival professor, Professor Samuel P. Huntington, telling you that we face a "clash of civilizations" and encouraging you to miniaturize yourself in exactly the way Professor Sen proposes you do not.

How to tell who is right and who is wrong? Are we plural selves who may have much in common with those we are asked to perceive as our Others, or are we singularities, closed to one another, hostile, and never more aggressive than when we believe we are being victimized? Who shall we follow, and—an even harder question—how shall we lead?

You are, or so the dictionary of contemporary received ideas tells us, "the leaders of tomorrow." If you look into the subject of leadership, you will be offered a great deal of instruction, from the unknown satirist who described a leader as someone who turns his back on the people and then claims they are all standing behind him, via the ruthlessness of Machiavelli's *Prince,* in which you will be told that fear is a more effective tool of governance than love, to President George W. Bush, who has memorably said that "a leadership is someone who brings people together" and that, in life, you can't have things both ways, you can't "take the high horse and then claim the low road."

How to distinguish the smart lesson from the dumb utterance? If this is the sort of question you have already been asking yourself, I congratulate you. If it's a line of inquiry you find to be of no value, then party on, dudes. If, however, you find yourself somewhere in between these two poles, then perhaps the following may be of some little use.

Thinking for yourself, the good idea I am here to recommend, is not a "given." You will find yourselves herded in many directions, encouraged or bullied to be a good member of various groups: your family, your country, your profession, your social class, your gender, your fellow baseball fans, your faith. There is a spirit abroad in the world that values collective responsibility more highly than individual liberty.

You will accordingly be urged to receive, and follow, the ideas of one or more groups that will claim you and that will all demand that you value your membership of that group more than any other: that, if offered a single ticket to the World Series on your wife's birthday, you should put your loyalty to your marriage above your love of your team, or the other way around; or, that in a conflict between your religious faith and your country, you should answer the demands of God and reject those of the state. We live in a time of competing group thought, and our ideas of right and wrong, of what is permissible and what must not be permitted, are shaped by such thinking to a degree so alarming that it may have stopped being funny.

In 1938, E. M. Forster wrote this, in "What I Believe": "If I had to choose between betraying my country and betraying my friend, I hope I should have the guts to betray my country." Which is to say that "elective affinities," Goethe's term for the allegiances we choose, rather than those that are foisted upon us, are the basis upon which each of us may construct a valuable, moral, and free self, if we only find in ourselves the courage to do so. And that it may be more instructive to take a look at the ideas and behavior of the unorthodox, the rebels and refuseniks of the world, than to admire those who have marched along with, or even at the head of, the crowd. In 1633 Galileo Galilei was forced by the Catholic Church to recant his heretical notion that the earth went round the sun, an idea it took the Catholic Church a mere 359 years to accept. (On October 31, 1992, Pope John Paul II expressed regret for Galileo's mistreatment.) Nelson Mandela spent twenty-seven years in jail for standing up against apartheid but emerged to change his country, and the world.

If individual freedom is what you're interested in, then heterodoxy, the ability to reject received ideas and stand against the orthodoxies of your time, may help you find your way there.

The power of orthodoxy has not diminished. Governments still routinely accuse their opponents of lacking patriotism, religious leaders are quick to anathematize their critics, corporations dislike whistleblowers and mavericks, the range of ideas available through the mass media diminishes all the time. Yet right and wrong, good and evil, are not determined by power, or by adherence to this or that interest group. The struggle to know how to act for the best is a struggle that never ceases.

Don't follow leaders. Look, instead, for the oddballs who insist on marching out of step. Thank you for listening, and good luck to you all.

# EMORY UNIVERSITY COMMENCEMENT ADDRESS, 2015

———

DEAR CLASS OF 2015, WE HAVE ONE THING IN COMMON: I'M leaving Emory today too, and may I say that I've been coming here a lot longer than any of you. Emory has been good to me, and I hope you think it has been good to you too. I've made good friends and learned a lot. I learned about that weird skeleton Dooley on my first day and I'm sorry not to see him here. Maybe he'll show up.

Thanks mainly to my students, I've been able to listen to music at Blind Willie's and eat tacos on the Buford Highway. Son's Place, where I was taken for great soul food within days of my arrival, is closed now, but I'm sure you've found other places.

On this day a little nostalgia is appropriate, because endings and new beginnings, no matter how exciting, also involve loss, the loss of the past, and it's right to take a moment and grant the past its due.

. . . Okay, now that that's over, I hope you're hungry, because your work here is done and it's time to go out there and swallow the world. That's a great big meal and so you'll need a big appetite.

Here's something Toni Morrison tells her students. "The world is interesting and difficult," she says. "Happiness? Don't settle for that." Now, I don't think Toni Morrison is actually telling you not to be happy—because after all, happiness, or at least the pursuit of happiness, is a constitutional right in America. I think she's telling you that happiness is not enough. Because, there it is, out there, waiting for you: the grand and appalling human reality, its elation, its despondency, its danger, its dentistry. Be greedy for it. Grab great handfuls of it and stuff it in your pockets, your mouths, or wherever you most like stuffing things. The best response to the vastness of the unknown is to be larger than life. If life is, as Toni Morrison says, difficult and interesting, be larger than that. Be more difficult, more interesting, and you'll be fine.

Try not to be small. Try to be larger than life.

One of the things I've learned as a writer is voraciousness. The novelist's art is in many ways a vulgar art, it's about life as it is really lived, it's the opposite of an ivory-tower form. The novelist's job, as I see it anyway, is to plunge his hands as deep into the stuff of life as he can, all the way up to the elbows, all the way up to the armpits, and come up with the stuff of life—what's really going on in people's heads, what music is in there, what movies, what dreams, which Kardashians—and then to deliver his reports.

It's not such a bad plan for life either. (Apart from the Kardashian part. If possible, avoid that part.)

Plunge in. Dive into the deep end. Sink or swim. Well, if possible, don't sink. If you learned anything at Emory, you should have learned how to stay afloat.

The world is full of siren songs luring unwary sailors onto rocks; false promises, fool's gold; foxes, cats, and coachmen luring young people to gluttonous, overindulging Pleasure Island, where, as you'll know if you've seen the movie of Pinocchio, the kids make jackasses of themselves.

Do not make jackasses of yourselves.

Let me tell you the tool you need to avoid that fate: skepticism. You need to have, and refine, and hone, what Ernest Hemingway said every writer needs: a good shit detector. (Once again, good advice for writers turns out to be excellent advice for life.) The world in which you have grown up is unusually full of crap. In the information age, the quantity of disinformation has grown exponentially. If you seek the truth, beware. Maybe you've come across the famous saying of President Abraham Lincoln. "The Internet," Lincoln said, "is full of false quotations."

Listen to your president. Be skeptical about what you swallow. It's good for the digestion. I sometimes think we live in a very credulous age. People are ready to believe anything. God, of course. Shocking how many Americans swallow that old story. Maybe you'll be the generation that moves past the ancient nonsense. Imagine there's no heaven, as John Lennon proposed. Try it. That's one antique truthiness that just maybe you can finally replace with the truth.

But it's not just God. There's also yoga, veganism, political correctness, flying saucers, birthers, 9/11 denialists, Scientology, and, for Pete's sake, Ayn Rand. When the Modern Library asked readers to vote for the best novels of all time, books by Ayn Rand came in at numbers 1, 2, 7, and 8, and books by L. Ron Hubbard—I was going to say fiction by L. Ron Hubbard, rather than nonfictional religious texts, but, hey, what's the difference?—came in at numbers 3, 9, and 10. The only other authors that made it into the top ten were Tolkien, Harper Lee, and George Orwell. If that isn't scary enough, opinion polls regularly show that the most trusted news network in the USA is Fox News. The American appetite for bad fiction, including very bad fiction indeed masquerading as fact—Iraqi weapons of mass destruction, for example, or Hillary Clinton's alleged Benghazi cover-up—seems to be inexhaustible.

Maybe you will be the beady-eyed generation that starts seeing through the disinformation, the badly imagined blah, the lies. If you can do that, if you can scrape away all the layers of gibberish that are being poured daily over the wonders of the world, maybe you'll be the generation that reminds itself that it is, indeed, a wonderful world and gets rid of the various kinds of snake-oil salesmen who are selling a world they made up for their own benefit.

I hope you are. We, my generation, we haven't made such a good fist of our time on earth, and it's right, I think, that I apologize to you publicly for the mess we are leaving, the whole ecological, fanatical, oligarchic mess, in which 1 percent of the country gets everything, while kids are daily being killed for the crime of being black; in which religious bigots in this country think Jesus wants them not to sell cupcakes to gay couples, while religious bigots elsewhere think their god approves of sawing off the heads of innocent men.

We thought of ourselves, my lot, as tolerant and progressive, and we are leaving you an intolerant and retrogressive world. But it's a resilient place, the world, and its beauty is still breathtaking, its potential still astonishing, and as for the mess we've made, you can change it, and I believe you're going to. I have a suspicion you're better than us, you care more for the planet, you're less bigoted, more tolerant, and your ideals may hold up better than ours did.

Make no mistake. You can change things. Don't believe anyone who tells you you can't. Here's how to do it. Question everything. Take nothing for granted. Argue with all received ideas. Don't respect what doesn't deserve respect. Speak your mind. Don't censor yourselves. Use your imagination. And express what it tells you to express.

You have been given all these tools by your education here on this beautiful campus. Use them. These are the weapons of the mind. Think for yourself, and don't let your mind run along tramlines someone else laid down. We are language animals. We are dreaming creatures. Dream. Speak. Reinvent the world.

What a piece of work is a man! How noble in reason, how infinite in faculty! In form and moving how express and admirable! In action how like an angel, in apprehension how like a god! The beauty of the world! The paragon of animals!

Believe it or not: That's you. Happy Commencement Day.

# PART
# FOUR

# THE COMPOSITE ARTIST: THE EMPEROR AKBAR AND THE MAKING OF THE *HAMZANAMA*

————

INDIA, IN THE MID-SIXTEENTH CENTURY. JUST THIRTY-ONE years have passed since a fierce Timurid warlord, Zahiruddin Muhammad Babar of Ferghana in what we would now call Uzbekistan, a descendant of Genghis Khan and Tamerlane and possessor of a surprising literary gift, was unhoused from his native land and swept down from the northwest to establish, by force of arms, a new kingdom in Delhi and to write a magnificent autobiography, one of the first ever written in Asia. Just fourteen years have passed since that warlord's less puissant son Humayun was deposed and fled into ignominious Persian exile, abandoning *his* infant son to be raised by an Afghan uncle. Just two years have elapsed since the fugitive's victorious return and the reestablishment of his dynasty, and just one since the returned monarch fell down a flight of steps and died in a moment of bathetic slapstick, leaving his thirteen-year-old son, the son who barely knew him, to ascend his father's precarious throne. What follows this period of near-perpetual upheaval, almost impossibly, is a time of political stability, economic prosperity, religious tolerance, cultural openness, the rule of law, and an artistic renaissance: the half-century-long reign of one of the most remarkable rulers the world has ever known. Jalaluddin Mohammed, known as "Akbar," "the Great," also called *jahanpanah*, the shelter of the world. In a portrait by one of Emperor Humayun's Persian master artists, Abdus-

Samad, the young Akbar is seen riding confidently in a bullock cart just before he became king. The kid was about to make quite a mark.

The second half of the sixteenth century was one of those exceptional periods, not unlike our own, when the whole world seemed to be changing rapidly, a "hinge moment" in history. The sixteenth century, perhaps unlike our own times, was also a hinge moment in the arts. Akbar's reign coincided almost exactly with that of Queen Elizabeth I of England; he ascended to the throne a year and a bit before her and lived a couple of years longer. In Italy this was the time of the High Renaissance, of Michelangelo and Titian and the poetry of Ariosto. In Spain it was the time of Cervantes and the two parts of *Don Quixote,* and in Elizabethan England, of course, it was the age of Shakespeare. What else of world-changing note? Yes: Sometime in the 1560s, the graphite pencil was invented and was used, originally, for the marking of British sheep.

(The New World, I'm sorry to say, lags behind a little; there is not a great deal of what one might call brilliance there at this time. Francis Drake initiated the slave trade with America in 1562, the Roanoke colony was established in 1584 and vanished by 1590. There is not much else to report.)

Mughal India is at once the "factual" territory of Akbar's court and also the highly fantasized space of the sixteenth-century imagination, filled with warrior princes, cross-dressing princesses, courtly knights, crafty spies, and any amount of witches, demons, and magic.

The West knew very little about the East then. In the poetry of the Renaissance—in, for example, the great narrative verse epic *Orlando Furioso,* by Ludovico Ariosto, and in its precursor, *Orlando Innamorato,* by Ariosto's fellow Ferraran Matteo Boiardo—fantasy makes up for ignorance. A prince can be described by Ariosto as the "ruler of India and Cathay," and it is assumed by the poet that such a nonsense will make enough sense to his readers to be plausible. Verisimilitude is unnecessary, and perhaps not even considered as an option, not even by Shakespeare. Othello, himself a Moor, speaks of meeting, on his travels, not only "Cannibals that each other eat, / The

Anthropophagi," but also "men whose heads / do grow beneath their shoulders." Across Europe, until as late as the seventeenth century, the legend of Prester John, a mighty Christian king whose lost kingdom, home of the Fountain of Youth, existed somewhere amid the Muslims and pagans of the East, was so widely believed that it had almost ceased to be fictional; except that no such king ever existed.

The Eastern imagination, as represented in its art, was as fond of such fancies as the West. Europe in the *cinquecento* was indeed busily exoticizing, "Orientalizing," the East; but that Eastern world was also happily fantasizing and exoticizing itself. Interestingly, the two imaginative universes are essentially the same, or at least overlap to a striking degree, with their mutual emphasis on gallantry and errantry (the hero must always be a wanderer), their fascination with the underhand worlds of the spy and the sorcerer, and their insistence on the physical enlargement of evil. Ogres and giants are to be found behind every rock, dragons fly down from the skies, and leviathans surge up from the deep. The occult arts are everywhere, and so too are echoes and mirrors of many Western folktales. A jinni released from a bottle grants wishes to his liberator, just as the Grimms' magic flounder seeks to please the fisherman who set him free. Magic words open a treasure cave in which a wicked magician will try to imprison the boy Aladdin, just as the Pied Piper of Hamelin's magic opens a rocky mountainside so that children can be captured inside it.

The overcoming of monsters, the desire for an idea of nobility, the love of magic, the need for a quest, the addiction to story: It may be that these are the things the human race has most profoundly in common, that in our dream lives and our waking imaginations we are indeed of one kind. Certainly this is the fabulous world of what may be the greatest artistic masterpiece ever created in India, one of the landmark achievements in the entire artistic canon, the astonishing sequence of fourteen hundred paintings, of which fewer than two hundred now survive, commissioned by the Emperor Akbar soon after his accession and created between 1557 and 1572: the "Adventures of Hamza," or the *Hamzanama*.

At the behest of a monarch who was only fourteen years old when he commanded it and twenty-nine when it was done, and under the supervision of two grand masters of Persian painting, more than one hundred Indian artists worked to complete fourteen large volumes containing one hundred folios each and in doing so created the distinctive manner, technique, and aesthetic of Mughal Indian painting—created it in an extraordinary collective act.

This is how I described it in *The Satanic Verses:*

The Mughals had brought artists from every part of India to work on the paintings; individual identity was submerged to create a many-headed, many-brushed Overartist who, literally, *was* Indian painting. One hand would draw the mosaic floors, a second the figures, a third would paint the Chinese-looking cloudy skies. On the backs of the cloths were the stories that accompanied the scenes. The pictures would be shown like a movie: held up while someone read out the hero's tale. In the *Hamzanama* you could see the Persian miniature fusing with Kannada and Keralan painting styles, you could see Hindu and Muslim philosophy forming their characteristically late-Mughal synthesis.

Akbar's reign was the pinnacle of the Mughal period. (A later Mughal emperor, Aurangzeb, sixth of the six "Great Mughals," Aurangzeb the iconoclast and temple-smasher, did a great deal to damage the culture of tolerance and ecumenicism that Akbar sought to create.) Also—as a footnote to my earlier text—while Akbar as emperor was indeed interested in Hindu philosophy as well as Muslim, and Christian philosophy too—he invited Portuguese Jesuit priests to visit his court from Goa so that his philosophers could engage them in debate—still Akbar as art patron was, I now believe, more interested in uniting all the *regions* of India, not the religions. In the art school and scriptorium we see a coming together of styles, much more important than beliefs.

BEFORE WE GO ANY further forward we must retreat, by several centuries, as a matter of fact, and ask: Who was Amir ("Lord") Hamza? Did he exist or was he a hero of fantasy, like Sinbad or Prester John? The answer is that he was a little of each. The most celebrated historical Hamza was Hamza ibn Abdul Muttalib, who lived in Arabia in the seventh century A.D. and was the beloved uncle, "milk brother," and close companion and adviser of the Prophet Muhammad. Although Hamza was the Prophet's uncle, the two were almost the same age and so grew up together. This Hamza was also much celebrated as a warrior; he was a hero of the Battle of Badr in A.D. 624 and a year later suffered a gruesome fate at the Battle of Uhud (A.D. 625). He was laid low by a javelin thrown by an Ethiopian slave named Wahshi, whose nephew had died at Badr. Then, it is said, the fearsome Hind, wife of the leader of Mecca, Abu Sufyan, cut open Hamza's dead body, took out his liver and heart, and ate them. She also cut off his nose and ears and some limbs and wore them as a victory necklace when she re-entered Mecca in triumph. These blood-soaked details are not without relevance. In the adventures of the fictionalized Hamza, there will be a great deal of bloody business of this type.

After his death, Hamza galloped quickly into legend and became "Amir Hamza," the itinerant hero of the fantastic tales that evolved into the *Qissa*, or history of Amir Hamza, a picaresque saga that never took definitive form and exists in different versions in different languages and countries. It is even possible that some of the Hamza stories predated the "real" Hamza, while others referred to another, quite different Hamza, who at the end of the eighth century battled the similarly legendary caliph of Baghdad, Harun al-Rashid, himself the hero of many tales in *The Thousand Nights and One Night*.

In spite of the association with the Prophet, the fictional Hamza's adventures are almost entirely secular in nature, more interested in sorcery than faith. One celebrated *Hamzanama* cloth—the pictures were, unusually, painted on cotton, not on paper—depicts the arch-villain Zumurrud Shah fleeing from the hero Hamza, flying through the air on an unusual form of transport: an enchanted flying urn sent to him by his sorcerer friends. There is very occasionally a mighty feat of piety. Another cloth shows Amir Hamza's ally, Prince Said Farrukh-Nizhad, singlehandedly lifting an elephant, a feat that so impresses two of his enemies that they straightaway convert to Islam; however, as you see, even in this story of belief conferring superhuman strength on the believer, the fabulous overwhelms the spiritual. For the most part, the spiritual dimension is absent from Hamza's adventures, both in story and picture form. The subject of Islam's victory over Zoroastrian sun-worshippers and other lowlifes is present as an underlying theme, but it rarely surfaces, though when it does, it does so in awe-inspiring fashion—for example, in the picture that shows the sea drying up, leaving behind all manner of fabulous, beached marine creatures, while pagan idols seem to voluntarily smash themselves, all this to celebrate the birth of the Prophet Muhammad.

In many of the surviving images, the faces have been erased. After the Mughals fell into decline, the seven books of the *Hamzanama* were broken up and the fourteen hundred pictures went on voyages as dangerous as those of the heroes and villains they depict. More than twelve hundred of the fourteen hundred have been lost, presumed destroyed. Of the surviving fewer than two hundred, many have been, literally, defaced, by the hands of adherents to a stricter idea of Islam than Akbar's, men—for they were surely men—opposed to the whole idea of representative art and determined to erase that most scandalous of things, the image of the human face. The defacings may not even have been officially ordered; some of the *Hamzanama* treasures ended up in public places, in cheap hostelries and coffeehouses across the Muslim world, and any angry hand could have scratched the faces away. The best-preserved of the surviving pictures are those that for a long time found safe haven in Persia, where, contrary to much present-day hullabaloo, few objections were made to the art of figuration, and even the Prophet himself was a frequent subject for painting.

The "frame story" of Hamza, such as it is, begins with a Mesopo-tamian king, Anoshirvan of Ctesiphon, who is told of a vision that a still-unborn child in Arabia will overthrow him. He sends a lieuten-ant on a terrible mission—to kill all the pregnant women in Arabia. Hamza is one of the lucky fetuses to escape this devastation. He grows up to become a master of the arts of war and Anoshirvan hears of him, lures him to his court, and even offers him his daughter's hand in marriage. The love of the princess Mihr-Nigar and Hamza will, however, remain unconsummated for about twenty years, partly because Anoshirvan sends him on a series of dangerous missions, and partly because—ahem—the hero spends eighteen years among the fairies and somewhat caddishly has a daughter with a fairy prin-cess named Asma, or Asman Peri. Eventually, however, Hamza and Mihr-Nigar are reunited.

The rest of the saga is a torrent of episodes of derring-do, in a world characterized by the frequent interventions of magic and also by the importance of *ayyars:* spies. In image after image of the *Ham-zanama,* spies enter palaces and decapitate guards, or bring vital in-formation back to their masters, and in general slither and hiss around the edges of the scene. In one tragic scene—the faces have been erased—an *ayyar* who has misunderstood his orders from King Anoshirvan of Ctesiphon enters the pavilion of the sleeping Qubad, Hamza's son, and cuts his throat. The *ayyar's* name, appropriately enough, can be translated as "Rug-" or "Cloth-Eared."

Sorcery and treachery are the true poles of this world, while faith and unbelief, good and evil, trail some way behind.

THE COLLECTIVIST APPROACH OF the emperor's painting studio and scriptorium may at first sight seem strange to students trained in the concepts and methods of Western art. The philosophy of Akbar's studio seems to offer a marked contrast to the humanist, individualist sensibility that had emerged as the dominant philosophy of the Re-naissance. In Renaissance Italy, the strength of the hand of the indi-vidual artist was everywhere celebrated and admired, and "genius" was a quality highly prized by patrons of the arts. There were many similarities between the two worlds, however: In both East and West, the artist still depended on the patronage of the powerful and high-born, of princes and popes. And all leading Renaissance artists had apprentices in their studios, apprentices who made their tools and mixed their paints for them—egg tempera in the early Renaissance, oil paint later on—and who were also permitted to work on minor parts of the masters' canvases. Leonardo da Vinci was apprenticed to Andrea del Verrocchio, and Michelangelo worked under Ghirlandaio. Nor was this kind of collective production limited to the world of painting. Elizabethan theater too was frequently collaborative, as we know; even Shakespeare collaborated, most probably with John Fletcher, on *Henry VIII* and *The Two Noble Kinsmen,* and a certain George Wilkins is the probable author of Acts One and Two of *Pericles.*

Still, an essential difference remains. European art in the sixteenth century already had what one might call an established star system. Giorgio Vasari's *The Lives of the Artists* deals constantly with the subject of fame, which turns out to be not as modern a preoccupation as one might think. "Michelangelo's fame," Vasari tells us, "was grown so great that in the year 1503, when he was twenty-nine years of age, [Pope] Julius II sent for him to come and build his tomb." Or again, soon after the painting of the *Mona Lisa,* Vasari has this to say of Leonardo da Vinci: "By the excellence of the works of this most divine of artists his fame was grown so great that all who delighted in art, and in fact the whole city, desired to have some memorial of it." Indeed, one of the underlying themes of Vasari's book is that the fame of artists could enhance the fame of their noble patrons, the cities where they lived, and the country itself.

Few of the hundred-plus artists assembled by Akbar the Great to work on the *Hamzanama* achieved anything remotely like this degree of personal celebrity. The two Persian grand masters brought to India by Akbar's father, Humayun, on his return from exile, and appointed by Akbar to supervise the studio, were certainly considered to be bright lights in Akbar's court of philosophical, musical, and political luminaries; but neither of them was named as one of the *Navratnas,* or "Nine Jewels," of Akbar's court, among whom were the noble and legendarily witty Birbal; Akbar's finance minister, Raja Todar Mal; his general Raja Man Singh; the historian Abul-Fazl; the poet Faizi; the musician Mian Tansen; the mullah Abul Hasan "Do Piaza" ("Two Onions"), priest, gourmet, and cook, creator of the famous dish Mutton Do Piaza . . . but no painters. In an early portrait, probably a self-portrait, the first head of the studio, Mir Sayyid Ali, showed how Indian Mughal painting would develop its own distinctive characteristics as it moved away from the formalist, decorative, "flatter" world of Persian art. In his work we see the beginnings of a third dimension, of spatial depth, and in the (Indian, not Persian) clothing and physical form of the figure we also see the arrival of volume. This is a key precursor to the style of the *Hamzanama* and establishes Mir Sayyid Ali as its prime begetter.

His fellow Persian, Abdus-Samad, was originally his deputy and then, in the closing years of the long project, took over as head of the studio when Mir Sayyid Ali asked for and received permission to make the pilgrimage to Mecca. He was fully equal to the task, as that early work depicting the boy king Akbar seated in a bullock cart showed. In the accurate but two-dimensional modeling of the animals, in the delicate patterning of the wooden screen around the seat, and in the style of the facial painting, we see that at this very early date Abdus-Samad is still using a more or less Persian style. At the other end of his life, two great masterpieces show how far he had come as a result of the *Hamzanama* project. A portrait painted after Akbar's death, during the reign of his son Prince Salim, who assumed the regnal title of Jehangir, is of the Persian king, Jamshid or Jamshed, who according to tradition was the builder of Persepolis. It shows figures with volume, faces full of depth and character, a genuinely three-dimensional depth of field, and a freedom in the nature painting that adds immensely to the life of the work; and in Abdus-Samad's delightful portrait of two camels fighting, the realistic energy of the combat has moved a long way from the stylization of the Persianate manner.

As for the rest of the artists, as we shall see, several do emerge as "named" painters credited with the major work on this or that *Hamzanama* painting, but undoubtedly the aesthetic, perhaps even the ethic, of this fourteen- or fifteen-year project was one that placed the value of the individual contribution beneath the value of the work as a whole. The artists of the *Hamzanama* did not attain anything like the social status of their Western counterparts, their rank being more like that of artisans, equivalent, for example, to the master masons who in this same period began the construction of an architectural masterpiece, the great sandstone miracle that is the palace-city of Fatehpur Sikri, the first permanent capital city that the Mughals ever built, today about an hour away from Agra by car. In many cases the artists ranked even lower than that; scores of the hardworking and highly skilled members of that studio and scriptorium remain forever nameless: many of the calligraphers who inscribed the tales of the adventures of Amir Hamza on the folios, many of the brilliant decorative artists who painted the spectacular borders around each image, and certainly all of the craftsmen who constructed these seven very complex volumes, setting the painted images (painted on cotton fabric) within the painted paper borders, affixing paper strips to both sides of the page to strengthen the joins, and placing three intermediate layers of paper, fabric, and paper again between the recto and verso sides of each folio for further reinforcement, and in general doing the work without which not even two hundred of the fourteen hundred images would have survived. All these must find their immortality where they can, in the living pages of the *Hamzanama* itself, but their stories are lost.

As a result of this emphasis on the group over the individual, we can perhaps say—as we cannot say of the patrons of Renaissance art—that the true "Overartist" of the *Hamzanama* project was none other than the Emperor Akbar himself. There is no answer in the historical record to the question of why the young king, newly ascended to the throne, made it his business so early in his reign to command so large an assembly of artists and then commission so massive a project. But there is, perhaps, an answer to be found in

Akbar's character and in his idea not only of the kind of ruler he wished to be but the kind of country he wished to rule over.

"Akbar," meaning "great," was not, let us remember, Akbar's name; yet from his youngest days it is what he was called, and legendary feats of physical prowess, even in childhood, were soon ascribed to him. "Greatness" was always at the heart of Akbar's project. He wanted to be a great man and a great king and understood that in order to be those things he must rule over a great people. Akbar, in other words, wanted to invent a kingdom worth ruling over, a kingdom whose pillars would be tolerance, reconciliation, and union. It is perhaps in that spirit that the studio and scriptorium were created; they formed, if you like, miniature models of the ideal state, in which creativity and genius were placed at the service of unity and togetherness. The "greatness" of the *Hamzanama* was to lie precisely in its plurality, in its multiplicity of talents, and in its ability to harness and shape those very diverse elements into a single harmonious whole. The task Akbar set Mir Sayyid Ali and Abdus-Samad was exactly the same, in its way, as the task he would set himself all his life, and the *Hamzanama* was the artistic reflection and glorification of his philosophy.

Why were the adventures of Hamza chosen as the subject for the grand undertaking? Clearly because he was a storied hero, perhaps also because his persona was part historical, part legendary—in other words, not at all dissimilar to the kind of "Akbar" that Akbar wished to create. Also, I think, because the tradition of the saga of the wandering hero, in which that hero overcomes great obstacles, defeats mighty foes, wins the hand of fair damsels, and triumphs over improbable odds is, inevitably, also a story of *becoming*, of attaining by deeds the stature, the worth, that only dragon-slayers and fairy-kissers can truly possess. Hamza's story is not a quest story in the traditional form and differs in this respect from, say, the Arthurian grail story or the Labors of Hercules or even the Persian quest myth, Attar's *The Conference of the Birds* (in which thirty birds set out to find their god, the Simurgh, and after many trials they arrive at the summit of Mount Qâf, where the god is said to live, to be told that the word "Simurgh" means "thirty birds"—i.e., that having made their great journey they have become the god they sought); but still it is a tale of magnification by one's works. Hamza's greatness is not merely shown in his deeds: It is actually the product of those deeds. Again, the fictional hero on his winged and three-eyed fairy horse, Ashqar, looks very like a model for the real boy king, as, for example, he sits upon his magic steed below the fortress of his enemy and challenges him to battle in the time-honored manner, that is, by the exchange of insults. (A convention that calls to mind the French abuse of the English knights in *Monty Python and the Holy Grail*, or its Broadway reincarnation as *Spamalot*: "Go and boil your bottom! . . . I blow my nose at you! . . . I don't wanna talk to you no more, you empty-headed animal-food-trough wiper! I fart in your general direction! Your mother was a hamster and your father smelled of elderberries!" Although I'm sure it was put more elegantly in Farsi.)

The Akbar who commissioned the *Hamzanama* was the king, but he was not yet the full master of his realm. For the first six years of his reign his territories were ruled by regents, first by his senior general, Bairam Khan, and afterward by his aunt and nurse Maham Anga and her son Adham, Akbar's foster brother. The machinations of the dreadful Maham Anga against the honorable Bairam Khan; Bairam's death, while he was traveling on the Haj, at the hands of a vengeful Afghan whose father had died in battle against Bairam years earlier; and the subsequent vile, rapist, bloodthirsty behavior of Adham Khan could all have come directly from the folios of the *Hamzanama*. The crisis came in 1562, when Adham Khan attacked Akbar's designated prime minister and then "laid hands" upon the nineteen-year-old emperor himself. Akbar was a big young fellow and did not lack the lethal decisiveness of a king. He knocked Adham Khan down, had him thrown off a building, and then, when that failed to kill him, ordered him to be thrown off again, headfirst this time. After that he assumed full control of the throne.

It will be seen from this that (a) real life in the sixteenth century was not so very unlike the artists' fantasy world and (b) that for six years the young Akbar had more time on his hands than he would ever have again once Adham Khan had taken his second dive. In that period of the regencies, the first half of the *Hamzanama* folios were completed, and as Akbar was always one for detail, always a hands-on ruler, one can with some certainty surmise that he was frequently involved in the supervision and criticism of the work in progress. Certainly he was becoming well acquainted with surreal levels of villainy. It's easy to believe that the fantastic nature of the *Hamzanama*, with its very Persian fondness for dragons, arose in response to a teenager's love of the fabulous and magical, a young fellow's interest in the wonder tale. Dragons were everywhere in the Persian literature of the time, and India's finest artists took to them with a will. In a picture designed and primarily drawn by one of the great discoveries of the Akbari school, the painter Dasavanta—originally a palanquin bearer's son fond of drawing graffiti on walls, graffiti that led Akbar to include him in the studio—we see a particularly magnificent dragon being slain by Hamza's great friend the spy, or *ayyar*, Umar, who throws a vial of naphtha at it and sets it on fire.

There is a conventional wisdom about the life of the emperor, which holds that while the young Akbar may well have been entranced by worlds of fantasy, he grew up to put aside such childish things, moving away from the dragon world to one of philosophy and wisdom. In other words, the "real" world supplanted that of dreams. I myself don't accept this somewhat simplistic portrait of a life, of any life, as a journey from childhood imagination to adult realism. In the first place, as I have tried to suggest, the "real" facts of Akbar's life make a picture of a "real" world containing most of the salient features of the *Hamzanama* cloths, give or take a dragon or two, a spotted ogre here and there. In the second place, as I've said, we are all dreaming creatures, who continually live, in part, in our dreams—dreams of what could be, for ourselves and our children, even our dreams of what is the case, dreams in which our husbands grow more charming, our houses finer, and our prospects richer than they are—dreams without which our daily lives might be intolerable. And to dream is also to create, and certainly no monarch as richly creative as Akbar could be said to have grown into a man who lost touch with his imagination. The *Hamzanama* should not be seen as depicting a boy's fancies but as a great man's grand, and often Machiavellian, vision of the world in which he lived.

THE PRINCIPAL ARTISTS OF the *Hamzanama,* other than Mir Sayyid Ali, Abdus-Samad, and the previously mentioned palanquin bearer's son and graffiti artist Dasavanta, were Basavana, Shravana, Madhava Khurd, Mahesa, and Kesava Das, followed in importance by Mah Muhammad, Tara, Jagana, Lalu, Mithra, and Mukhlis.

(Mah Muhammad, one of the secondary artists, is interesting because of his gift for painting architecture. In his fantasy palaces we see the birth of the style that would become reality at Fatehpur Sikri.)

The collaboration on a single image could be very close indeed. In a picture of the giant Landhaur from Sri Lanka being abducted in his sleep by a *dev,* or bad fairy, the collaboration is between Dasavanta and Shravana. In this case Dasavanta is responsible for the design, for the clothing of the sleeping Landhaur, with its three-dimensionality and brightly colored and patterned pajamas, and for the figure of the *dev,* one of the many *Hamzanama* beasties or wild things of which Maurice Sendak would have been proud. Shravana is responsible for the painting of the bed on which Landhaur sleeps and probably for the softly modeled rocks in the corner of the painting. The flat Persianate plant life may be by yet a third hand. So we begin to see how these disparate talents come together.

One of the most famous *Hamzanama* images, in which a sea monster attacks Hamza and his men, is a collaboration between Basavana and Shravana. (Hamza has fired an arrow at the creature, and it has lodged in its eye, enraging it.) The human figures are by Shravana, and the clothing and the sea monster by Basavana.

One of Hamza's greatest adversaries in the *Hamzanama* is the giant Zumurrud Shah, the "king of the East." He suffers a number of terrible adversities at the hands of Hamza and his allies. In one well-known image he has mysteriously fallen into a large hole and is being beaten by "suspicious gardeners." The ingenious design, which places Zumurrud Shah in a circular frame (the hole) within the larger frame of the picture, and the figure painting are the work of Kesava Das. The rest of the picture is by other, unidentified hands. Once again, we see that this many-handed approach fails to create the messy effect one might expect; the different skills—the landscape painting, the figure painting, the architecture painting, the modeling of the clothes—all merge seamlessly into a whole. Sometimes, as the artists study one another, their talents begin to blend, and it is difficult to identify which hand is at work. One of the great achievements of the *Hamzanama* to my mind lies in its discoveries about the representation of non-solid, mutating things like water and clouds. The techniques by which fluidity was represented were a genuine innovation of Akbar's studio, and all the artists seem to have wanted to try their hand at the new method. In one image of a flood released by an enemy into Hamza's camp, the floodwaters are expressively painted by Jagana; in a closely succeeding picture, the foe, Tayhur Shah, has been slain, and this time the floodwaters are the work of Shravana. And in a picture showing the rescue of an abandoned baby, the water and the majority of the picture (though not the background architecture) are by a third artist, Kesava Das. Showing his mastery of all fluid forms, Kesava Das also offers an extraordinary cloudy sky above an image of an unidentified and somewhat overweight hero killing a big-eared female demon. The brilliance of the sky, with its sinuous, abstract forms of cloud and air, draws the eye toward it, actually overwhelming the scene below.

Finally, even Mah Muhammad, usually limited to architecture painting, gets into the act, and in an image of the heroine and famous archer Mihrdukht, Hamza's daughter-in-law, escaping in a boat from unwanted suitors (having told them she will have whichever one first retrieves an arrow she has fired), the water and landscape painting is by Mah Muhammad; the figures are attributed to another *Hamzanama* artist, Banavari.

It would be wrong to omit the many daring and often bloody acts of the *ayyars,* spies, from any study of the work of the *Hamzanama* "composite artist." We have already spoken of the murder of Hamza's son Qubad by one such *ayyar;* again, in an unusually beautiful image notable for Dasavanta's modeling of the seawater—it's Dasavanta this time—the *ayyar* Umar, one of Hamza's closest allies, embarks on a search for the hero, who has at this point in the story been taken captive. Umar, always drawn as rather an elegant young man, is capable of rough work. In a scene outside Fulad Castle, he is shown by Kesava Das (the figures) and Mah Muhammad (the architecture, inevitably) kicking a soldier to extract information from him. And Umar's colleagues, Hamza's other *ayyars*, are perfectly ready to kill, sneaking into an enemy palace and decapitating the guards.

Even female *ayyars* such as Mahiya, a spy for another of Hamza's sons, Prince Ibrahim, are enthusiastic murderers. In a spectacular image by Jagana and Kesava Das, Mahiya is seen at the very center of the picture cutting one man's throat while two others lie decapitated and no fewer than five more are scattered around, slain. All this on one of the most ornately beautiful pieces of mosaic and other decorative patterning to be found in the entire work.

Another female *ayyar*, Khosh-Khiram, wanders through a wood, idly holding the severed head of yet another spy, Kajdast, in a beautiful composition, part sylvan, part palatial, created by Basavana and Mukhlis.

You get the picture.

IN THE UNIVERSE OF the *Hamzanama*, opposites coexist: violence and beauty, realism and phantasmagoria, heroism and villainy. This too is an attempt to create a composite: not only a composite artist but a composite world. In these exquisite folios the project seeks to depict all that life itself contains, and much that the living can only imagine in nightmares or in dreams. And much ogre life, and animal life, and a little divine life as well.

The hero Hamza is also a composite self—not only created by the joining of several different "originals," he is in part a man of the world, seeking to overcome the obstacles placed in the path of his true love for the princess of Ctesiphon, Mihr-Nigar, and in part a wanderer in a faery realm, lover of *peris*, fairies, and enemy of their rival *devs*. His fairy love, Asma, or Asman Peri (*asman peri* means "heaven fairy"), represents his love of the world of fancy, just as his earthly love represents his love of the real world; and in this too he represents the king who commissioned the work that was to become, exactly as Akbar had planned, one of the great ornaments and glories of his reign.

ALL THESE THINGS HAPPENED a very long time ago. But history is a contested space, nowhere more so than in India (but by no means only there). The battle over the past is inevitably a battle for the present. The history of the Muslim conquests of India, of which the Mughal Empire was the last and most illustrious, has become in recent times the subject of much bitter dispute. The growth, in the past three decades or so, of a form of aggressive Hindu revisionism has led to claims that Muslim India was somehow *inauthentic*, that the Muslim dynasties crushed and stifled the "true" Hindu India and had an effect that was both crippling and distorting. This highly negative view of the period has even begun to find its way into textbooks. As part of its Hindu supremacist project, the BJP government is seriously, deliberately, engaged in the business of rewriting and falsifying history. And in an age when the militancy of modern Islam may persuade some people that perhaps those Hindu revisionists were not so very wrong, the *Hamzanama* images become important evidence in the debate.

In the reign of the Emperor Akbar, Indian civilization rose to heights it had never before attained, and to say this is not to undervalue the achievements of, say, the great southern Hindu kingdom of Vijayanagar, which was declining as the Mughals rose. And thanks to the exceptional personality of the king, that civilization was marked by, and is still remembered for, a spirit of genuine philosophical inquiry, an atmosphere of tolerance, and a process that included all Indians, of all regions, and all religions. India without its Mughal past would be much less than it is today. Whether the reign of Akbar was a brilliant interlude or an important landmark is a subject for another day. Until that day, the many-headed, many-brushed composite artist of the *Hamzanama* stands before us as a sign of what human beings can achieve when their creativity is brought together in a common cause.

# AMRITA SHER-GIL:
# LETTERS

———

IN THE EARLY 1990S, WHEN I BEGAN TO THINK ABOUT MY novel *The Moor's Last Sigh*, I soon realized that it would contain an account of the character (and also the work) of an entirely imaginary twentieth-century Indian woman painter. I thought about my friendships and acquaintanceships with a number of fine contemporary artists—Krishen Khanna, Bhupen Khakhar, Gulam Mohammad Sheikh, Nilima Sheikh, Nalini Malani, Vivan Sundaram, Anish Kapoor—and of others I did not know personally but whose work I admired—Pushpamala N., Navjot, Sudhir Patwardhan, Gieve Patel, Dhruva Mistry, Arpana Caur, Laxma Goud, Ganesh Pyne. The work of all these painters helped me think about the pictures my fictional "Aurora Zogoiby" might create. But the figure that, so to speak, "gave me permission" to imagine her personality, to invent a woman painter at the very heart of modern art in India, to believe in the possibility of such a woman, was an artist I never met, who died tragically young, and whom I first encountered in a luminous painting by Vivan Sundaram, her nephew. That artist was Amrita Sher-Gil.

The painting is of a family at home. A male figure stands brooding in the background, a Western woman sits stiffly on a chair (and there is a pistol on a table at her side). The room is rich in furnishings and art, and the whole is portrayed in a palette of glowing oranges and golds. But for all the lushness and mystery of the scene, the eye is drawn to the young woman in the foreground, strikingly beautiful, faintly smiling: an intelligent, amused face. This is Amrita.

I did not know much about her in those days. I knew she was half Hungarian, and I had seen some of her paintings of scenes of village life—storytellers, young girls—both in the National Gallery in Delhi and at Vivan's home. And while I was writing my book I resisted knowing more. I conjured up an imaginary Amrita for myself—a woman much influenced by Gandhian ideas, who dedicated herself to painting the "true" life of India, the life of the villages—and decided that my Aurora would be in many ways her antithesis, an unrepentant urbanite and sophisticate. It was only after the book was done that I permitted myself to know the real Amrita a little better, and I discovered at once that she and my Aurora had much more in common than I suspected. Indeed, in some ways—her sexual proclivities, for example—Amrita Sher-Gil was a more bohemian, less inhibited figure than the flamboyant woman I had made up.

In her letters, the real Amrita leaps from the page. "You will think I am self-opinionated," she writes in 1934, aged just twenty-one, "but I will stick to my intolerant ideas and to my convictions." Her outspokenness, which makes her so very much the sister, not the antithesis, of Aurora Zogoiby, is one of the most delicious aspects of her correspondence. She praises Rabindranath Tagore, but she also says, "His eminence is due to the surrounding flatness of the country." Her anger at the philistinism of the nizam of Hyderabad leads her to speak bluntly to his face:

> He has millions of rupees worth of *junk* at the same time as beautiful jade and good Mogul and Rajput paintings in his palace . . . and when I saw the Lord Leightons, the Wattses, the Bouguereaus amassed there and everybody in the party spouted admiration and praise, I felt so sick that when he asked me what I thought of them I asked him in return how on earth anybody with any taste could buy Leighton, Bou-

guereau and Watts when there were Cézannes, Van Goghs and Gauguins in the market.

After this he unsurprisingly refuses to buy her two "Cubist" pictures, and she is "of course furious."

Writing to her close friend and ally Karl Khandalavala, she talks about his art criticism in terms that might have damaged a lesser friendship:

One has an impression of a lucid impersonal account written by an objective person, the possessor of a calm and collected mind. And while one is reading it one is inclined to say aloud "quite so" but as soon as one has laid it aside one forgets it. That is to say "it creates no powerful or lasting impression on the mind." It is too moderate in its *mode* of expression (perhaps the fault lies in your choice of words).

Her most heightened contempt is reserved for the artists of the Bengal School, whom she compares dismissively to the ancient Ajanta cave painters:

Ajanta is painting with a *kernel*, the painting of the Bengal School has only got a shell, it is a lot of things built round nothing, a lot of unessential things and it would cease to exist if those unessential things were taken away from it.

She admits that Jamini Roy has "a certain talent" but refuses to allow his line to be compared to the masters of Ajanta either.

This ferocity of mind and sharpness of tongue, combined with an unashamed openness about her own behavior and an insistence on her right to behave as she chooses, are also present in her thoughts about her family and friends. When her father ("Duci") hesitates about her proposed return to India from Europe and accuses her of lacking interest in India, she delivers herself of an extraordinary text that is at once an artistic testament and an assault on her father's narrower mores of social and sexual conduct:

> I wish to return primarily in interest of my artistic development. . . . How utterly mistaken you are when you speak of our lack of interest in India, in its culture, its *people*, its literature, all of which interest me profoundly. . . . Our long stay in Europe has aided me to *discover*, as it were, India. Modern Art has led me to the comprehension and appreciation of Indian painting and sculpture. It seems paradoxical, but I know for certain that had we not come away to Europe I should perhaps never have realized that a fresco from Ajanta or a small piece of sculpture in the Musée Guimet is worth more than the whole Renaissance! In short, now I wish to go back to appreciate India and its worth. . . . I was rather sad to realize that you place the conservation of your good name above your affection for us. I was also disappointed to know what a place of importance you give to the bickering of public opinion. . . . I don't in the least consider myself an immoral person, I am *not* immoral. . . . Besides I think you are rather dramatizing the situation (a thing you are apt to do at times) when you say that the ruin of your good name is synonymous with our returning to India. Fools and mischief-makers will always talk, even if one doesn't give them food for it. And there are narrow-minded, prejudiced and fanatical people all over the world, in India too (as you found out at your expense) but need one bother about *them*?

She chides her mother too, first for maltreating servants and later, as that troubled lady descends into mental instability, for her lies.

> She charges us indiscriminately with every vice, criminal ingratitude being the least of them, of filth, sloth and abnormal sexual manias.

Caught between a cold, conventional father and an increasingly deranged mother, Amrita takes refuge in an artistic vision remarkable not only for its outspokenness but for its passionate love of what is beautiful. In a letter to her sister Indu, she tells of frescoes found in Cochin:

I spend my days from morning till evening—that is to say till the light fails—at a deserted palace here. It contains some perfectly marvelous old paintings that haven't been "discovered" yet. Nobody knows about them and the local people—even so-called responsible people like the Diwan—would destroy them I am sure if that were in their power because some of the panels depict erotic scenes. Animals and birds are copulating with the utmost candor but curiously enough the human figures are never depicted in the act. . . . It is only when one starts copying them that one realizes what an astounding technique these people had and what an amazing knowledge of form and power of observation they possessed. Curiously enough unlike the slender forms of Ajanta the figures are extremely massive and heavy here. The drawing perhaps the most powerful I have ever seen.

The Cochin frescoes return in a passionate letter to Karl Khandalavala, and it is clear they influenced her deeply, just as Brueghel did, and Renoir. She became convinced that "*all art, not excluding religious art,* has come into being because of sensuality: a sensuality so great that it overflows the boundaries of the mere physical."

Her taste in art is impeccable, whether it be European literature (Rousseau, Verlaine, Proust) or the majesty of the Ellora carvings and Ajanta cave paintings ("Dear Karl, ELLORA, AJANTA. Revelation"). Her taste in human beings is good too: "I have met a wonderful woman at last, Sarojini Naidu. And her two interesting daughters. One . . . who is intelligent and witty, and her younger sister who looks the older of the two—a strange wild creature, *sympathique comme tout.*" (Sarojini Naidu was an important figure in the independence movement, a political activist and a poet whose work earned her the nickname "the Nightingale of India.")

A woman like Amrita could perhaps not be expected to be happy in such a time. She writes to Indu in March 1941:

> I . . . have passed through a nervous crisis and am still far from being over it. Feeling impotent dissatisfied irritable and unlike you not even able to weep. There seem to be forces at work—elemental forces—disrupting, throwing things out of equilibrium. The chaos and darkness of the lives of individuals—the wars earthquakes floods—all seem to be indefinably interconnected. We are not alone. I see it everywhere.

(But then, a few lines on, she finds time to criticize her sister's handwriting—"you must make an effort to render it *lisible*"—and to be glad that a new divan "looks lovely.") Six months later she was dead, aged just twenty-eight, of a cause that remains uncertain.

It is immensely moving to encounter, in Amrita's letters, this impassioned, opinionated, brilliant voice that spoke so clearly but for such a brief time. To return to her paintings after this reading is to find new depth in her somber palette, all earth tones and shadows. She writes, only partly ironically, of choosing to depict

> principally the sad aspects of Indian life . . . It may be that the sadness; the queer ugliness of the types I choose as my models (which to me is beauty that renders insipid all that which according to the standards of the world goes under the category of the word "Beautiful") corresponds to something in me, some inner trail in my nature which responds to things that are sad, rather than to manifestations of life which are exuberantly happy or placidly contented.

Amrita Sher-Gil's is an art that moves naturally toward the melancholy and tragic, while keeping its eye fixed firmly on high ideals of beauty. That it, and she, were so often misunderstood is poignant, but not, perhaps, surprising. In a letter from abroad, written to her parents in August 1938 after they had burned a "roomful" of her letters, including old love letters, she resigns herself to a

> bleak old age unrelieved by the entertainment that the perusal of old love letters would have afforded . . .

and ends, piteously, in Hindi: *Me kohi aysi baat nahin kahungi ya karungi jisse aap ko dukh pahunje.* "I will not say or do anything which may cause you pain."

She was denied old age, bleak or otherwise, but neither her exuberant, magnificent self, nor the work it made, contained anything for which she needed to apologize. Time has passed, and her art endures. As Moraes "Moor" Zogoiby wrote of his mother, Aurora: "Even now, in the memory, she dazzles, must be circled about and about. We may perceive her indirectly, in her effects on others . . . Ah, the dead, the unended, endlessly ending dead: how long, how rich is their story. We, the living, must find what space we can alongside them; the giant dead whom we cannot tie down, though we grasp at their hair, though we rope them while they sleep."

# BHUPEN KHAKHAR
## (1934–2003)

—

I FIRST MET BHUPEN KHAKHAR IN THE EARLY EIGHTIES. IT was at the Riverside Studios in Hammersmith, London. There was a gathering at which writers and artists visiting from India were given the opportunity of meeting writers and artists of Indian origin based in London. Bhupen and I hit it off immediately and became friends. He said he had read and enjoyed my books, in part because he saw a connection between them and his pictures. I had the same feeling, in reverse. There was a rapport between us artistically, a sense that each of us knew what the other was trying to do, that we were trying to achieve the same ends but in different art forms.

In my early work I tried to base my writing on the colloquial street language of Bombay. Similarly, Bhupen drew on the visual language of the Indian street—painted storefronts, trucks and rickshaws, hand-colored movie posters—for many of his works.

Visiting Bhupen at his home in Baroda, in the Indian state of Gujarat, was like entering his pictures. He'd take you down a back alley into a watch repair shop, and suddenly you were in one of his canvases, filled with bold colors.

He was a storyteller, using the old traditions of narrative painting much as I was trying to use a version of the Indian oral storytelling tradition. The more you look at his images, the more you see going on. Often a whole tale plays out in one canvas, as in the title work of his 2016 Tate Modern retrospective, *You Can't Please All*, in which a father and son taking their donkey to market appear several times.

A year or so after we first met, I visited him at the Knoedler Kasmin gallery on Cork Street in London, where he had a show. As it happened, I had just sold a short story to an American magazine and the check was in my pocket. There was a painting in the show with which I instantly fell in love, *Second Class Railway Compartment*. I didn't think I would be able to afford it but asked the price anyway, and discovered it was exactly the same figure as the one on the check in my pocket. (Only about £1,500 or so—Indian art was still ludicrously cheap back then.) I loved the idea of turning my story into his painting. So that's what I did. I bought it, and it remains one of my most treasured possessions.

*Second Class Railway Compartment* is not a part of the Tate Modern show, but two other works I own are: the oil painting *Window Cleaner* and a limited-edition art book we made together, *Two Stories*, in which he illustrated a couple of my stories, "The Free Radio" and "The Prophet's Hair," with woodcuts and linocuts.

I think of Bhupen as the best of a fascinating generation of artists who tried to find and forge new languages for Indian art, a "middle generation" preceding the current stars (such as Subodh Gupta, whose work sells for high prices and who regularly cites Bhupen as an influence) and following the earlier masters who had been powerfully influenced by Western art. The horses of M. F. Husain, for example, jump straight out of Picasso's *Guernica*, while the work of many other big names (such as S. H. Raza) was deeply indebted to developments in Western abstraction. That middle generation of artists such as Arpita Singh, Nilima Sheikh, Nalini Malani, and others was extraordinary, with Bhupen perhaps its leading light.

I actually sat for Bhupen in 1995. The BBC was making a documentary about my novel *The Moor's Last Sigh*, a novel inspired by my friendships with Indian artists including Bhupen. (There's a character in the novel, a painter known as "the accountant," that's a deliberate reference to him. He worked as an accountant some of the time.) The BBC thought it would be a nice idea to have my portrait painted as a segment of the program, so I immediately suggested Bhupen, who came to London to do the portrait. He borrowed a friend's studio in Edwardes Square, off Kensington High Street. Barely had we sat down than Bhupen took out his charcoal and drew a single-line profile portrait that was the most exact likeness you could ever have imagined. He then did the painting on top, with characters from the book depicted around me. But I'd love to have an X-ray of that painting and see the drawing underneath again.

(*The Moor's Last Sigh* is a novel about a painting hidden under another painting, so it's appropriate, I suppose, that there's a drawing hidden under this painting too.)

In the finished image, he took his lead from classic Indian portraiture but gave it a modern twist. In the royal portraits of sixteenth- and seventeenth-century Indian princes, the body faces the viewer while the head is in profile. Bhupen painted me the same way—the joke, however, is that while the princes of yesteryear wore elaborate muslin shirts in the finest fabric, I'm shown wearing a cheap nylon shirt. These days the painting hangs in the National Portrait Gallery in London. He's the only Indian painter with a work there, and I'm very proud that it's a portrait of me.

Bhupen Khakhar was a superb painter, and a brave one. He revealed his homosexuality on canvas and dealt openly with gay themes, never a simple matter in India, where it was then illegal to be gay. In his early pictures, he was indirect and allusive, but as he grew older and more confident, his work became much more sexually explicit. In an Indian context these works were, and perhaps remain, shocking.

Bhupen died of cancer in 2003. He was a huge figure in the history of Indian art. The Tate retrospective brings him a whole new level of international appreciation, something he richly deserves.

# BEING
# FRANCESCO CLEMENTE:
## *SELF-PORTRAITS*

---

*Gagosian Gallery, London, 2005*

J UST AS WE ALL HAVE SOVEREIGN INDIVIDUAL SELVES, OR SO
the Renaissance taught us, so also are our faces possessed of a sovereign individuality. We all carry within ourselves self-portraits that are, for the most part, portraits of our faces, though there must be, there *are*, cases in which we, some of us, see ourselves in other parts of our bodies; a muscleman's self-image may be the picture of a biceps, a dancer may see herself as existing most fully in her feet, a gigolo in his genitalia, or a pianist in her hands. But mostly it is in our faces that we face ourselves, and in this regard the invention of the looking glass is an event of some importance, making possible as never before the prolonged daily study of the self, the self as face, the self as reflected self from which that further reflection, the self-portrait, can be born. We should not, however, overstate the importance of this moment, because before the looking glass there were earlier proto-mirrors; the Incas had mirrors of a sort, could not do without them, even though they never learned the secret of the wheel. And in Greece and Rome there were polished shields, such as those in which it was safe to behold the Gorgon, and glassy pools, such as the one by which Narcissus, perhaps the first self-portraitist, lay in eternal contemplation of his beauty.

Nor is the availability of a reflection essential. We know ourselves whether we see our mirror images or not. "Man cannot understand without images," Aquinas said, and our minds are programmed to construct those images, even without the help of our eyes. The consequence of the gift of self-consciousness, the gift that makes us human, is the invention of the self-image. Blind men have painted self-portraits, and sculptors who never saw their faces nevertheless carved them in stone. Almost three and a half thousand years ago, Bak, the chief sculptor of the pharaoh Akhenaten, made stone carvings of himself and his wife, Taheret or Taheri. At that time portraiture was a commissioned art, yet Bak felt the need, without hope of financial reward, to portray himself and his beloved. Phidias, it's said, was jailed for the blasphemy of carving the image of his own face on Athena's shield in the Parthenon. He must have known of the taboo he was breaking, yet he broke it, yielding to the ancient, potent urge to be seen by others as one sees oneself.

To take a walk along the famous Vasari Corridor in Florence, the covered walkway built by Giorgio Vasari in 1565 to allow Cosimo de' Medici to walk unobserved between the Uffizi Gallery and the Pitti Palace, which now houses perhaps the world's greatest collection of self-portraits, is to witness many comparable acts of self-revelatory bravery. Here the minatory patriarchal hauteur of Lucas Cranach the Elder seems to terrify the haunted, youthfully uncertain Filippino Lippi; the swagger of Velázquez's stance and the suspicion in his eyes are answered by Rembrandt's serene undefended acceptance of the passage of the years. Chagall reveals himself as a blue wizard, with one of his airborne ladies at his brow, while the Swedish painter Carl Larsson is a clown, in a clownish hat, holding a clown doll. To make a work of art one must use a form of double vision, looking simultaneously outward and inward, making naked what is clothed and telling what is secret, and revealing how the interior world of sensibility, memory, and fear is linked to what is shouted aloud and paraded before our eyes in the world all around, which is so brightly illumined but which remains, nevertheless, opaque, until the artist's nakedness provides the key that unlocks its mystery. This is what we mean when we say that art is an act of courage and why the success of a great self-portrait feels almost heroic, because this is the form that is, perhaps, the *locus classicus* of the meeting between the interior and exterior worlds; failures of self-portraiture, the preening reluctances one encounters all too often, are evidence of a type of cowardice.

The self-portrait is the interrogation of what the artist knows best, but it is also the most polymorphous of forms, emphasizing continuity or change, surface or depth, mask or skull. And sometimes the artist is merely the model—though perhaps the artist when serving as his own model is never "mere": Caravaggio, painting himself as the decapitated head of Goliath, was himself a falling giant nearing the end of his life; Artemisia Gentileschi lending her big, strong features to her ferocious heroines also intended something personal, as, no doubt, did James Montgomery Flagg when he used his own features to create the ultra-patriotic image of "Uncle Sam."

If Rembrandt's long study of himself over time stands at one end of the spectrum of self-portraiture, then Warhol's representation of the artist as product stands at the other, and in between are the morbid, perhaps over-revelatory introspections of Kahlo and the enigmatic, opaque gestures of Gilbert and George; the performances of Cindy Sherman, the artist as role-player, and the documentary quality of Nan Goldin, and then there is the case of Sam Francis, who painted self-portraits that didn't look like him at all, pictures in which his face might become female or even Japanese, and whose subject, he said, was metamorphosis. He needed otherness in order to find his way back to himself. The more one looks at self-portraits, the more one begins to feel that metamorphosis, the art of the protean, may lie closer to the truth about the form than representation, and this, finally, is why Francesco Clemente's new pictures of himself are so interesting. Clemente is a metamorph *par excellence*—actor, clown, mask, avatar, and as slippery as the legendary Old Man of the Sea. He wriggles hard when you try to pin him down. You have to hold on tightly, and for a long time, while he mutates ceaselessly to elude your grasp, and only at the very end, when you are both exhausted, does he give up his secrets and tell you what you need to know.

"All things flow, nothing abides," wrote Heraclitus, and the idea of change as the only constant later became one of the dominant concepts of the Roman Empire. Ovid, in his *Metamorphoses,* offered a brilliant gloss on this theme. Yes, change was everywhere—it could be playful, extraordinary, or grotesque—but it was not random. Endangered women and assaulted emperors alike metamorphosed not according to their fancy but in response to the crises of their lives, and their metamorphoses were not games or disguises but revelations. Ovid's characters changed, one might say, into themselves. The chameleon, after all, does not change color whimsically but to protect himself, to survive. His changes too reveal his slow and guarded nature.

Clemente and the chameleon are two of a kind. Here they are, united in a single mysterious, even mystical image, the green creature curling over the artist's head like a second self and refusing, no doubt for aesthetic reasons, to adopt the coloration of the field against which it poses. Which is the self-portrait in this self-portrait, one might well ask, the image of the reptile or the man?

In Indian mythology and philosophy too, the idea of the changeable self, of gods as well as men, lies close to the heart of things. I myself have always been strongly attracted to metamorphs, and I suspect that this Indian interest in all that is mutable accounts for Clemente's long, passionate response to India, of which there is so much evidence in his new self-portraits, in the bright bleeding-Madras pink of the *Self-Portrait with Smoke,* set against the human figure's somber tones; in the *Tantric Self-Portrait;* and again in the transfigured *Self-Portrait as a Bengali Woman,* reminiscent of those Sam Francis self-alterations. But beneath these obvious Indian signs there is something more deeply subcontinental in Clemente by now, something more than simple referentiality—an acquired or developed or discovered feeling for an Indian rhythm of life. Set these portraits beside the work of a major contemporary Indian artist like the late Bhupen Khakhar and the echoes are there for all to see. Khakhar, seeking an Indian "voice" that was imitative neither of the West nor of traditional Indian miniature-style painting, found inspiration in the contemporary, in the visual furniture of the Indian street, in the color palette of storefronts and billboards, and constructed from these materials his own, increasingly passionate, increasingly explicit, increasingly erotic world. Clemente, no slouch at the erotic himself, likewise takes inspiration from—seeks the eternal in—the Indian contemporary; his fish-eating cat, his spiraling smoke-self, the bountiful patternings and colors of his beautifully lurid caged bird, his Tantric meditation and his yin-yang mandala are similar to what one might find on India's ubiquitous calendars of the gods, or matchboxes, and equally ubiquitous political posters deifying their subjects, as well as the bright-yellow ghee canisters, the cobalt-blue cheese tins, and the purple-and-vermilion saris drying on the dark *dhobi-ghat* rocks.

What is it about Italians and Indians? Because if the best kind of comedy is the comedy of recognition, the laughter that comes when we think, yes, it is like that, things are so and we are thus, then in India there is often a recognition-comedy of this sort between Indians and Italians, because sometimes Indians, when looking upon Italian visitors, feel that we are looking into a sort of mirror, as if we were seeing ourselves in translation; we recognize something, perhaps, in the gesticulations, or the volubility, or the love of mothers, or the poetry, or the gusto of the eating, or the high pitch of the speech, or the caste system, or the vehemence, or the quickness of the temper, and we think, some Indians think, that perhaps, if only we drank wine, we would be those people, perhaps Italians are just Indians who drink wine. Consequently in India it is sometimes said to Italians that they, the Italians, are the Indians of Europe. Usually it is said to make these visitors feel at home and so it is a form of Indian politeness—and there are so many forms of Indian politeness, including ones that are really insults—but this one contains enough truth to merit repetition. And if the Italians are the Indians of Europe, then the Indians are the Italians of Asia, and not only because we are both Southerners, Indians and Italians, not only because we each hang off the bottom of our continent of origin, Italy like a giant leg, India like a giant, dripping nose. And standing upon the Italian–Indian border, that fantastic frontier, straddling, or, better, leaping back and forth across this imaginary borderline, smiling his wicked commedia dell'arte smile, at once satyr-like and iconic—*satyriconic*—is Francesco Clemente, mingler of the two worlds, artist of spiritual cynicism and erotic chastity, or perhaps of cynical spiritualism and chaste eroticism, his face hanging hugely above his dreamscapes like the moon.

There is a story by Italo Calvino about a time when the moon was closer to the earth than it is today, when lovers could leap off the earth to walk upon its satellite and look up at their home planet hanging upside down above their heads. Separation, inversion, the fascination of the leap: These are the characteristics of Clemente's paintings. His is a traveler's art. "In each place where I was," he says, "the continuity of memories, the tradition of the place, has been broken, somewhere, sometime; I don't know why. Really, you can't look at any place in the world from the place itself. You have to look from somewhere else to see what is there." These ideas, of the fragmentation of cultures and of the creative benefits of displacement, are close also to my heart. "The only people who see the whole picture," one of my characters says in *The Ground Beneath Her Feet*, "are the ones who step out of the frame." Fragments are what we have left, and the artist must assemble them into meaningful form, so that they can reveal some, at least, of their broken mysteries, the way the shards of Heraclitus's lost book still, after two thousand years, retain the power of significant speech. The *Self-Portrait with Smoke* reassembles a fragmentary self in just this way, uniting the artist's dissociated and replicated physical elements with the most transient and evanescent of bonds.

These paintings are more playful, less somber than the great "grisaille" series of a few years ago, offering, in place of the grave, unflinching self-examination of those earlier pictures, a quasi-mystical vision of the artist as present in all things, just as all things are present in the artist. Clemente is the cat with the fish in its mouth (but he might as well be the fish); he is the pig with the Clemente mask as well as the artist with the pig mask. He is in a wisp of smoke, and a godlike being riding a priapic phallus, and the dreamer, perhaps the conjurer, of an aerial apocalypse. Cinematic parallels present themselves: of the menacing Agent Smith in *The Matrix*, taking over and transforming into his own image whatever body he chooses to occupy; or of the sequence in *Being John Malkovich* in which, in the actor's interior universe, all of reality has been Malkoviched, all faces are Malkovich's face, and the only word in the only known language is "Malkovich." There is a delicious narcissism at work in Clemente, but it is redeemed by what one may call his Hindu insistence on the underlying principle of unity in the universe, *Tat Tvam Asi*, "Thou Art That," as the wise father, Uddalaka, explains to his son Svetaketu in the *Chandogya Upanishad*, meaning, approximately, that the Self is a part of, or one with, the Ultimate Reality, which is the origin of everything.

The "transformational grammar" of these paintings (to borrow Chomsky's term) seeks to connect the deep structure of the images embedded, as Aquinas understood, in our essential, unconscious natures to the surface structure of our visual perceptions. And at the collection's heart, less antic than the other pictures, darker and more melancholy, is the extraordinary *Self-Portrait from a Family Photograph*, a picture that hides the family's eyes from us, but even so, even though we cannot look into the soul's windows, manages to convey love, intimacy, pain, loss, and other emotions for which there are no names; a painting in which the hidden world behind the eyes is perfectly revealed through what is seen of faces, gestures, and touch: a masterpiece.

# TARYN SIMON:
## AN AMERICAN INDEX
## OF THE HIDDEN
## AND UNFAMILIAR

———

*Whitney Museum, New York, 2007*

"OUR INTEREST'S ON THE DANGEROUS EDGE OF THINGS," the poet Robert Browning wrote in "Bishop Blougram's Apology" (1855). It's a line that inspired writer Graham Greene, who said in his 1971 memoir *A Sort of Life* that it could serve as an epigraph to all his novels. It could equally well serve as an introduction to the photography of a woman whose aesthetic is one of stretching the limits of what we are allowed to see and know, of going to the ambiguous boundaries where dangers—physical, intellectual, even moral—may await. She doesn't think twice about entering the mountain cave of a hibernating black bear and her cubs or a room filled with nuclear-waste capsules glowing blue with radiation that, were you not shielded against it, would kill you in seconds. Taryn Simon has seen the Death Star and lived to tell the tale.

I am always immensely grateful to people who do impossible things on my behalf and bring back the picture. It means I don't have to do it, but at least I know what it looks like. So one's first feeling on looking at many of these extraordinary images is gratitude (followed quickly by a momentary pang of envy: the sedentary writer's salute to the woman of action). I once knew a sports photographer who bribed a course attendant at Aintree Racecourse in Liverpool, England, to allow him to sit wedged in at the foot of the giant fence, Becher's Brook, which is the most dangerous obstacle in the four-and-a-half-mile Grand National Steeplechase, so that he could bring back "impossible" photographs of the mighty racehorses jumping over his head. If one of them had fallen on him, he would almost certainly have been killed, but he knew, as Taryn Simon knows, that one of the arts of great photography is to get yourself into the place—the radioactive room, an animal disease center, the racecourse fence—in which the photograph is about to occur, and seize it when it does.

Look at these innocent orange and yellow cables coming up through the floor in an almost empty room in New Jersey, protected only by the simplest metal cage: they have traveled four thousand miles (actually, 4,029.6 miles: Simon likes to be precise) across the ocean floor from Saunton Sands in the United Kingdom to bring America news from elsewhere—60,211,200 simultaneous voice conversations, Simon says. But the point about the transatlantic cables is that you might have guessed that such things probably existed, but you almost certainly had no notion of where they were, or how many, or how thick, or what color, until you saw this picture. You could not have imagined your own voice into this banal yet magical room, but it has been here, transformed into little digital parcels of energy. Every day we pass through secret worlds like the worlds inside these cables, never suspecting what is happening to us. Which, then, is the phantom world and which the "real": ours, or theirs? Are we no more than the ghosts in these machines?

Ours is an age of secrets. Above, beneath, and beside what Fernand Braudel called the "structures of everyday life" are other structures that are anything but everyday, lives about which we may have heard something but of which we have almost certainly seen nothing, as well as other lives about which we have never heard, and yet others in whose existence it is hard to believe even when we are shown the pictorial evidence. Would you have believed in the existence, for example, of an edition of *Playboy* magazine in Braille? Well, here it is, bunny ears and all, published by a branch of the Library of Congress, no less. And here too is a photograph looking for all the world like a slightly stagy Hitchcockian crime scene. It's a picture of a young boy's corpse rotting in a wood, taken at a research facility in Tennessee set up specifically to study how bodies decompose in different settings. Here, Simon tells us, there are up to seventy-five cadavers at any given time, decomposing across a six-acre site. Maybe Patricia Cornwell or the folks at *CSI* knew about this kind of cutting-edge forensic research, but I didn't, and even as one looks at Taryn Simon's preternaturally beautiful picture, with its bare glistening branches and fallen leaves and rich autumnal palette, one finds oneself wondering at human beings' limitless ingenuity, our need to know, in which cause even our own dead bodies might someday be pressed into service to decay in a woodland glade.

How do you get into some of the world's most secret places and get out again with the picture? The great journalist Ryszard Kapuściński says that he survived the world's most dangerous war zones by making himself seem small and unimportant, not worthy of the warlord's bullet. But Taryn Simon doesn't deal in stolen images; these are formal, highly realized, often carefully posed pictures, which require their subjects' full cooperation. That she has managed to gain such open access to, for example, the Church of Scientology and MOUT, an inaccessible simulated city in Kentucky used, for training purposes, as an urban battlefield, and the Imperial Office of the World Knights of the Ku Klux Klan with its wizards and nighthawks and kleagles, looking like characters from a Coen Brothers movie, and even the operating theater in which a Palestinian woman is undergoing hymenoplasty, a procedure generally used to restore virginity, is evidence that her powers of persuasion are at least the equal of her camera skills. In a historical period in which so many people are making such great efforts to conceal the truth from the mass of the people, an artist like Taryn Simon is an invaluable counterforce. Democracy needs visibility, accountability, light. It is in the unseen darkness that unsavory things huddle and grow. Somehow, Simon has persuaded a good few denizens of hidden worlds not to scurry for shelter when the light is switched on, as cockroaches do, and vampires, but to pose proudly for her invading lens, brandishing their tattoos and Confederate flags.

Simon's is not the customary aesthetic of reportage: the shaky handheld camera, the grainy monochrome film stock of the "real." Her subjects—gray parrots in their quarantine cages, marijuana plants grown for research purposes in William Faulkner's hometown of Oxford, Mississippi, the red-hot form of Dirty Harry's .44 Magnum shot in the heat of the forge, a pair of Orthodox Jews United Against Zionism—are suffused with light, captured with a bright, hyperrealist, high-definition clarity that gives a kind of star status to these hidden worlds, whose occupants might be thought to be the opposites of stars. In her vision of them, they are dark stars brought into the light. What is not known, rarely seen, possesses a form of occult glamour, and it is that black beauty that she so brightly, and brilliantly, reveals. Here is the beach house at Cape Canaveral where astronauts go with their spouses for a last private moment before they blast off into space. Here is a man skewered through the chest, hanging in the air, during the Lone Star Sun Dance. Here is the floodlit basketball court of the Cheyenne Mountain Directorate in Colorado, a surveillance post designed to survive a thermonuclear bomb. One can only imagine what strange postapocalyptic one-on-one games, what last-ever turnaround jump shots, might be attempted here if things go badly wrong for the rest of us. This is the way the world ends: not with a bang but a skyhook. (No, on reflection, there would probably be a bang as well.)

Simon uses text as few photographers do, not merely as title or caption but as an integral part of the work. There are images that do not reveal their meaning until the text is read, such as her photograph of the flowing Nipomo Sand Dunes in Guadalupe, California, beneath which, she tells us, lies one of the most extraordinary film sets ever built, the City of the Pharaoh created for Cecil B. DeMille's 1923 silent version of *The Ten Commandments*, and deliberately buried here to prevent other productions from "appropriating his ideas and using his set."

There are (rare) instances when the text is more bizarrely interesting than the image. Cataloging the confiscated contents of the U.S. Customs and Border Protection Contraband Room at John F. Kennedy Airport, Simon offers up a kind surrealist fugue, an ode to forbidden fruit (and meat) that outdoes even her cornucopia of an image: "African cane rats infested with maggots," she sings, "African yams (Dioscorea), Andean potatoes, Bangladeshi cucurbit plants, bush meat, cherimoya fruit, curry leaves (murraya), dried orange peels, fresh eggs, giant African snail, impala skull cap, jackfruit seeds, June plum, kola nuts, mango, okra, passion fruit, pig nose, pig mouths, pork, raw poultry (chicken), South American pig head, South American tree tomatoes, South Asian lime infected with citrus canker, sugar cane (Poaceae), uncooked meats, unidentified subtropical plant in soil."

For the most part, however, her images easily hold their own, even when accompanied by the most astonishing information. The smoky, white-on-white portrait of the degree-zero cryogenic preservation pod in which the bodies of the mother and wife of cryonics pioneer Robert Ettinger lie frozen is beyond spooky, speaking so eloquently of our fear of death and our dreams of immortality that few words are necessary. The top-shot of a mass of infectious medical waste achieves the abstract beauty of a Jackson Pollock drip painting, or, perhaps, a Schnabel smashed crockery piece.

There are images of deep humanity, such as the portrait of Don James, a terminal cancer patient, taken just after he received a prescription for a lethal dose of pentobarbital, for which he had successfully fought under Oregon's Death With Dignity Act. There are mind-numbing grotesques, such as the picture of Pastor Jimmy Morrow the Serpent Handler of Newport, Tennessee, holding a lethally poisonous southern copperhead snake just above a Biblical text instructing us to "Call His Name Jesus." And there are mind-expanding epic images, such as a roseate portrait of a star-forming region, the Pacman Nebula, nine and a half thousand light-years away. (That's slightly less than 57,000,000,000,000,000,000 miles, by my calculation: a long way to go for a good picture.)

And in at least one instance there's a remarkable piece of "found" art. Who could have predicted that those ninety stainless-steel capsules containing radioactive cesium and strontium submerged in a pool of water and giving off that blue radiation would so closely resemble, when photographed from above, the map of the United States of America? When a photographer comes up with an image as potently expressive as that, even a dedicated word-person such as myself is bound to concede that such a picture is worth at least a thousand words.

# KARA WALKER
# AT THE HAMMER MUSEUM,
# LOS ANGELES, 2009

---

Aaccording to pliny's *natural history*, painting "began with tracing an outline around a man's shadow," a theme treated by Vasari, Murillo, and many others. If the shadow is the body's representation, the silhouette is a representation of that representation, and in it are contained many of the most profound themes of art: light and darkness, good and evil, the self and the shadow self, the body and the soul. We have never ceased to see ourselves as shadows, never forgotten the shadows in ourselves, and have depicted them over and over, from the figures frozen on Keats's Grecian urn, his "bold lover" who can never kiss his beloved, whose beauty can never fade, to the abstract color forms of Matisse's *papiers coupés;* from the female figures prancing through the title sequences of Bond movies to the little male and female figures on toilet doors; from Fred Astaire dancing with his shadow in the movie *Swing Time* to the haunting shadow-play cutouts of Lotte Reiniger's animation masterpiece *The Adventures of Prince Achmed.*

In the strange German tale of Peter Schlemihl, the devil gives a poor boy a never-emptying purse of gold coins but takes away his shadow, which makes the poor youth repulsive to all men in spite of his newfound wealth. In Hans Christian Andersen's even stranger story about a shadow that escapes the man to whom it belongs, the shadow becomes more powerfully alive than its former owner and eventually takes his place. As Eliot wrote in "The Hollow Men":

"Between the idea / And the reality / Between the motion / And the act / Falls the Shadow."

Such is the ancient theme that Kara Walker has chosen with such flair and brilliance to reinvent and reanimate. Her sorcerer's wand is not a paintbrush but a knife. With it, and with a profound awareness of the old shadows behind her new shadows, she enters a world that, while bygone, has by no means lost its power, a world once real, much mythologized, which retains, in her astonishing silhouettes, a shocking reality and a mythic force, and to which she adds extraordinary dimensions of line and wit. The antebellum era of the American South is reborn with a visionary mastery and freighted irony that is entirely of today. Kara Walker's ample, kerchiefed women and bony, angled girls move with grace, terror, innocence, and mischief through landscapes in which they encounter dancers, lovers, rapist slave owners, and sometimes nooses slung over the branches of cruelly spreading trees. There is a dark humor at work here, and a self-examining intelligence too. "It's all about absence," Kara Walker has said of her work, and it is her genius to inhabit the shadow world of slavery so potently that it shines more brightly than the bright, columned mansions of the masters. Her images are often shocking. A sword penetrates a vagina, a slave weeps, a child watches another child being lynched. But they are redeemed by an almost musical delicacy. Like Andersen's rebel shadow, Kara Walker's shadows triumphantly take center stage; liberated by her sensuous, lyrical freedom of form and line, their joy and pain, their secrets and lies, dance darkly and dangerously across white voids of paper, walls, and cloth.

It has been, to recap briefly, a brilliant career. At just twenty-seven, Kara became the youngest-ever recipient of a MacArthur Fellowship, the so-called "Genius Grant." She was the Hammer Museum's very first Hammer Projects artist and has gone on to exhibit more than forty solo shows around the world. In 2007 her retrospective *My Complement, My Enemy, My Oppressor, My Love* received raves from critics, and from the public as well. She has worked in video and watercolor as well as cutouts. *Time* magazine named her one of the hundred most influential people in the world.

Kara Walker is a history artist. She has always reminded us that we can see the way forward only by gazing truthfully and unsparingly at the past. Slave songs, minstrel shows, the lost narratives of the South, the complex malign narrative of racism, the intimate oppressions taking place each day and night between master and slave—all these inform her work. She reimagines America unsparingly, with savagery and wit. She can approach horror almost playfully, can look unflinchingly at eroticism and brutality, and has made and is making us see America's original sin of slavery through her unflinching, lyrical art. She is one of the most important artists at work today.

# SEBASTIÃO SALGADO

———

WHEN WE CONFRONT A WORK OF ART WE LISTEN FOR THE artist's voice. The greater the artist, the stronger and more distinct is the voice we hear. Only Mozart sounds like Mozart, only Hemingway sounds like Hemingway. This is one of the chief satisfactions of the artistic experience: to hear a voice speaking as only that voice can speak. And when the voice is exceptionally strong, it can exalt its material and allow us to experience the rarest of joys: that of transcendence.

The visual arts have voices too, soaring in the case of Brancusi, polyphonic in the case of Picasso. Photography is no less capable of speech. Cartier-Bresson's photograph of a dancing crowd on India's independence day, Arbus's unquiet Americans, Avedon's unforgiving portraits, the view from the workroom window of Nicéphore Niépce in 1826 (the "First Photograph," which started it all)—these images are anything but silent, or, at least, their silences are as eloquent as any spoken words.

Sebastião Salgado's is one of the most powerful voices in contemporary photography, capable of harshness in its unflinching examination of men and women at work, of epic grandeur in its statements about the mass movements of human beings across the earth, and of lyric beauty in its images of the natural world. He is the poet of the open air, of figures in landscapes, and, most recently, of landscapes from which human figures are absent so that more primordial matters can be revealed: the flick of a whale's fin against a lucent sky, the mysterious intimacy of a five-fingered reptilian hand, the *mille-feuille* striations of ancient stones.

He is not just another photographer. He is a superstar, a celebrity, and that brings criticism. Ingrid Sischy compared him unfavorably to Walker Evans, because, she said, Salgado brought "the unrelenting application of the lyric and the didactic to his subjects." And yes, Salgado's work is didactic. It is not like Walker Evans's. But that does not, to my eye, necessarily diminish it. The French critic Jean-François Chevrier was harsher, calling Salgado's work "sentimental voyeurism . . . an exploitation of compassion." Why? Because they are *too beautiful*. But beauty is not sentimentality, nor is it glamour. Salgado's work does have great formal beauty. So do Renaissance paintings of the Crucifixion. Nothing is sentimentalized in Salgado's portraits of poverty and work, nothing is glamorized, and yet, time and again, the organizing power of his eye adds meaning to what he documents. The cry bursting from the gaunt mouth of an Indian *dhobi* at the washing *ghat* is dramatically amplified by the arc of water flying from the cloth he is thrashing against stone. The exploding water is that cry made visible. Children strike attitudes on bare white tombs and make us think of the saints they are not and the ghosts they will become. Figures at the edge of a cloud-filled abyss stretch out their arms to fly, playfully, fantastically, hopelessly. Nobody has ever taken better pictures of dust, sweat, and mud, or of the exhaustion, determination, and despair to be found on the faces of the muddy, the perspiring, and the parched. Oil soaks human beings as if they were dying birds.

In his pictures of journeyings, Salgado captures one of the great themes of our time, the migrations that our age has made possible and necessary, the migrations that in their turn have shaped and defined our time. Men and women who have left all they had and knew cluster on hillsides like an ancient army going to war, like pilgrims without a sacred place to hope for. Humanity swarms, teems, struggles, sinks, rises again. There are many crowds in these images, but these are not anonymous crowds. The individuality of men and women is not lost. Here are their faces, their sinews, their needs. And when they do, on occasion, blend into a filthy, striving mass, still the mass has shape and movement. It has, we can say, character.

In these images of fortress cities and gold mines, of fishing nets and oil wells, of steaming volcanoes and spouting sea lions, Sebastião Salgado has given us a portrait of our world that speaks in the rarest voice of all, the voice that tells us things we did not want to know, things, perhaps, we did not know how to know, but that, when we are told of them, we instantly recognize as the truth.

# THE
# UNBELIEVER'S CHRISTMAS

———

WHEN I WAS GROWING UP IN BOMBAY (WHICH WASN'T Mumbai then, and still isn't in my personal lexicon), Christmas wasn't really a thing. Not only were we not Christians, we weren't a religious household, and so December 25 was just that: the twenty-fifth of December. New Year's Day was much more significant.

The above paragraph is not completely true. For one thing, the school I went to was called the Cathedral School, or, in full, the Cathedral and John Connon Boys' High School, run "under the auspices," whatever "auspices" were, of the Anglo-Scottish Education Society, whatever that was. As a result, there were hymns at assembly every day of the year and regular school trips to the Anglican St. Thomas' Cathedral, and "O Come, All Ye Faithful" and "Hark! The Herald Angels Sing" in December, and all of us—Hindu, Muslim, Sikh, Parsi—had to sing along. And because we were after all schoolboys, we learned the comic version of "Hark" also.

Hark! The herald angels sing
Beecham's pills are just the thing.
If you want to go to heaven
take a dose of six or seven.
If you want to go to hell,
take the whole damn box as well.

Also, my sisters and I had a wonderful Christian ayah, Mary Menezes from Mangalore, a devout Roman Catholic who helped to raise us and because of whom my mother put up a (very small) tree and made us sing carols to her on Christmas morning. Other than the brief appearance of the very small tree and the compulsory singing, though, there was nothing. Turkey? Mince pies? Brussels sprouts? Of course not. We had much tastier food to eat. And presents were for birthdays and Eid.

After St. Thomas' Cathedral in Bombay there was boarding school in England, Rugby School, with compulsory attendance at services in William Butterfield's Rugby Chapel, and the whole of Rugby School having to sing Handel's *Messiah* as a special Christmas "treat." Hallelujah. And some of the Christmas carols were in Latin now.

> *Adeste fideles,*
> *laeti triumphantes,*
> *venite, venite, in Bethlehem.*

*Venite* was pronounced "wenite" because that was the posh British way to say it. Slightly disappointing that the Latin for "Bethlehem" was *Bethlehem* and not something more Roman-sounding, but oh well.

This pretty much atheistic boy of Indian Muslim heritage sang, along with everyone else, about the adoration of a Middle Eastern boy who had been born the king of angels. While I sang, I looked at the thing that pleased me most in the chapel: the marble memorial to a great Old Rugbeian, the Reverend Charles Lutwidge Dodgson, a.k.a. Lewis Carroll, containing silhouettes of the Tenniel illustrations of his immortal characters, black silhouettes set in white marble, white silhouettes set in black. I was not a fan of Rugby Chapel. It was much later that I learned to appreciate Butterfield's neo-Gothic building. But I liked it that the creator of Alice had been there before me. That was better than Christmas.

Then I was at King's College, Cambridge, in the presence of King's Chapel, perhaps the most beautiful building in England. One day I went with a few other lucky Kingsmen up a narrow spiral staircase in a corner, led by John Saltmarsh, the history don with the muttonchops who was the great expert on the chapel. We came at last to a shadowy space beneath the roof but above the famous fan vaulting, which stretched away before us like the skeleton of a giant beast. "Be careful," Mr. Saltmarsh said, "because there are places where the stone is less than half an inch thick, and if you step on it you'll fall through and leave a nasty hole. It's eighty feet down, and in addition, people will be very cross with you."

In the chapel was the famous choir, and at Christmas there was the famous Festival of Nine Lessons and Carols, and even an ungodly undergraduate could not help but appreciate the beauty of the singing—except during the term in which my room was in the college's Peas Hill Hostel, whose other occupants were all members of the choir and practiced incessantly. Several hours a day of beautiful singing next door will do a lot to erode your belief in beauty, especially if your own voice happens to be a wretched tuneless wail.

For some years after I settled in London, I would join with other Christmas refuseniks and go out for an Indian meal on December 25, often at the Gaylord restaurant on Mortimer Street. No presents, no stuffing, lots of irreverent fun and tandoori chicken. Then came marriage and children.

Children change Christmas. My sons, Zafar and Milan, wanted a proper Christmas. So did my nieces, my sister Sameen's daughters, Maya and Mishka. So now does my daughter-in-law, Zafar's soprano wife, Natalie. They are all—well, no, not all—Christmas fundamentalists. Sameen and I have given in to their demands, and so for many years now there have been tall trees decked with ornaments, and holly, mistletoe, turkey, stuffing, bread sauce, cranberry sauce, brandy snaps, crackers, the whole nine yards, even the brussels sprouts. (Once or twice lately we have broken with tradition and eaten Sameen's delicious Indian food instead.) There is the queen on TV. There is an annual ocean of wrapping paper. There are stockings. There are Christmas sweaters. My sister and I look at each other from opposite ends of the groaning dining table and ask, silently, how did this happen to us? We allow ourselves only two small rebellions. One: We don't like Christmas pudding and won't eat the stuff. And two: I don't give her a Christmas present and she doesn't give me one. That is our small acknowledgment of the people we used to be.

We have a grand time. We are, I think, a funny bunch, we Rushdies, and so the day is full of laughter. We are not like those movie families (and not just movie families) whose get-togethers are like little wars. We all get along and have a great day and if, in some way, it's all because of the baby Jesus, then we agree not to mind. Thank you, baby Jesus, from this godless bunch. We don't believe in you but here we are anyway, celebrating family and fellowship and love, and that is an annual bright deed in a darkening world.

# CARRIE FISHER

———

Back in 1977, while driving from Chicago to New York, "Harry Burns" (Billy Crystal) told "Sally Albright" (Meg Ryan) that "Men and women can't be friends, because the sex part always gets in the way." (To clarify: It was 1977 *in the movie*. Rob Reiner's romantic comedy *When Harry Met Sally* was actually released in 1989.)

When I saw the movie, I felt strongly that Harry's assertion was wrong. I grew up with three sisters and no brothers and consequently I've had always had at least as many women friends as men. I say "consequently" because I've always thought that that family circumstance was the reason for my many female friendships. Then, in 1997, I met one of the co-stars of *When Harry Met Sally,* and the closeness that developed between us became perhaps the best rejoinder to Harry's proposition. That actress—that extraordinary individual—was Carrie Fisher.

We met in London in 1997, as guests on Ruby Wax's late-night talk show *Ruby,* sitting around a dinner table talking and pretending to eat, and we got on so well that soon afterward Ruby invited the two of us to dinner at the River Café. Now, it's possible that Ruby thought she might be matchmaking (I don't know, I've never asked her), but I was happily married and my son Milan was about to be born, so that wasn't an option. At the restaurant I put my "banana phone" down on the table and said, "If that phone rings I'll have to leave, because it will mean the baby is on the way." That took care of romance. Instead, we became, and remained, the closest and deepest of friends.

I have so many happy memories of our friendship. I remember a dinner in New York with Peter Farrelly of the Farrelly Brothers (and, recently, of *Green Book*) at which I told Carrie and Peter about a dentist who had recently died in New Jersey, leaving behind a macabre collection of arcane objects, including the bloodstained shirt worn by President Lincoln at Ford's Theatre and, even more wondrous, the penis of Napoleon Bonaparte, with a full provenance authenticating it. Immediately Carrie imagined a documentary. We would acquire the detached organ and bring it ceremoniously to Paris and place it with all due solemnity on Napoleon's tomb in the Hôtel des Invalides, making the emperor whole once more. It would be our gift to the French people in return for the Statue of Liberty. Peter's producer and friend Charlie Wessler tried to acquire the penis. He failed.

When Chiwetel Ejiofor and Ewan McGregor were playing Othello and Iago at Donmar Warehouse, Carrie got herself and me a couple of hard-to-get tickets by calling Ewan and using the *Star Wars* connection. Afterward, Ewan, Carrie, and I had dinner at the Ivy, and Ewan suddenly asked her about the famous speech in the original *Star Wars* movie, the one hidden inside R2-D2. "Do you remember it?" he asked her. "Of course I fucking remember it," she said. "Can you do it, then?" he asked her, and without missing a beat she went into Princess Leia mode and did the speech with full dramatic intensity. "Help us, Obi-Wan Kenobi," she finished, "you're our only ho!" Then she explained, "You see, the recording was cut off before I could finish saying 'hope.'"

Another time in London we got photographed coming out of a restaurant and the next day a newspaper ran the photo with the headline SALMAN RUSHDIE AND MYSTERY BLONDE. I can't remember why her hair was blond then, but it was, and amazingly it meant the newspaper failed to recognize her. She was overjoyed, got hold of a copy of the paper, framed the article, and put it in pride of place in her home. After that for a time she signed her messages to me "Mystery Blonde."

And . . . we had dinner together in New York on Halloween. And, because neither of us felt like dressing up, we told people we were there as each other. And ... we went to George W. Bush's White House together during the National Book Festival, and Carrie was magnificently, regally disdainful, as if she were Leia scorning Jabba the Hutt. And ... she practiced her material on me, so long before I saw her triumphant one-woman show, *Wishful Drinking*, I knew, for example, that when she asked George Lucas why there weren't any bras and panties for her to try on during her first *Star Wars* costume fitting, he answered, as if he knew: "Carrie, there's no underwear in space."

Behind the comedy was fragility, and her close friends all felt very protective of her. She was open about her difficulties—a history of drug abuse as well as acute bipolar disorder—using comedy to triumph over adversity. She had shock therapy regularly, and even though that disturbed me, and others, she swore by it and said it helped, though, as her phone message told us, it meant she probably didn't remember who we were. So, fragility, yes, but also immense courage.

We were a motley crew, the princess's courtiers—*Bridget Jones's Diary* creator Helen Fielding, the filmmaker and actor Griffin Dunne, the actors Craig Bierko and Tracey Ullman, the novelist and screenwriter Bruce Wagner, the comedian and comedy writer Kevin Nealon, and several more—but we all loved her and guarded her fiercely. It wasn't always easy. Sometimes she was despairing and wild. Sometimes she was at the bottom of a dark well. Often, she ranted, and we had to hear her out. There were days when I visited her gloriously eccentric home on Coldwater Canyon and found her manic, bad-Carrie side in charge. (To see her, you usually went to her place; she often seemed reluctant to leave that gated redoubt.) I recall one afternoon when I was sitting on her bed, as her friends did, while she soliloquized about whatever was eating at her for two long (very long) hours. Then abruptly she stopped, grinned wickedly at me, and said, "So! And how are *you*?"

She befriended my sons as well as me. She met Milan when he was still very young but already a major *Star Wars* aficionado, and she started sending him the most delightful gifts: a Chewbacca rucksack, a flip-top R2-D2 dustbin. She showed up at Zafar's engagement party. She showed up for us all, as if we were family, and that's how we thought of her. Carrie was family.

In October 2016 I sat with her at the New York Film Festival premiere screening of the documentary *Bright Lights,* about her relationship with her mother, Debbie Reynolds, who in her later years would telephone her daughter every morning from her house at the bottom of Carrie's garden and say, "Good morning, Carrie. This is your mother, Debbie." As if she needed to introduce herself. There's a clip in the documentary that shows the teenage Carrie being summoned onstage by Debbie and told to sing—whereupon she sings "Bridge Over Troubled Water," revealing a great, powerful voice. "I never knew you could sing like that," I said to her. "Why haven't you done it more?" "Oh," she said, "I always thought singing was my mother's thing." After the film, Carrie complained that she didn't look good in it but eventually conceded that it was a touching record of an exceptional mother–daughter bond. Now that they are both gone, the film seems even more precious than it did then.

She had a love-hate relationship with Los Angeles. In some ways she was the ultimate Hollywood insider, she knew everything about everybody, but she also hated all the bullshit. She loved London and wanted to spend more time there, rummaging about on Portobello Road. Just two months after that New York premiere, we were both in London, she breaking the journey on her way back to L.A., I to see my family for Christmas, and she summoned me to her hotel, the Chiltern Firehouse. It was Thursday, December 22. I found her in the residents' bar with Sharon Horgan, with whom she had been making the TV series *Catastrophe.* I remember thinking that she seemed really well, in fine, lively, good-Carrie form, and that she was very excited about having bought herself a London base, a house on Old Church Street, and was full of London plans. Then she went to bed because she had to catch a plane the next day. And the next day, she caught her flight to nowhere.

I loved her, and I believe she loved me. I offer this account of our friendship as my answer to Billy Crystal/"Harry Burns." It was a friendship. Nothing else. And that was plenty.

# PANDEMIC

———

*A Personal Engagement
with the Coronavirus*

On MONDAY, MARCH 9, 2020, MY EDITOR, ROBIN DESSER, came over to my place to go over her editorial comments on the manuscript of this book. The world was still "normal" then, but my instincts told me it wouldn't remain that way for long. I was booked to fly to London to see my family three days later, on March 12, during the New York University spring break. (For the past six years I have been teaching a graduate seminar in narrative nonfiction at NYU during the spring semester.) After Robin left, I canceled my London flight. I hadn't seen my sons since Christmas, but they agreed it was a sensible decision. One week later I began running a fever and it rapidly became plain that the coronavirus had come to call. I was seventy-two years old and had asthma, which made me a prime target. March 16 is one day later than the Ides of March, but, then again, I'm no Julius Caesar.

UNTIL THAT DAY I had had only two serious illnesses. Unsurprisingly, I found myself thinking about both.

The first illness: In 1949, when I was still under two years old, I fell ill with typhoid fever. The medications that were prescribed all failed, and the family doctor told my parents that I would probably die very soon. My anguished father demanded, "There must be something else to give him." The doctor told him, "There is a new antibiotic called Chloromycetin. There's very little information on its effectiveness, but you might as well try it, because he's dying anyway." It was evening and my father drove around Bombay to find an open pharmacy. He came home with the medicine and it cured me very rapidly. After that, Chloromycetin became and remained for decades the standard treatment for typhoid, at least in that part of the world. I owe my life to it.

(This is the way the story has taken shape in my memory. I'm sure it has been dramatized and embellished—the doctor coldly announcing my imminent death, my father driving at speed around the city at night, searching frantically for an open drugstore. Maybe the doctor was less brutal, and the medication more readily available, perhaps at the nearby Thomas Kemp & Co., the pharmacy that gave its name to what is still called Kemps Corner. Maybe it all happened in the afternoon. But it's true that I had typhoid, and that Chloromycetin was very new in 1949, and that it saved me.)

The second illness: In London in 1984, I somehow contracted double pneumonia. Nobody ever worked out how I got it, but I was hospitalized for two weeks in a public ward for patients with chest troubles, at University College Hospital. All around me were people much more unwell than I was, many of them cancer patients. Almost every day, screens were put up around a nearby bed because somebody had died. After that for a short time there would be an empty bed, and then it would be occupied again.

(In those days I was a heavy smoker, and I have always believed I was cured of that habit by the use of a metaphor. The doctor attending to me asked me if I liked movies and when I said I did, he replied, "Think of lung cancer as a movie. Imagine that it's a feature film. In which case, what's happening to you now is that you are watching the trailer. So, while you're having your fifteen-minute convulsive coughing fits and bringing up the green slime, you should think about if you would like to see the movie.")

I emerged from the typhoid experience without any lasting damage. My asthma, however, was the universe's gift to me for recovering from pneumonia and giving up smoking. And now, three and a half decades later, here I was in the COVID-19 danger zone: a "senior" with an underlying condition.

FOR THE NEXT TWO WEEKS and more, I felt groggy, I coughed, and my fever took me on a roller-coaster ride, getting up as high as 103.5 degrees, swooping down to normal, and then, just as I thought I might be getting better, climbing back up again. It was dispiriting, but I was lucky. The illness never reached my lungs. My excellent primary-care physician was in touch with me most days—I'm aware that I was privileged to have such a doctor, and good health insurance. Each time, he asked if I felt any tightness across my chest and if I was short of breath. When I said I didn't and wasn't, he told me that in that case my life wasn't at risk, and I should stay away from hospitals and stay home in bed, take the Tylenol and the cough syrup, and, in his words, "tough it out."

Reader: I tried. I'm not sure how tough I was. I've never been a good patient. A bad cold reduces me to a grumpy, petulant wreck. Luckily for me I had a deeply caring partner looking after me. She got sick too but somehow managed to shrug it off in a few days. It took me seventeen.

Since then, I've come to understand exactly how lucky I was. I've watched with growing horror and grief as the numbers of the dead have grown and as the even larger numbers of the bereaved, the orphaned, the kinfolk of the dead, have fought to come to terms with those endings, the dying unable to be comforted by their loved ones as they died, the living denied the painful closure of a funeral. I've also found out how scared my family really was about my sickness. Everyone put a brave face on it when they spoke to me on our daily video calls, but behind their confident, reassuring expressions, they were terrified. If I'd known that, I'd have been terrified too.

John Prine died. He was a year older than me and I had loved his music ever since his debut album in 1971, and was fortunate enough to meet him once, when I was a member of the jury that presented him with a PEN Song lyrics of Literary Excellence Award in 2016. My friend the legendary music producer Hal Willner died. A friend's mother died. Another friend's father died. But there were also friends who fought the thing off. Writers and publishers, photographers and restaurateurs I knew survived. My old pal Marianne Faithfull fought the virus off in a London hospital, in spite of her checkered medical history. Every day brought bad, and some good, news. The horrifying numbers kept climbing, and the pressure on the already crumbling healthcare system kept growing.

IN HER CELEBRATED BOOK *Illness as Metaphor,* Susan Sontag—herself a cancer survivor, who years later succumbed to a different cancer—warned us against seeing ill health as a figure of some other social ill.

> My point is that illness is *not* a metaphor, and that the most truthful way of regarding illness . . . is one most purified of, most resistant to, metaphoric thinking.

As the global pandemic raged, many people failed to take her advice. Voices including an ISIS spokesman, Hulk Hogan, and a conservative pastor from Florida named Rick Wiles declared that the virus was a punishment from God. Other, greener voices suggested it was nature's revenge on the human race—though, to be fair, there were louder voices warning against anthropomorphizing "Mother" Nature. The old science-fiction idea that the human race is the virus from which the earth is trying to recover got some airtime too. Politicians characterized the pandemic as a war. Arundhati Roy called it "a portal, a gateway between one world and the next."

And sales of Albert Camus's 1947 novel *The Plague* went through the roof.

I didn't buy any of it, the stuff about divine or earthly retribution, or the dreams of a better future. Many people wanted to feel that some good would come out of the horror, that we would as a species somehow learn virtuous lessons and emerge from the cocoon of the lockdown as splendid New Age butterflies and create kinder, gentler, less greedy, more ecologically wise, less racist, less capitalist, more inclusive societies. This seemed to me, still seems to me, like Utopian thinking. The coronavirus did not strike me as the harbinger of socialism. The world's power structures and their beneficiaries would not easily surrender to a new idealism. I couldn't help finding strange our need to imagine the good emerging out of the bad. Europe in the time of the Black Death, and later London during the Great Plague, weren't full of people trying to see the positive side. People were too busy trying not to die. Like the characters in Eric Idle's *Monty Python* spin-off *Spamalot*, not being dead was all there was to celebrate:

> I am not dead yet
> I can dance and I can sing
> I am not dead yet
> I can do the Highland Fling
> I am not dead yet
> No need to go to bed
> No need to call the doctor
> Cause I'm not yet dead.

We are not the dominant species on the planet by accident. We have great survival skills. And we will survive. But I doubt that a social revolution will follow because of the lessons of the pandemic. But yes, sure, one can hope for betterment, and fight for it, and maybe our children will see—will *make*—that better world.

It is a part of our tragedy that in this time of crisis we are cursed, in many countries, including all three of those I have most cared about in my life, with leaders of astonishing cynicism and bad faith. In India, Narendra Modi's government used the pandemic to put the blame on Muslims. In the United Kingdom, Boris Johnson (in spite of having had and recovered from the virus himself) handled the crisis with stunning incompetence, at first downplaying the dangers (like Trump), reacting too little and too late (also like Trump), and continuing to play the Brexiteers' anti-immigrant card (like Trump yet again), in spite of the fact that both the primary carers who looked after him in the hospital were immigrants and the British National Health Service as a whole depends on their skills and courage. And in Trump's America, where nothing was unthinkable, in that country without a moral floor, so that no matter how low he and his followers sank, there was always a lower level to sink to—in Trumpistan, the virus (like everything else) was politicized, minimized, called a Democrat trick; the science was derided, the administration's lamentable response to the pandemic was obscured by a blizzard of lies, wearers of masks were abused by wearers of red hats, and the mountain of the dead went on growing, unmourned by the self-obsessed charlatan who claimed, in the face of all the evidence, that he was making America great again.

To repair the damage done by these people in these times will not be easy. I may not see the wounds mended in my lifetime. It may take a generation or more. The social damage of the pandemic itself, the fear of our old social lives, in bars and restaurants and dance halls and sports stadiums, will take time to heal (although a percentage of people seem to know no fear already, as we see on beaches, in parks, and at protests). We will hug and kiss again. But will there still be movie theaters? Will there be bookstores? Will we feel okay in crowded subway cars?

The social, cultural, political damage of these years, the deepening of the already deep rifts in society in many parts of the world, including the United States, the UK, and India, will take longer. It would not be exaggerating to say that as we stare across those chasms, we have begun to hate the people on the other side. That hatred has been fostered by the cynics who rule over us, and it bubbles over in different ways almost every day. It isn't easy to see how that chasm can be bridged—how love can find a way.

I WAS SURPRISED BY how many people said to me when the lockdown began, "Well, of course, after the Iranian *fatwa* against *The*

*Satanic Verses,* you know all about lockdowns, so this must be familiar to you." I decided not to argue the point, because if people couldn't see that an assassination threat aimed at an individual by a foreign government for religious reasons was *not the same* as a global pandemic—in the way that, for example, a stone thrown at a man's head in a village square is not the same as a lethal avalanche of boulders descending upon that village and destroying it—then I probably couldn't help them.

Other people said, "This must be a great time for you, because you can just stay home and write a novel." And again, I forbore to reply, because my reply would have been heavily sarcastic. "You're so right about that—there are already well over a hundred and ten thousand dead people in the United States alone, but my goodness, what a good time to be a novelist." In reality I found it hard to write. I started something and, after writing over a hundred pages, abandoned it as a foolishness. It took me months to embark, tentatively, on something else. Many other writers to whom I spoke also told me that it was hard to work. The roar of the real world was deafening and left no quiet space in which an imagined world might grow.

AS WELL AS CAMUS, many readers turned to Daniel Defoe's *A Journal of the Plague Year.* My NYU seminar discusses works of journalism that use the techniques of novelists to tell true stories (Truman Capote's *In Cold Blood,* Svetlana Alexievich's *Voices from Chernobyl,* John Edgar Wideman's *Writing to Save a Life,* Isabel Wilkerson's *The Warmth of Other Suns*). Some of the most interesting writing of the last fifty years stands at the blurred frontier between fact and fiction, and the results are sometimes dazzling (as in Katherine Boo's portrayal of life in a Mumbai slum, *Behind the Beautiful Forevers*) and sometimes problematic (as in *The Emperor,* Ryszard Kapuściński's account of the Ethiopian court of Haile Selassie and of his downfall, a book so beautifully written, its world so richly created, that one wants to overlook the serious questions of veracity the text raises, and to which it gives no satisfactory answers).

Daniel Defoe's book does the reverse of the texts above. It uses the techniques of journalism—and presents itself as a journalistic text—but it is in reality a work of the imagination. Defoe published it in 1722, anonymously, ascribing its authorship to "a Citizen who continued all the while in London." He was sixty-two, which meant that at the time of the Great Plague in 1665, he would have been five years old. He may, as a child and teenager, have heard stories of the plague from his uncle Henry Foe, but this essentially is a novel, not a work of reportage.

Both *The Plague* and *A Journal of the Plague Year* are fine books and well worth reading, but for myself I've turned more than once to William Golding's dark fable, *Lord of the Flies,* finding, in Golding's account of the fragility of civilization and the ease with which that veneer can be destroyed to reveal the barbarism beneath, a terrible and relevant truth. Then in May 2020 I read an article by Rutger Bregman in *The Guardian* about a real-life version of the Golding saga. In 1965 a group of Australian schoolboys were marooned on an island in the Pacific Ocean, south of Tonga. And unlike Golding's young savages, these castaways

> "set up a small commune with food garden, hollowed-out tree trunks to store rainwater, a gymnasium with curious weights, a badminton court, chicken pens and a permanent fire, all from handiwork, an old knife blade and much determination." While the boys in *Lord of the Flies* come to blows over the fire, those in this real-life version tended their flame so it never went out, for more than a year.
>
> The kids agreed to work in teams of two, drawing up a strict roster for garden, kitchen and guard duty. Sometimes they quarreled, but whenever that happened they solved it by imposing a time-out. Their days began and ended with song and prayer. . . .
>
> [One of the boys] slipped one day, fell off a cliff and broke his leg. The other boys picked their way down after him and then helped him back up to the top. They set his leg using

sticks and leaves. "Don't worry," [another boy] joked. "We'll do your work, while you lie there like King Taufa'ahau Tupou himself!"

In other words, there was no descent into savagery. They behaved like civilized young people, worked together, cared for one another, and survived because of it. They were rescued after a year and a half and were found to be in pretty good shape. The broken leg had healed perfectly.

The Golding novel and this Australian news story have come to represent to me the essential truths of how human beings react to crisis. Crisis shines a very bright light on human behavior, leaves no shadows in which we can hide, and reveals, simultaneously, the worst of which we are capable and our better natures as well. We have seen a great deal of the best of humanity, in the work of the front-line warriors, doctors, nurses, and hospital staff, and in the round-the-clock efforts around the world to find a vaccine. And we have seen the worst too, in the degeneration of parts of society into an ignorant, bigoted rabble. Golding's masterpiece turns out to be untrue about human nature and also true about it, at exactly the same time.

IN MY FOUR DECADES of being a parent, there has never been a period of more than half a year during which I haven't seen my children. I have learned all about Zoom, which is helpful but not enough. Now that I'm well, this physical distance from them is the greatest hardship.

THINK ABOUT IF YOU *would like to see the movie.*
I've been filling the empty evenings by rewatching the great movies I first saw in my youth, the films that made me fall in love with cinema as an art form. If my next novel is influenced by the French New Wave, as I believe it just might be, then it's the lockdown that's to blame, because I watched Jean-Luc Godard's *Bande à part* ("Band

of Outsiders") and *Vivre sa vie* ("Her Life to Live"), both starring the luminous Anna Karina, and was excited, all over again, by the *nouvelle vague* techniques of long takes, frame-breaking moments, crash cuts between scenes, and alienation techniques such as title cards that describe the action before it's shown. Eric Rohmer made six "Moral Tales," all with essentially the same plot—a character is involved with another character, is tempted by a third character, but in the end returns to his or her former life—and I watched the two best of those films, *Le Genou de Claire* ("Claire's Knee") and *Ma Nuit chez Maud* ("My Night at Maud's").

I ventured beyond France to explore that great age of World Cinema. I studied the indolent, drifting, sensual narrative structure of Michelangelo Antonioni's *L'Avventura* ("The Adventure"), the film that made Monica Vitti a star. I looked closely at Akira Kurosawa's samurai movie *Yojimbo,* and at Fellini's *8½,* and at *Xala,* by Ousmane Sembène, a Senegalese comedy about impotence.

There were nights of English-language entertainment too—Hitchcock's delicious *The Lady Vanishes,* peak-period Marilyn (*Some Like It Hot, Gentlemen Prefer Blondes*), the comic escapism of *High Society, Funny Face,* and *Bringing Up Baby.* This private film festival is what has made my creative juices start flowing again. When I was young, movies inspired me at least as much as books. It's rather wonderful that at this later stage of life, they are doing it again.

AFTER I REGAINED MY HEALTH and strength, I walked the streets, properly masked and gloved, to renew my relationship with this city, New York, which I have always loved, ever since I first visited it in the early 1970s. I stood completely alone in the great hall of Grand Central Station, which was eerie. I saw the heart that had been mown into the grass of the Bryant Park lawn as a tribute to the front-line workers, and the emptiness of Fifth Avenue, and a white-haired gentleman on a bench in Madison Square Park, quietly playing his guitar. I saw Times Square without any people in it. And I paid my respects to the deli that used to be the legendary Max's Kansas City.

The deli was closed now, as Max's had closed long before. Would it reopen? Impossible to know. Maybe the past would return as if by magic and the ghosts of Lou Reed and the Velvet Underground would play upstairs at Max's again, and Bowie and Warhol would be sitting in the back room, and Debbie Harry would be waiting tables.

And then the city changed again, as a second crisis arrived, and for a time, at least, it was as if the pandemic had ceased to exist.

A DIFFERENT KIND OF social revolution began in the aftermath of the murder of George Floyd by Minneapolis police officers led by Derek Chauvin on May 25, 2020, and maybe that crime, more than the pandemic, will prove to be the tipping point. The streets were suddenly full of people, crowded together, as if the pandemic had been a bad dream. As the huge protests triggered by George Floyd's death unfolded, night after night in city after city, I recalled Peter Finch in the 1976 movie *Network,* shouting, "I'm as mad as hell, and I'm not going to take this anymore." And I remembered Toni Morrison saying, "White people have a very, very serious problem and they should start thinking about what they can do about it," and "If you can only be tall because somebody is on their knees—then you have a serious problem." And in the eyes and faces of the protesters— some masked, some not—I saw a determination that said, "This time it's different."

Time will tell if the protests give new energy to the pandemic. Time will tell too if America can indeed be different and the wanton murder of black men and women by police officers and other armed white supremacists can come to an end. By the time you read these words we will know if there's a new president in America, and the dawn of a better day. I dearly hope that will be so. If it isn't, the God in whom I don't believe will need to help us all.

ON WEDNESDAY, JUNE 3, I went to the offices of my primary-care physician and gave blood for an antibody test. On Friday, June 5, I got the result. Antibodies have been detected! When I was told, I experienced a kind of exhilaration. It was possible to walk down the road or enter stores or other rooms with less fear. It was possible to contemplate the slow restart of a life with other people. The idea of getting on a plane was less alarming. Life beyond the virus was perhaps beginning again.

The American medical authorities seem reluctant to say definitively if antibodies confer immunity. Some prominent German authorities, however, say that there is immunity for at least a year, and the presence of antibodies means you can't be a carrier or a spreader either. Right now I trust the Europeans more than the Americans, if only because there doesn't seem to be any political meddling in the medical side of things in Europe.

I guess I'm immune. I told a few friends and more than one replied, "So now you're Superman." I don't feel very super. And I know that for every Superman there is also a rock of green Kryptonite.

We shall see.

# THE PROUST
# QUESTIONNAIRE:
## *VANITY FAIR*

—

WHEN AND WHERE WERE YOU HAPPIEST?
*Now, and here.*
On what occasions do you lie?
*These.*
What is your current state of mind?
*Singing.*
Which talent would you most like to have?
*The ability to sing.*
What do you consider your greatest achievement?
*To have continued.*
What do you consider the most overrated virtue?
*Faith.*
What is the trait you most deplore in yourself?
*Talkativeness.*
What is the trait you most deplore in others?
*Silence.*
What is your greatest extravagance?
*Linguistic.*
What is your most marked characteristic?
*Droopy eyelids.*
What is your most treasured possession?
*Reasonably good health.*
What do you regard as the lowest depth of misery?
*Any illness, however trivial.*

What is the quality you most like in a man?

*Warmth.*

What is the quality you most like in a woman?

*Humor.*

Who are your favorite writers?

*My friends.*

Who is your favorite hero of fiction?

*Leopold Bloom, Gregor Samsa, Bartleby the Scrivener.*

Who are your heroes in real life?

*Tennis players, baseball players, guitar players.*

Where would you like to live?

*On bookshelves. Forever.*

If you were to die and come back as a person or a thing, what do you think it would be?

*A city street.*

If you could choose what to come back as, what would it be?

*A city.*

How would you prefer to die?

*I would prefer not to.*

# ABOUT THESE
# TEXTS

────────

"Wonder tales," "proteus, "heraclitus," "autobiography and the Novel," "Adaptation," "The Liberty Instinct," and "The Composite Artist" have all been adapted from lectures originally given at Emory University. "Gabo and I" is a new version of a lecture delivered at the Ransom Center of the University of Texas at Austin. "Hans Christian Andersen" is from a lecture given in Odense, Denmark, on the occasion of receiving the Hans Christian Andersen Literary Prize.

"Another Writer's Beginnings" is a somewhat expanded version of the inaugural Eudora Welty Lecture at the National Cathedral in Washington, D.C. "Philip Roth" was delivered as part of the Philip Roth Lecture series. "Kurt Vonnegut and *Slaughterhouse-Five*" was a lecture for the Vonnegut Library in Indianapolis.

"Samuel Beckett's Novels" originally appeared as the introduction to that volume of his Complete Works. "Cervantes and Shakespeare" is a revised version of the introduction to a collection of stories inspired by those writers. "Harold Pinter" combines two pieces to form a new piece. "*The Paris Review Interviews, The Art of Fiction, Vol. IV*" was the introduction to that volume. "Notes on Sloth" appeared in *Granta* magazine. "*King of the World* by David Remnick" was an introduction to that book. "Very Well Then I Contradict Myself" appeared in *The Times* (U.K.)

"Truth" originally appeared in *Svenska Dagbladet*. "Courage" and "The Pen and the Sword" originally appeared in *The New York Times*.

"Christopher Hitchens" originally appeared in *Vanity Fair*. "The Arthur Miller Lecture" was published in *The New Yorker* under the title "On Censorship." "Osama bin Laden" was published in *The Daily Beast*. "Ai Weiwei and Others" originally appeared in *The New York Times*. "The Half-Woman God" was first published in *AIDS Sutra*, an anthology dealing with the AIDS crisis in India.

"*Taryn Simon: An American Index of the Hidden and Unfamiliar*" and "Being Francesco Clemente: *Self-Portraits*" were written as introductions to the catalogs of those two exhibitions. "Bhupen Khakhar" appeared in *The Daily Telegraph*. "Amrita Sher-Gil: Letters" was written as an introduction to that book. "Sebastião Salgado" was an introduction to a volume of the photographer's work. "Kara Walker" was a tribute on the occasion of an award to her at the Hammer Museum, Los Angeles. "The Unbeliever's Christmas" and "Carrie Fisher" appeared in British *Vogue*. "The Proust Questionnaire: *Vanity Fair*" was published in *Vanity Fair*.

"The Pen and the Sword," "The Birth of PEN World Voices," "PEN World Voices Opening Night 2014," "PEN World Voices Opening Night 2017," "Nova Southeastern University Commencement Address, 2006," "Emory University Commencement Address, 2015," and "Pandemic" are published here for the first time.

All the pieces in this book have been thoroughly revised. None of them appear in their original form.

PHOTO: © RACHEL ELIZA GRIFFITHS

SALMAN RUSHDIE is the author of fifteen novels: *Grimus, Midnight's Children* (which was awarded the Booker Prize in 1981), *Shame, The Satanic Verses, Haroun and the Sea of Stories, The Moor's Last Sigh, The Ground Beneath Her Feet, Fury, Shalimar the Clown, The Enchantress of Florence, Luka and the Fire of Life, Two Years Eight Months and Twenty-Eight Nights, The Golden House, Quichotte,* and *Victory City.*

Rushdie is also the author of a book of stories, *East, West,* and five works of nonfiction: *Joseph Anton: A Memoir, Imaginary Homelands, The Jaguar Smile, Step Across This Line,* and *Languages of Truth.* He is the co-editor of *Mirrorwork,* an anthology of contemporary Indian writing, and of the 2008 *Best American Short Stories* anthology.

A fellow of the British Royal Society of Literature, Salman Rushdie has received, among other honors, the Whitbread Prize for Best Novel (twice), the Writers Guild Award, the James Tait Black Prize, the European Union's Aristeion Prize for Literature, Author of the Year prizes in both Britain and Germany, the French Prix du Meilleur Livre Étranger, the Budapest Grand Prize for Literature, the Premio Grinzane Cavour in Italy, the Crossword Book Award in India, the Austrian State Prize for European Literature, the London International Writers Award, the James Joyce Award of University College Dublin, the St. Louis Literary Prize, the Carl Sandburg Prize of the Chicago Public Library, and a U.S. National Arts Award. He holds honorary doctorates and fellowships at six European and six American universities, is an honorary professor in the

Humanities at M.I.T., and is a university distinguished professor at Emory University. Currently, Rushdie is a distinguished writer in residence at New York University.

He has received the Freedom of the City in Mexico City, Strasbourg, and El Paso, and the Edgerton Prize of the American Civil Liberties Union. He holds the rank of commandeur in the Ordre des Arts et des Lettres—France's highest artistic honor. Between 2004 and 2006 he served as president of PEN American Center and for ten years served as the chairman of the PEN World Voices International Literary Festival, which he helped to create. In June 2007 he received a knighthood in the Queen's Birthday Honours. In 2008 he became a member of the American Academy of Arts and Letters and was named a Library Lion of the New York Public Library. In addition, *Midnight's Children* was named the Best of the Booker—the best winner in the award's forty-year history— by a public vote. His books have been translated into over forty languages.

*Midnight's Children* has been adapted for the stage. It has been performed in London, Ann Arbor, and New York by the Royal Shakespeare Company. In 2004, an opera based upon *Haroun and the Sea of Stories* was premiered by the New York City Opera at Lincoln Center. In 2016, an opera based upon *Shalimar the Clown* was premiered at the Opera Theatre of Saint Louis.

A film of *Midnight's Children,* directed by Deepa Mehta, was released in 2012.

*The Ground Beneath Her Feet,* in which the Orpheus myth winds through a story set in the world of rock music, was turned into a song by U2 with lyrics by Salman Rushdie.

salmanrushdie.com

Facebook.com/salmanrushdieauthor

Twitter: @SalmanRushdie